Kobe University Monograph Series in Social Science Research

The Kobe University Monograph Series in Social Science Research is an exciting interdisciplinary collection of monographs, both authored and edited, that encompass scholarly research not only in the economics but also in law, political science, business and management, accounting, international relations, and other sub-disciplines within the social sciences. As a national university with a special strength in the social sciences, Kobe University actively promotes interdisciplinary research. This series is not limited only to research emerging from Kobe University's faculties of social sciences but also welcomes cross-disciplinary research that integrates studies in the arts and sciences.

Kobe University, founded in 1902, is the second oldest national higher education institution for commerce in Japan and is now a preeminent institution for social science research and education in the country. Currently, the social sciences section includes four faculties—Law, Economics, Business Administration, and International Cooperation Studies—and the Research Institute for Economics and Business Administration (RIEB). There are some 230-plus researchers who belong to these faculties and conduct joint research through the Center for Social Systems Innovation and the Organization for Advanced and Integrated Research, Kobe University. This book series comprises academic works by researchers in the social sciences at Kobe University as well as their collaborators at affiliated institutions, Kobe University alumni and their colleagues, and renowned scholars from around the world who have worked with academic staff at Kobe University. Although traditionally the research of Japanese scholars has been publicized mainly in the Japanese language, Kobe University strives to promote publication and dissemination of works in English in order to further contribute to the global academic community.

Yuka Kaneko · Teuku Alvisyahrin ·
Taqwaddin Bin Muhammad Husin ·
Jianping Wang · Ebinezer R. Florano
Editors

Recovery of Disaster Victims

Results of Joint Survey in East Japan, Aceh, Sichuan, and Tacloban

KOBE UNIVERSITY

Springer

Editors
Yuka Kaneko
Center for Social Systems Innovation
Kobe University
Kobe, Japan

Taqwaddin Bin Muhammad Husin
High Court of Aceh
Banda Aceh, Indonesia

Ebinezer R. Florano
National College of Public Administration and Governance
University of the Philippines Manila
Quezon City, Philippines

Teuku Alvisyahrin
Graduate Program in Disaster Science
Syiah Kuala University
Banda Aceh, Indonesia

Jianping Wang
School of Law
Sichuan University
Chengdu, China

ISSN 2524-504X ISSN 2524-5058 (electronic)
Kobe University Monograph Series in Social Science Research
ISBN 978-981-99-2956-6 ISBN 978-981-99-2957-3 (eBook)
https://doi.org/10.1007/978-981-99-2957-3

This Springer imprint is published by the registered company Springer Nature Singapore Pte Ltd.
The registered company address is: 152 Beach Road, #21-01/04 Gateway East, Singapore 189721, Singapore

Contents

Editors and Contributors

About the Editors

Yuka Kaneko LL.D., Professor and deputy executive director, Center for Social Systems Innovation, Kobe University, Japan. She is active in the field of Asian comparative law and legal sociology. Her edited books include *Asian Law in Disasters: Toward a Human-Centered Recovery* (Routledge, 2016), *Civil Law Reforms in Post-Colonial Asia: Beyond Western Capitalism* (Springer, 2019), *Land Law and Disputes in Asia: In Search for an Alternative Development* (Routledge, 2021), *Build Back Better: Issues of Asian Disaster Recovery* (Springer, 2021), *Insolvency Law Reforms in the ASEAN Emerging Economies: Consequences of the Donor Model Designed for Economic Crises* (Springer, 2022). She is a Editor-in-Chief of *Asian Journal of Law and Society.*

Teuku Alvisyahrin Ph.D. in Crop, Soil, and Environmental Sciences (University of Arkansas). Lecturer, Graduate Program in Disaster Science and Soil Science Department, and also the former Head of Division in charge of international collaborations and partnerships at Tsunami and Disaster Mitigation Research Center, Syiah Kuala University, Indonesia. Visting Lecturer and Guest Instructor at the Geophysics Department, Stanford University (2016) and Visiting Professor at the Graduate School of International Cooperation Studies, Kobe University (2018).

Taqwaddin Bin Muhammad Husin LL.D. (North Sumatra University). Justice at High Court of Aceh, Indonesia. Former Ombudsman in Aceh Province. He is the lecturer at Syiah Kuala University, and also the expert at the Aceh Province House of Representative, WWF, and the Social and Religion Activist (Muhammadiyah) of Aceh. His publications include a chapter included in *Asian Law in Disaster,* edited by Kaneko, Matsuoka and Toyoda, Routledge, 2016; *Kapita Selekta Hukum Adat Aceh*, Bandar Publishing, Banda Aceh, 2016; *Sisi lain Bekerjanya Hukum dalam Masyarakat*, Bandar Publishing, Banda Aceh, 2018; and *Catatan dari Ombudsman*, Bandar Publishing, Banda Aceh 2022.

Jianping Wang Ph.D. in Economics, Professor, School of Law, Sichuan University, China. Also, professor of disaster law at the Institute for Disaster Management and Reconstruction of Sichuan University—Hong Kong Polytechnic University. He is the chief expert, Natural Disaster Emergency Management and Disaster Recovery Research Think Tank in Sichuan University and is a council member of civil law in the China Law Society. He has published a study of structural control of risk of listed companies and studies on codification of civil law, the traps, and risks in contract law in practice, and legal regulation of securities market risk.

Ebinezer R. Florano Ph.D., Professor IV and U.P. Scientist I (2020–2022), National College of Public Administration and Governance, University of the Philippines. Visiting Professor at the Graduate School of International Cooperation Studies, Kobe University (2021–2022).

Contributors

Teuku Alvisyahrin Graduate Program in Disaster Science, Syiah Kuala University, Banda Aceh, Indonesia;
Tsunami and Disaster Mitigation Research Center, Syiah Kuala University, Banda Aceh, Indonesia

Ebinezer R. Florano National College of Public Administration and Governance, University of the Philippines, Quezon, Philippines

Yegane Ghezelloo Architecture and Urbanism, Graduate School of Engineering, Kobe University, Kobe, Japan

Akihiko Hokugo Graduate School of International Cooperation Studies, Graduate School of Engineering, Research Center for Urban Safety and Security, Kobe University, Kobe, Japan

Yuichi Honjo Graduate School of Disaster Resilience and Governance, University of Hyogo, Kobe, Japan

Taqwaddin Husin Faculty of Law, Syiah Kuala University, Banda Aceh, Indonesia; High Court of Aceh, Banda Aceh, Indonesia

Yuka Kaneko Center for Social Systems Innovation and the Research Center for Urban Safety and Security, Kobe University, Kobe, Japan

Jingyi Liao Sichuan University—The Hong Kong Polytechnic University Institute for Disaster Management and Reconstruction, Chengdu, Sichuan, China

Rizki Wan Oktabina Health Polytechnic, Ministry of Health, Banda Aceh, Indonesia

Abel Táiti Konno Pinheiro Disaster Reduction and Human Renovation Institution, Kobe, Japan

Yumi Shiomi Asian Disaster Reduction Center, Kobe, Japan

Risma Sunarty Aceh Disaster Risk Reduction Forum, Banda Aceh, Indonesia

Toshihisa Toyoda Graduate School of Disaster Resilience and Governance, University of Hyogo, Kobe, Japan;
Kobe University, Kobe, Japan

Jianping Wang Sichuan University—The Hong Kong Polytechnic University Institute for Disaster Management and Reconstruction, Chengdu, Sichuan, China

List of Figures

Introduction: Comparing the Prioritization in Post-disaster Life Recovery

Resident Questionnaire Survey on the Lives and Livelihoods Recovery in the Devastated Area After Ten Years from the Great East Japan Earthquake and Tsunami: Overall Results Review

Survey Results on the Recovery Perception of the Commercial and Industrial Entities as of the 10th Anniversary of the East Japan Earthquake

List of Tables

Resident Questionnaire Survey on the Lives and Livelihoods Recovery in the Devastated Area After Ten Years from the Great East Japan Earthquake and Tsunami: Overall Results Review

Survey Results on the Recovery Perception of the Commercial and Industrial Entities as of the 10th Anniversary of the East Japan Earthquake

Aceh Post 2004 Tsunami Recovery: Strategies and Implications

Recovery Status from the 2013 Typhoon Yolanda: Results of a Survey in Two Typical Barangays in Tacloban City

Introduction: Comparing the Prioritization in Post-disaster Life Recovery

Yuka Kaneko

Abstract This volume presents the results of an international joint survey conducted as of the 10th anniversary of the 2011 East Japan Earthquake, based on the same questionnaire answered by the disaster affected populations in each area affected by recent mega-disasters in Asia, as an international joint research among the researchers from Syiah Kuala University in Aceh, Indonesia since the 2004 Indian Ocean Tsunami, Sichuan University since the 2008 Sichuan Earthquake in China, and University of the Philippines since the 2013 Typhoon Yolanda. The purpose of joint survey was to ascertain and compare the status of recovery after a long run of each different choice of prioritization among plural policy goals of disaster recovery. One of the findings was the difficulty of a concurrent achievement of safety and livelihood, especially for the vulnerable groups of people who tend to sacrifice their safety in order to achieve survival. The best policy mix cannot be reached without realizing substantive participation with disclosure of information to local communities.

1 Purpose of the Joint Survey

This volume presents the results of a joint survey conducted during the years 2020 through 2021, as of the tenth anniversary of the 2011 East Japan Earthquake, by an international research group consisting of researchers representing the major universities affected by recent mega-disasters in Asia, as a product of the interdisciplinary project on disaster mitigation and post-disaster recovery at the Kobe University Center for Social System Innovation (hereinafter "KUSSI"). From among the members of such research collaboration, this volume collects the contributions by the researchers from four countries, namely, the research group at KUSSI, Japan, as well as Dr. Teuku Alvisyahrin, Dr. Taqwaddin Husein and their colleagues at the Graduate Program in Disaster Science, Syiah Kuala University in Aceh, Indonesia; Dr. Wang Jinping and his colleagues at the Institute for Disaster Management and Reconstruction of Sichuan University, China; and Dr. Ebinezer Florano at the National

Y. Kaneko (✉)
Center for Social System Innovation, Kobe University, Kobe, Japan
e-mail: ykaneko@kobe-u.ac.jp

Y. Kaneko et al. (eds.), *Recovery of Disaster Victims*, Kobe University Monograph Series in Social Science Research, https://doi.org/10.1007/978-981-99-2957-3_1

College of Public Administration and Governance of University of the Philippines, the Philippines.

The authors of this volume already conducted a series of joint surveys from 2012 to 2016, toward the fifth anniversary of the East Japan Earthquake, in order to ascertain the common policy goals of post-mega disaster recovery as well as the procedures for establishing a justifiable priority among them, the result of which was jointly published as *Asian Disaster Law: Toward a Human-Centered Recovery* (Routledge, 2016). One of the major findings was a variation of legal procedures for the decision-making of post-disaster town-planning, by either central government's discretion, local initiatives, or community autonomy. The 2011 Law on Post-East Japan Earthquake Recovery Special Zone in Japan was a typical mechanism for central government's discretion to expedite the post-disaster public construction works by excluding the application of existing laws meant for policy adjustments and civic participation, which invited a heavy infrastructure centered recovery principle prioritized throughout the ten year reconstruction period, and was in a quite contrast to the regulatory experience in the post 1995 Hanshin-Awaji Earthquake recovery where the Kobe city's ordinance led a participatory town-planning involving disaster-affected communities. The post 2004 Indian Ocean Tsunami recovery in Aceh, Indonesia was guided by a series of Aceh provincial ordinances (qanun) which mandated the traditional villages (gampong) for autonomous decision of either relocation to highland or reconstruction in inundated areas, or in other words, a choice between safety and livelihood, which was an opposite model to the state-led East Japan Earthquake, even though both cases were tsunami disaster. The post 2008 Sichuan (Wechan) Earthquake recovery in China was another unique attempt under the central umbrella ordinance that mandated the "twin assistance" or a coupling between the donor provinces from rich east coast areas of the country with each affected municipalities in Sichuan, with a full discretion given to each such coupled governments for town-planning, which resulted in a speedy completion of physical reconstruction within a few years, but questions remained for other recovery policy goals, particularly the livelihood recovery of affected people who were isolated from the access to original means of livelihood due to relocation. The post 2013 Typhoon Yolanda recovery can be characterized as an experiment of the functioning of the country's 1992 Local Autonomy Law which emphasizes the autonomy of village communities (balangay), while the town-planning was led by the political line of central-municipal relation over the allocation of recovery budget. A hypothetical view obtained from this variation of decision-making process among target countries was that, while there are plural policy goals in disaster recovery, a different choice of decision-making can result in different prioritization among such goals.

After five years, the same research group has now intended to conduct another review of the subsequent stages of post-disaster recovery, particularly for the purpose of observing the outcomes of each different choice of the priority of recovery goals.

Accordingly, this volume attempts the evaluation of the status of post-disaster recovery in the same target countries in Asia in the long term, with a particular focus on the human life recovery of disaster-affected people and communities, for the ultimate purpose of reviewing and comparing the outcomes of different prioritizations among the plural goals of disaster recovery. Through such a review, the authors intend to induce policy implications to guide a better recovery process with lesser impact on the human life recovery in the future disasters that we humans are destined to meet. The target areas were selected based on the aforementioned hypothetical view obtained from the previous survey of the authors in regard to the deferent procedures of recovery decision-making, and includes 16 districts in Iwate and Miyagi prefectures in Japan, all seriously affected by tsunami in the 2011 East Japan Earthquake, as well as three villages in Banda Aceh and its outskirts, Aceh Special Province, Indonesia, 17 years after the 2004 Indian Ocean Tsunami; two districts in Mianyang city in Sichuan, China, 13 years after the 2008 Sichuan (Wenchuan) Earthquake; and two village communities in Tacloban, the capital city of Leyte island hit by the 2013 Typhoon Yolanda.

This volume is a result of the Japanese government's Kaken grant in aid for scientific research (B) No. 17H04507 (for the fiscal years 2017–2020) titled "A Comparative Research on the Social System for the Promotion of Community-Based Disaster Mitigation in Asian Disaster Affected Regions".

2 Method of the Joint Survey

The methodology of this joint survey is an empirical approach based on the perception of the disaster affected population through a common questionnaire sheet, which consists of four parts (see the Attachment in this volume), namely, Part I on the status of individual life recovery particularly in terms of housing and livelihood reconstruction (10 questions), Part II as the "Recovery Calendar" or a time scale of the progress of disaster recovery viewed from multiple factors (12 questions), Part III on the perception on the status of reconstruction of regional economy (9 questions), and Part IV on the recovery of community functions (12 questions).

A unique attempt of this survey is an evaluation of overall recovery status based on the perceptions of the people in the disaster affected areas, instead of depending on the outside databases. This is due to the authors' concern that many of governmental and scholarly projects of evaluating the post-disaster recovery tend to select the data from outside sources to introduce a favorable result. By simply depending on the answers directly obtained from the people affected in disasters, who are the very addressees of the post disaster recovery planning, we will be able to come closers to the facts of the disaster recovery. For this purpose, the questions were asked about not only the status of each life recovery of disaster affected people, but also their perceptions on the statuses of local economy and the community.

Together with individual questions asked about the recovery status, the "Recovery Calendar" in Part II has been an established method of disaster recovery evaluation by disaster-affected citizens, on the 12 policy goals developed through the accumulation of research by disaster sociologists after the 1995 Hanshin-Awaji Earthquake in Kobe, Japan. Such an elaboration of a perception-based methodology was started with the "seven elements of life reconstruction" developed through a series of community-based workshops in Kobe city and allied to the fifth anniversary survey on the recovery status conducted in 2000 by the city government. The Hyogo Prefecture government has also developed the recovery evaluation methods, including "three indicators on the perception of life recovery" applied in its tenth anniversary survey in 2005. There is a stream of preceding research which have elaborated the applicability of these indicators developed from the post Hanshin-Awaji Earthquake recovery to other disaster incidents.[1] Between them, the "Recovery Calendar" has shown particular validity in reflecting the perception of a disaster-affected population based on twelve factors representing different aspects of disaster recovery,[2] namely, (1) grasped overall damage, (2) thought it is now safe, (3) resolved to live an inconvenient life, (4) restarted work, (5) have finally resolved housing problems, (6) household budget has recovered, (7) daily life has settled down, (8) local activities have returned to normal, (9) self-perception as a disaster victim has disappeared, (10) regional economy has escaped the effects of the disaster, (11) local roads have been repaired, and (12) local schools have recovered. It has often been applied for a comparative purpose between different areas or across different disasters, by comparing the time point which the majority of the interviewees answer affirmatively, and was also utilized by the national government in the fifth anniversary recovery evaluation after the East Japan Earthquake.[3]

The authors of this volume together express the special gratitude to all who have contributed to the implementation of the joint survey with great teamwork and utmost caution under the risks of the COVID-19 pandemic. The authors also extend special thanks to Mr. Peter Cassidy, attorney at law in Australia, for his enormous help in this publication.

3 Post-east Japan Earthquake Recovery: Prioritization of Public Works

Chapter 2 of this volume introduces the results of the questionnaire survey conducted by the research team at KUSSI in 2020, toward the 10th anniversary of the 2011 East Japan Earthquake that occurred on March 11th, 2011, which took more than 20,000 lives due to the millennium-scale tsunami caused by the magnitude 9.1 shock. The questionnaire was distributed to 7,895 households in 16 areas chosen among the districts most seriously affected by tsunami inundation in Iwate and Miyagi prefectures, where large-scale governmental construction works have been implemented as a part of the "multiple Approach to Disaster Prevention (*Taju Bosai*)" policy of the national government, which highlights the combination of a "hard approach" standardized at the level-1 class tsunami (1929 tsunami class) through the construction

---

[1] See Hayashi (2000), and Tachiki (2013), etc.

[2] See Kimura et al. (2001).

[3] See Recovery Agency Great East Japan Earthquake Life Recovery Evaluation Team (2016).

of 400 km long great seawalls covering the entire coastlines of the affected prefectures, land-readjustment projects for land-filling, relocation from designated high risk areas, as well as the "soft approach" or community-based disaster risk management for the level-2 class tsunami (2011 East Japan Earthquake class). Answers were obtained from 1,273 households, with a response ratio of 16.1%. While the detailed analysis is yet to follow, Chap. 2 intends to place the immediate results of simple tabulations.

The intention of this survey to focus on the directly affected population in 2011 Tsunami was proven to be met by the survey result that 75% of the answering households were heavily affected in terms of the governmental certificate on housing loss (Table 6 of Chap. 2). While 75% of the answering households used to own each house on the self-owned land (Table 5 of Chap. 2), the status of housing recovery after ten years is that 40% of such households have chosen to be a lessee of the governmental apartments (Table 7 of Chap. 2). A cross tabulation of housing recovery with the residing areas revealed significant differences (Table 8 of Chap. 2) which seems to reflect the different mode of town-recovery projects, either the land readjustment projects for land-filling works which resulted in the suspension of housing reconstruction of disaster affected households for several years until the work completion, the government-sponsored relocation projects which were available only for the residents in the designated disaster risk areas, the government sponsored apartment complex in the inland, or the individual relocation areas where each household chose to relocate in safe places outside of the government sponsored projects. Similarly, the results of the question No. 5 in the "Recovery Calendar" which was asked about the timing of housing reconstruction show significant differences between the residing areas (Figs. 2 through 17 in Chap. 2), such that the households which reconstructed by the individual relocation as well as the households chose to end up with the lessee status of public apartment have achieved an early housing recovery, while the housing reconstruction of the households which waited until the completion of the governmental town recovery projects show an obvious delay, such as the Otsuchi town answers showing only 40% achievement of housing reconstruction as of the year 2020.

As for the livelihood reconstruction, 73% of the works or business of the answering households were affected by the 2011 disaster (Table 18 of Chap. 2), while 32.4% of them maintained the original works or businesses, and a total of 27.1% experienced the temporary or permanent cessation of their works or businesses (Table 16 of Chap. 2). Less than a half of the answering households have restored the pre-2011 status of the business performance (Table 19 of Chap. 2), on which significant differences are observed in a cross tabulation with the category of industries (Table 25 of Chap. 2). The status of housing income, expenditure, saving and borrowings are deteriorating by 40–60% compared to the pre-disaster situation (Table 30 through 32 of Chap. 2). While the results of the question No. 4 in the "Recovery Calendar" on the timing of work reconstruction does not show much difference between the areas nor industries, the results of the question No. 6 on the timing of household's income recovery show significant differences between the residing areas (Figs. 2 through 17 of Chap. 2), with an implication that the households which got involved in the governmental town recovery projects had to endure an obvious delay, as typically seen in the answers in Otsuchi town, Rikuzen-Takata city, etc. where the households answers showing only 50% achievement of household's income recovery as of the year 2020.

Perhaps, one of the most fundamental goals of the disaster recovery is the "safety" toward the next disasters, as envisaged in the article 3 of the Law on Recovery from the Great Disasters. However, the results of the No. 2 question on "safety" in the "Recovery Calendar" of this survey reveals a significant dismal in almost all areas, which leaves the question of what is the adequate standard of safety for the local residence in the disaster recovery, which are the questions to be further studied for the betterment of future disaster recovery.

Another peculiar tendency of the result of the "Recovery Calendar" is the particularly low achievement of the question No. 9 on "overcoming the self-recognition as a disaster victim" across the different areas. While there is a basic tendency of the recovery curb for this No. 9 answer that follows the recovery curbs of No. 5 on housing reconstruction and No. 6 on the timing of household's income recovery, there are some areas where the the No. 9 curb does not improve even after many years of the achievement of housing reconstructions, such as in the curb of Kuwagasaki in Miyako city, which requires a further investigation on the causes.

As for the status of local economy, significant differences are seen in the answers on the recovery of local economy in regard of the residing areas (Table 37 of Chap. 2), which again implies the effect of the prolonged governmental town recovery projects. Similar results are seen on the answers on the status of the reactivation of the local merchant streets (Table 39 of Chap. 2). A significant relation was found between these answers on the local economy and the answers on the status of population recovery (Table 45 of Chap. 2). This tendency also corresponds to the lowest achievement of the question No. 10 "economic recovery" among 12 questions of the "Recovery Calendar," which reveals a particularly worst result in the commercial spots in the rural aquaculture-based economy. An implication is the inapplicability for the rural economy of the urban-oriented town-reconstruction model established in Japanese disaster recovery that prioritizes the residential area's reconstruction while entrusting the livelihood and economic matters to the capacity of urban industries. A concurrent focus on both residential and livelihood reconstruction must be required for the disaster recovery in the rural socio-economy.

4 Post-east Japan Earthquake Recovery Viewed from Economic Entities

Chapter 3 describes the results of another questionnaire conducted in the areas affected by the 2011 East Japan Earthquake, which targeted the business sector in the municipalities of Miyako city, Yamada town, Otsuchi town and Kamaishi city in Iwate prefecture, for the purpose of ascertaining the status of economic recovery and reconstruction. The questionnaire was distributed to 2,766 businesses which belong to the local chambers of commerce and industry, while answers were obtained from 568 businesses among them with a response ratio of 20.5%.

Major findings include a significant gap between the regions due to the different forms of reconstruction, such as land-fill projects to raise the elevation, which arose from differences in the recovery construction policies applied by the government, and also a significant gap between the regions in the degree of business recovery, as well as a significant difference in perceptions of the status of the local economy and population drain. There is a clear tendency for business recovery to be largely dependent upon the special procurement demand generated by government construction projects, and also a tendency of slower business recovery by smaller-scale businesses, heavily damaged businesses, and businesses with no option other than to reconstruct in designated disaster risk areas and areas subject to land-filling projects. Another tendency was that more heavily damaged industries obtain more government subsidies.

The "recovery calendar" of each region (Figs. 2 through 5 in Chap. 3) shows a similar tendency of "No.10 Regional Economy" having the most obvious delay in recovery, followed by the delay in the recovery factors "No.9 Self-perception as a disaster victim," "No.6 Recovery of Household Livelihood", and "No.2 Safety". While the delay in achieving "(10) local economy" was similarly identified in the prior research following the Great Hanshin-Awaji Earthquake, the delay concerning "(9) self-perception as a victim" has been a peculiar tendency in this survey on businesses affected by East Japan Earthquake, and may require further investigation on the difference in the nature of recovery between these two disasters.

The fact that "(2) safety" had the lowest result in this survey, along with "(10) regional economy" and "(9) self-perception as a disaster victim", can be read as an expression of doubts by businesses about the adequacy of the government's safety measures, even though they required a decade long suspension of normalization of economic activities. One of the lessons learned from this survey is that recovery policy planning should be carried out through the full disclosure of information and in a participation way that reflects the reasonable consideration of local businesses.

5 Recovery in Post-indian Ocean Tsunami Aceh: Isolated Safety

Chapter 4 of this volume presents the results of the interview survey conducted by the research group led by Dr. Alvisyahrin and Dr. Taqwaddin at Syiah Kuala University, 17 years after the Indian Ocean Tsunami that occurred on December 26th in 2004 and took 100,000 lives in Aceh.

According to the previous study conducted by the authors, a characteristic of the post-tsunami recovery in Aceh is the autonomy given to the basic level of traditional villages (*gampong*) in choosing the mode of village reconstruction; the land adjustment works known as the RALAS project conducted by the international donors' alliance headed by the World Bank, relocation to higher grounds, or any other choice. Such self-determination was made possible by a series of provincial ordinances introduced amid the post-Soeharto reformation under the 1999 Law on Local Autonomy of Indonesia, which restored the legal status of traditional villages as formally autonomous bodies.[4] If so, then what about the outcomes of each different choice made by such autonomous villages? To observe the status of community recovery after nine years of post-tsunami reconstruction, in 2013 a joint research team from Kobe University and Syiah Kuala University conducted an interview survey in six villages and identified certain challenges which can be summarized as a trade-off of safety and livelihood; the villages which chose to reconstruct in the original area to maintain access to the basis of their livelihoods, such as fishery ports and coastal aquaculture fields, have faced the same disaster risks as before, while the people who chose to leave such villages to seek a safer reconstruction in the higher ground are isolated from the economy.[5]

After six years from the survey in 2013, in December 2019, the same research group again visited the same villages in Aceh to prepare for a structured interview, and then proceeded on to the survey in February 2020. A focus was made on three target villages representing each different mode of recovery, namely, Lambada Lhok village which chose to reconstruct the whole village on the waterfront and accepted the implementation of the land-readjustment project named "RALAS" led by the international donor group headed by the World Bank; Lambung village which accepted the implementation of the safety plan provided by the Japanese ODA which included a land-readjustment project and the construction of a tsunami evacuation tower; and Neuheun village (known by its nickname "Jackie Chan village") which chose to relocate the entire village to a collective relocation spot constructed with the aid of the Chinese government in the hillside, 17 km away from the central part of Aceh. The interviews were conducted with a total of 99 randomly-selected households.

As for the housing recovery, while all interviewed households answered they had their houses driven away by tsunami, and almost all of them answered that they were offered new houses within one to two years by the donors, the mode of such reconstruction differed between the three villages. In Lambada Lhok village, 80% of interviewees reconstructed on their original land lot after land measurement was conducted by the donors' RALAS project. In Lambung village, all who answered had their house reconstructed in a compact complex site created by the Japanese-led land readjustment, as a result of the landowners' dedicating 20% of their original land area as land reduction (*genbu* in Japanese). In Neuheun village, which chose the mountainside relocation, while the original property-owning status was divided 50:50 between the land and house owners and tenants, all of the relocated households received an equal allocation of a governmental land for construction purposes (*hak guna bangnan*) with the houses provided by the donors with a common spec. On the

[4] See Taqwaddin and Alvisharin (2013, 2016).

[5] See for the major results of the 2013 survey, (Kaneko 2016).

other hand, the results of "Recovery Calendar" on the timing of housing recovery (Question 2 (5)) revealed a diversity between the three villages.

As for the household budget status, the tendency in the three villages is the same in that 70–80% of the interviewed households experienced the impact of the disaster on their family budget. When asked about their household income level, the tendencies in the three villages show a certain difference, such that the decrease of income is evident in 40% of the interviewees in Lambada Lhok village, and 80% in Neuheun village, while an income increase is reported by more than 60% of interviewees in Lambung village. On the other hand, the results of "Recovery Calendar" on the timing of household budget recovery (Question 2 (6)) revealed a slowest process of recovery in Lambung village. This gap could be explained by the differences in the village economies, where the primary source of household income in Lambada Lhok village is the fishery industry, while the occupations of the residents in Lambung village varies, including business owners and public officers with a stable salary.

The status of the local economy also reveals a gap. While about 50% of the interviewees in Lambada Lhok village and Neuheun village think their economy has recovered to the pre-disaster level, more than 70% of interviewees in Lambung village think their economy is higher than the pre-disaster level (Figs. 1, 2 in Chap. 4). Also noticeable is a gap in the access to governmental support, in that 70% of the interviewees in Lambada Lhok village and Lambung village have received certain governmental support, but 50% of the respondents in Neuheun said that they never received any governmental support (Figs. 3, 4 in Chap. 4).

As for population recovery, the majority of the respondents in Lambada Lhok village said that their population is merely 40–50% of the pre-disaster level, but the most frequent answers in Neuheun village report a population increase, while the answers in Lambung village report not much change.

Based on these results, it seems that, after 17 years from the tsunami event, the tendency of the trade-off between safety and livelihood that was detected in the 2013 survey of the authors' team has deteriorated over the long run. Residents in Neuheun village that prioritized safety through relocation to a remote mountain have resulted in sacrificing their livelihoods, as shown by having the worst level of livelihood recovery among the three target villages in the survey results. Though the post-disaster relocation merely targeted housing, the authors of the Chapter induced a lesson that the relocation should be designed for a balance of both housing safety and livelihood.

On the contrary, in Lambada Lhok village, which chose to reconstruct in the disaster risk area for the benefit of their fishery-based livelihoods, the "Recovery Calendar" shows a delay in the recovery of feeling safe (Question 2(2)), which took three years for the majority to feel so, while the other two villages took merely one year or so. A question remains whether the choice of Lambung village has proven to be a correct one in terms of concurrently aiming for safety and livelihood recovery. It seems as if the village achieved economic recovery by choosing to remain in the coastal area near the city center, while concurrently securing safety by accepting JICA's construction works such as the tsunami evacuation tower. However, negative evidence against such an assumption is the remarkable slowness of the population recovery in Lambung village that was revealed in this survey, despite the economic success, which is in quite contrast to the population increase in Neuheun village despite its failing economic recovery. One interpretation of this paradox could be that JICA's safety project in Lambung village was merely addressed to the formal landowner class who were afford to wait until the completion of the construction works, while those who used to have customary residential rights were destined to leave due to being treated as a landless class, which is a hypothetical view already obtained in the 2013 interview of the authors' joint research.[6]

Another interpretation is the negative effect caused by the pinpointed intervention by JICA's safety project in Lambung, which caused an increase in land prices until the ordinary income class could not afford to remain in the area. Meanwhile, the land price in Neuheun village is becoming affordable to the middle-income class who choose absolute safety rather than seeking easier access to their livelihood in the lower land. In the long run, safety will be a luxury that only certain income classes can afford. This paradox might teach us the risk of partial intervention by the donors on a safety choice, without considering equal access to a certain minimum standard. It also reminds us of what we found in the questionnaire surveys in East Japan on the population drain invited by governmental construction works, where lower income households that were unable to fund themselves until the completion of lengthy construction works had no other choice but to leave their old town to seek work outside.

6 Sichuan Earthquake Recovery: Questions Remained for Agricultural Livelihood

Chapter 5 of this volume is the product of the research team at Sichuan University headed by Prof. Wang Jinping, on the status of life recovery of the victims of the Sichuan Earthquake that occurred on May 12th in 2008 and resulted in 69,000 casualties, 18,000 missing, 370,000 injuries, and material damage amounting to 800 billion yuan. The recovery process was led by the three-year plan based on the Regulation on Post-Wenchuan Earthquake Restoration and Reconstruction and introduced within one month from the disaster. Such speedy completion of reconstruction has been highly appreciated as a result of a unique recovery method known as "coupling assistance" that individually matched wealthy provinces along the Chinese coast with each affected municipality in Sichuan. The field survey conducted in August 2014 by a joint team from Kobe University and Sichuan University identified, however, certain difficulties experienced by the farming households who were obliged to leave their ancestral farmland due to the government-led relocation of housing to remote areas, without involving the transfer of farmland.[7] Wang (2021) referred to the issues

[6] See Kaneko (2014).

[7] See Li (2016) and Hayashi (2000).

of the decision-making process in the rural society's system as a background reason of such isolation of the disaster-affected population from their means of livelihood.

In 2020, a follow-up survey was conducted by the team led by Prof. Wang at Sichuan University with the purpose of identifying a variety of elements of post-disaster recovery in the long run, based on the perception of the disaster-affected people particularly in the autonomous areas of the Qiang ethnic group. Specifically, the team conducted interviews with a total of 183 randomly selected households in Beichuan district and Anzhu district in Mianyang city. Beichuan lost 15,000 people, or 40% of the total population of 35,000, due to the landslides triggered by the earthquake, and its city center was targeted for complete relocation to a safer area 20 km away via the coupling assistance provided by Shandong province. Conversely, Anzhu district was reconstructed in the same location based on the coupling assistance provided by Liaoning province, even though it was one of the most devastated areas with 1,500 casualties. From the comparison of these two districts sharing the common characteristics of an agriculture-based local economy colored by traditional Qiang ethnic culture, as well as the impact of the Chinese government's growth-oriented economic policies as represented by the one-belt one-road concept, Prof. Wang implies that the Beichuan district has shown a lesser degree of recovery in this survey, probably as a result of the policy design of the relocation.

As for the housing recovery, in both districts, the majority of the interviewed households had a certification of housing damage at the level of entire destruction, and 80% of them successfully achieved housing reconstruction within three years, but the mode of such reconstruction differs between the two districts. Namely, 30% of interviewees in Beichuan districts were involved in the collective relocation, while 20% came under the land-readjustment project. In Anzhu, merely 5% of interviewees were involved in the collective relocation, and merely 6% participated in the land-readjustment, while the rest of the households reconstructed on the original ground (Chap. 5 , Fig. 2).

Such difference in the mode of reconstruction was a result of top-down decisions by the governmental plan, instead of the choice of individual households. But 70% of the interviewees answered positively about such governmental leadership (Chap. 5, Fig. 3). On the other hand, the same survey detected deteriorating community bonds, as identified by the fact that merely 14 among the total of 183 households answered that they participate in the local disaster prevention activities. Prof. Wang assumes that the top-down approach constantly taken by the government in the recovery process might have impeded the recovery of the autonomous functioning of each community.

As for the economic recovery, 50% of the interviewees answered that the local economy has grown to better than the pre-disaster period (Chap. 5, Fig. 4). Among the 106 households which answered that their business was affected by the earthquake, 46 said their status has improved due to the growth of the regional economy (Chap. 5, Fig. 5). However, if we turn our eyes to the situation of each individual household, while 60% of the interviewees restarted their job within one year from the earthquake, and 60% among them could maintain the same job they used to have, 30% of them stated their business has not recovered to the pre-earthquake level, and 25% of the interviewees remained silent (Chap. 5, Fig. 6).

As for the population change, the gap between the two districts is evident. In Beichuan, 70% of the interviewees answered that the local population has decreased, while 30% in Anzhu answered similarly (Chap. 5, Fig. 7). Such perception of the local people also corresponds to the census. Prof. Wang tends to estimate that the gaps in several aspects of Beichuan's recovery reveals the limitations of the recovery planning designed by the government, which lacked sufficient consideration on the aspect of livelihood. If a participatory approach had been taken in the process of recovery planning, more consideration for the economy and livelihoods could have been incorporated in the succeeding steps.

7 Typhoon Yolanda Recovery: Resilience of Informal Sector

Chapter 6 of this volume is a report from Tacloban, the capital city of Leyte island in the Philippines and one of the areas most seriously damaged by Typhoon Yolanda, which hit the country on November 7th through 8th in 2013 and took more than 8,000 lives nationwide. The research team at the University of the Philippines headed by Prof. Ebinezar Florano conducted a questionnaire survey in February through March in 2020, under a special permit by the city government of Tacloban, with 100 randomly selected households in two village communities (barangay) which were subject to the construction ban within 40 m from the coast line, for the purpose of ascertaining the status of life recovery of the village population in the long run.

Earlier in March 2014, four months after the typhoon, the joint research team of Kobe University and the University of the Philippines conducted a field survey in Tacloban, which identified different contexts of gaps between the barangays with different demographic structures: barangays consisting of low income households often lacked formal title for residing in the coastal area and were facing the risk of compulsory eviction under the construction ban, despite their livelihood being linked to the seaside, while the barangays of richer classes were critical of the scarcity of governmental support that only focused on housing support for the low income population affected by the dwelling construction ban. In other words, low income barangays were faced with the dilemma of safety versus livelihood, while the rich barangays were critical of the redistribution policy-oriented usage of the disaster recovery budget.

The joint research team has formed a hypothetical view that the autonomy of the basic level of barangays secured by the 1991 Local Government Code of the Philippines has enabled each barangay, whether it is for the rich class or for informal residents, a chance for collective decision-making on the community's recovery, which may have resulted in the different status of life recovery of each village's population in the long run.

Accordingly, after eight years along each community's recovery path, this interview survey in 2020 was conducted by the leadership of Prof. Florano with a focus on two barangays, namely, Barangay 60A which used to have a population of 1,600, including those who resided in the coastal area without formal title in order to make a living in fishery or ran a small-scale business as their livelihood, and Barangay 90 which used to have a population of 400 mostly middle- to high-income class residents, including the Tacloban mayor's family. Both barangays were equally seriously damaged by the storm surge brought by the Typhoon that reached nearly one kilometer inland, in response to which the construction ban of 40 m from the coast was equally applied by the Tacloban city government.

According to the interview results, housing recovery shows a different status between the two target barangays (Chap. 6, Table 3). Prior to the typhoon, in terms of the status of property ownership, more than 50% of interviewees in Barangay 60A answered that they lacked formal title or in other words were squatters, while almost all interviewees in Barangay 90 were formal landowners. All interviewees in both barangays lost their houses in the typhoon, and all of them have reconstructed their housing by now.

As for the household economy, 40% of the interviewed households in Barangay 60A have seen an increase in income compared to the pre-disaster period, while only 30% answered their income decreased. But in Barangay 90, 70% of the interviewees reported a decrease in income. The results of the "Recovery Calendar" also revealed a difference between the two barangays, such that the majority of the interviewees in Barangay 60A felt attaining safety (Question 2 (2)) and the settling of daily life (Question 2 (7)) within one year from the typhoon, while the interviewees in Barangay 90 took four years in many aspects of the "Recovery Calendar" (Table 7 of Chap. 6).

However, the perception of interviewees in the two barangays differ on the status of regional economy to the converse. The most frequent answers in Barangay 60A said that the recovery of the regional economy is merely 40–50% of the pre-typhoon status, while the answers in Barangay 90 described it as 60–80% (Table 8 of Chap. 6). While 70% of the answers in Barangay 60A and 80% of the answers in Barangay 90 equally emphasized the role of the government to guide the economic recovery, the ratio of households which had access to governmental support was limited to 14% in Barangay 60A and 8% in Barangay 90 (Table 9 of Chap. 6).

The government census tells that the population change during this period of post-typhoon recovery shows a remarkable decrease in both barangays: from 1,640 to 923 in Barangay 60A, and from 382 to 61 in Barangay 90. Asked about the causes of this population drain, the most frequent answer in Barangay 60A was the shortage of job opportunities, while the answers in Barangay 90 referred to the lack of infrastructure for living (Table 8 of Chap. 6). Asked about the community activities, answers in Barangay 60A described an active status of various communal functions such as joint efforts for environmental conservation and town-planning, while an 80% majority of the answers in Barangay 90 reflected the desire of residents to restore traditional festivals, as if reflecting a pessimistic view on the continuation of old customs due to the serious post-disaster population drain.

Thus, the survey by the team led by Prof. Florano has identified a unique contrast between Barangay 60A as a typical low income area and Barangay 90 as a typical high class area, and he tends to explain this difference as evidence of the resilience of the communities which have been facing difficulties since a long time before the disaster and hence have developed a community culture to jointly overcome the difficulties. Another implication may be the effect of the social-oriented recovery policy of the city government of Tacloban toward considerations for the vulnerable class. A remaining question is the outcomes of the drastic population drain, especially in the high-income village of Barangay 90 that saw an 80% decrease, which may invite a debate on the validity of the safety measure which merely applied the construction ban of 40-m width without providing any support or guidance for collective relocation. It is assumed that most of the communities put under such a ban without support will result in an inevitable disintegration of resident numbers, unless such a community has maintained a particularly strong bond as seen in Barangay 60A.

8 Implications from a Comparative Perspective

(1) Trade-off Between Safety and Livelihood

A comparative perspective in this volume, covering the recovery experience from mega-disasters across Asia, has enabled us to induce certain common lessons for the policy prioritization for the betterment of recovery planning toward the future. A recurring issue across the target Asian cases has been the trade-off between safety and livelihood that many of the affected households and communities were destined to face. That is, whether to leave a disaster risk area and choose safety at the sacrifice of their livelihood, or to stay in such area in order to continue making a living for survival. The result of such a choice seems to inevitably differ between the high-income class which can afford to choose safety (as seen in the cases of Neuheun village in Aceh and Barangay 90 in Tacloban), and the low-income class who have the indispensable basis of their livelihood in a high-risk area (as seen in Lambada Lhok village in Aceh and Barangay 60A in Tacloban). Governmental intervention is supposed to be designed to mitigate such a gap, so as to avail access to both safety and livelihoods for vulnerable populations and communities.

However, the joint survey has identified the tendency that most governments act toward the deterioration of the conflict between safety and livelihood. In East Japan, post-disaster public works have been constantly prioritizing the construction of safety infrastructure since the 1923 Great Kanto Earthquake, which compels the long-term suspension of housing and livelihood reconstruction of disaster-affected people who must either continue to stay in temporary shelter for several years or decide to leave the community; the surveys in this volume (Chaps. 2 and 3) have revealed the negative outcomes of this on livelihoods in terms of deteriorating household income and regional economy. The Sichuan Earthquake is another example of government prioritization of safety infrastructure in many "twin assistance" cases, which despite its evident superiority in terms of speed, was even more severe given the more compulsory nature of the governmental decision. In the results of this joint survey in Beichuan district, where the relocation of an entire city was forcibly implemented, the difficulties placed on household livelihoods were evident compared to Anzhu district, where individual construction was conducted on the original land. Similarly, in Tacloban in the Philippines, the governmental safety standard that imposed the 40-m construction ban seemed to have triggered the serious population drain.

In Aceh after the Indian Ocean Tsunami, even though the initial safety blueprint presented by the central government was rejected by the local communities, which instead each chose their own ways of pursuing safety, the outcomes seem to be similar to other countries' cases in the sense that the choice was between either safety or livelihoods. Even in the case of Lambung village, where the Japanese ODA seemed to have provided a choice of both safety and livelihood, this joint study has detected an implication that there has been a population drain, particularly of the vulnerable population who lacked formal title or could not afford to remain, which reminds us of the similar phenomenon frequently observed in East Japan.

(2) Implication from the Recovery Calendar on Time Factors

Such tendency of a deteriorating trade-off between safety and livelihood can be learned from the time frame suggested by the results of "Recovery Calendars". Among the 12 indicators included in the "Recovery Calendar," if we assume that: Question 2 (11) "local roads have been repaired" represents the progress of the post-disaster public works for safety, while Question 2 (2) "thought it is now safe" represents the attainment of safety; Question 2 (5) "have finally resolved housing problems" represents the attainment of housing recovery; Question 2 (6) "household budget has recovered" represents household livelihood recovery; Question 2 (7) "daily life has settled down" and Question 2 (9) "self-perception as a disaster victim has disappeared" represents the status of psychological recovery, while Question 2 (8) "local activities have returned to normal" represents community reconstruction; and Question 2 (10) "Regional economy has escaped the effects of the disaster" as an indicator of local economy, then we may describe the similarities and differences of the recovery path of each case of Asian disaster recovery more visibly.

In Aceh, for example, obvious delay was seen in Lambung's "Recovery Calendar" (Fig. 10) in the timing of attainment of the completion of infrastructure (Question 2 (11)), and also the attainment of housing recovery (Question 2 (5)), livelihood

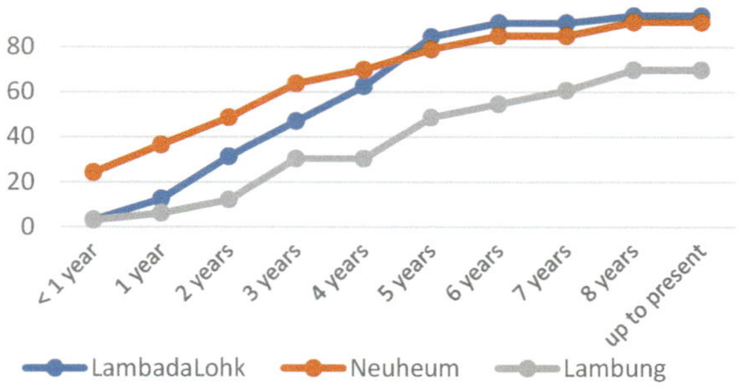

Fig. 1 Aceh recovery calendar: "Safety" (Question 2(2), %)

recovery (Question 2 (6)) as well as the community reconstruction (Question 2 (8)), when compared to other villages (Figs. 8 and 9). In particular, Neuheun village shows the earliest attainment in most of the elements of "Recovery Calendar", except the slowness of local economic recovery which may naturally reflect the geological distance from the commercial center of the Aceh city (Figs. 1, 2, 3, 4, 5, 6 and 7).

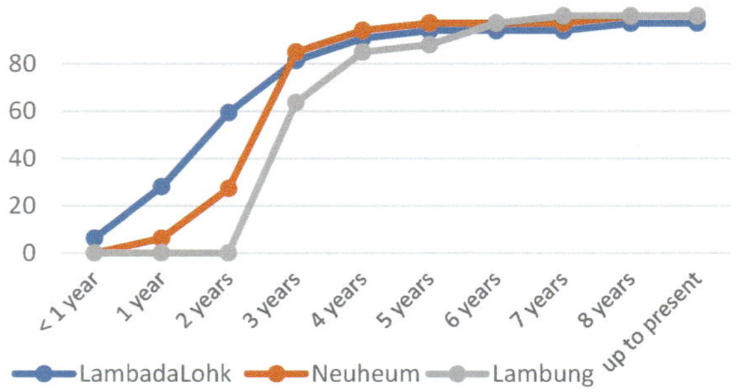

Fig. 2 Aceh recovery calendar: Housing (Question 2(5), %)

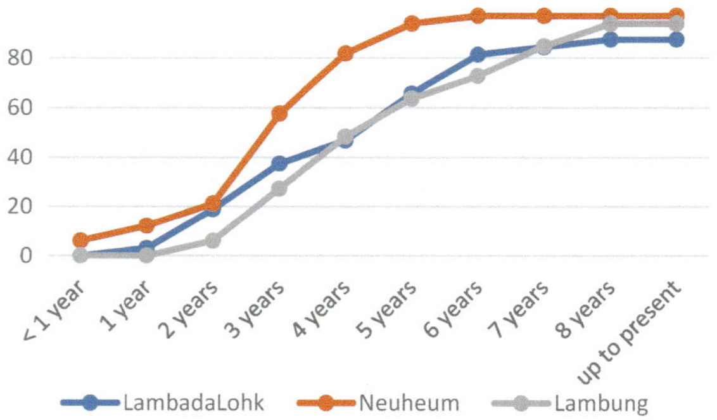

Fig. 3 Aceh recovery calendar: Household budget (Question 2(6), %)

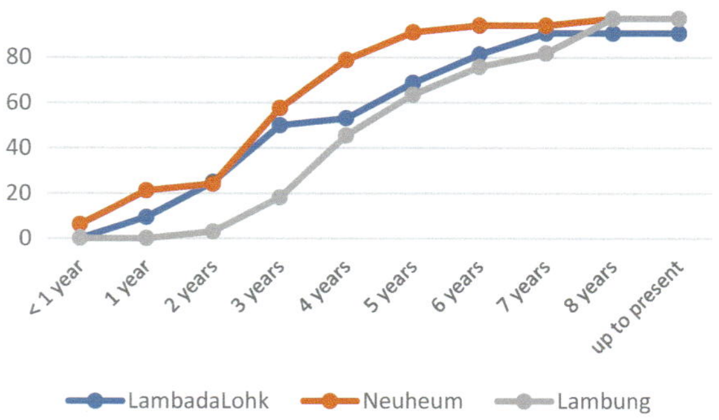

Fig. 4 Aceh recovery calendar: Community (Question 2(8), %)

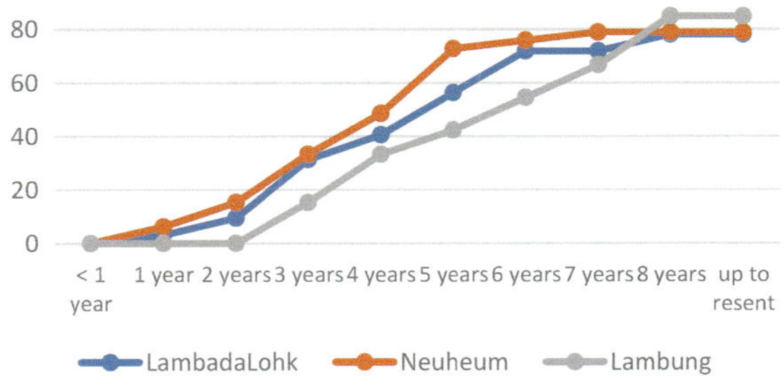

Fig. 5 Aceh recovery calendar: Perception as a victim (Question 2(9), %)

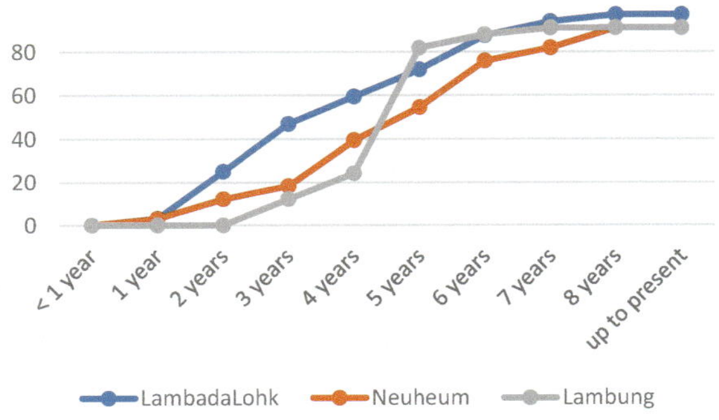

Fig. 6 Aceh recovery calendar: Local economy (Question 2(10), %)

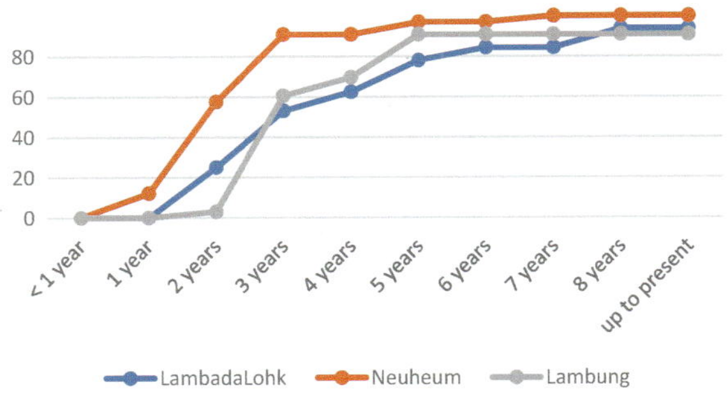

Fig. 7 Aceh recovery calendar: Infrastructure (Question 2(11), %)

Also in Sichuan Earthquake affected areas in China, almost all factors of the "Recovery Calendar" reveals the slowness of the recovery progress in Beichuan district where the entire city relocation was conducted by the governmental recovery plan, compared to these of Anzhu district which selected the reconstruction in the original place (Figs. 11, 12, 13, 14, 15, 16, 17, 18, and 19). Even the perception of safety (Question 2 (2)), which has been the primary goal of the entire relocation of Beichuan, has revealed the slower progress compared to Anzhu. The mental recovery

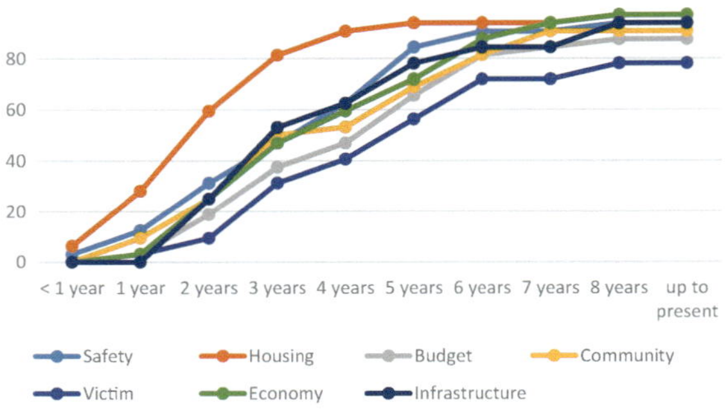

Fig. 8 Aceh recovery calendar: Lambada Lohk (RALAS) (%)

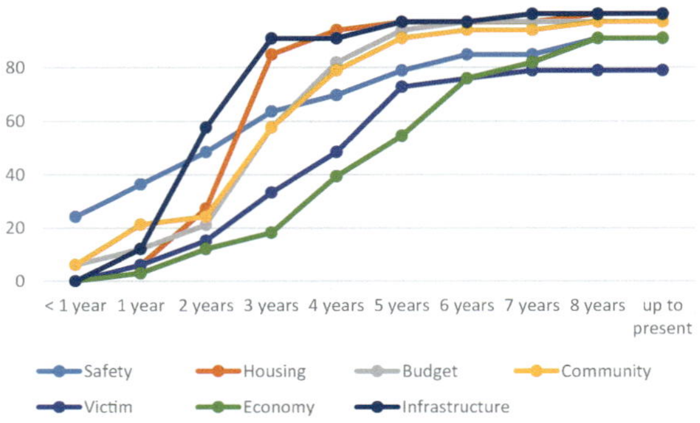

Fig. 9 Aceh recovery calendar: Neuheum (Relocation) (%)

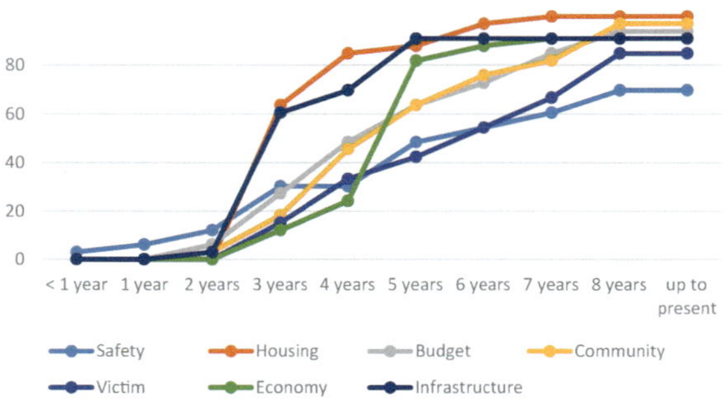

Fig. 10 Aceh recovery calendar: Lambung (Land Readjustment) (%)

represented by the cessation of perception as a disaster victim (Question 2(9)) was a rare element that Beichuan showed a better recovery than Anzhu in the early stages, but has result in a reverse in a long run.

In Tacloban where the permanent dwelling ban has been applied to the coastal areas, Barangay 60A as a lower income community shows a quicker recovery in

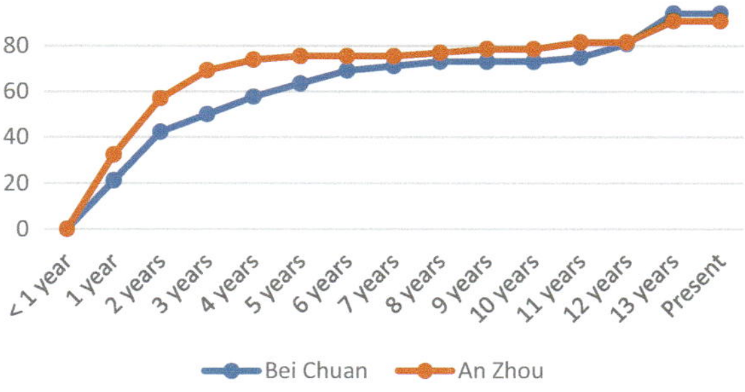

Fig. 11 Sichuan recovery calendar: "Safety" (Question 2(2), %)

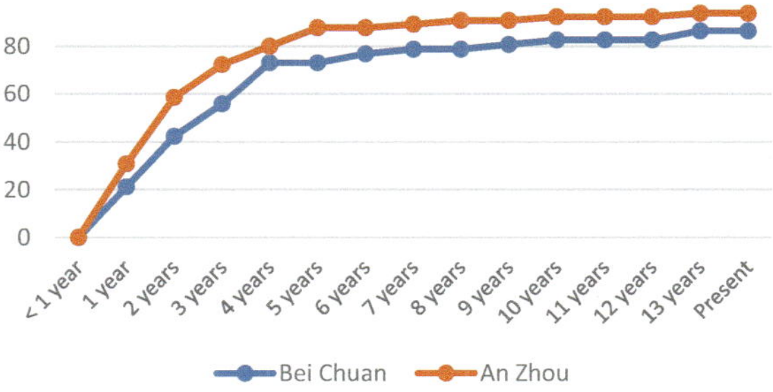

Fig. 12 Sichuan recovery calendar: Housing (Question 2(5), %)

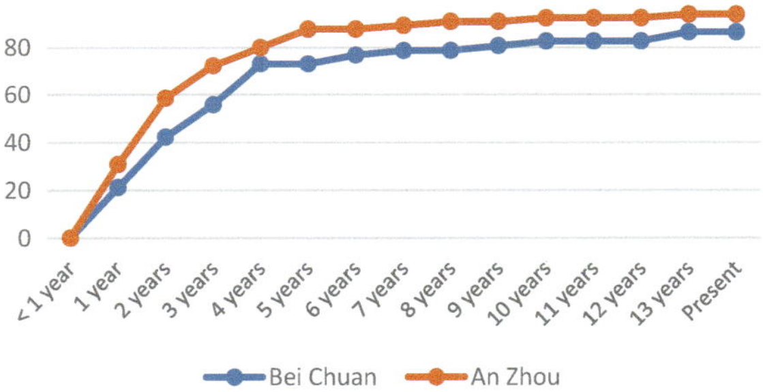

Fig. 13 Sichuan recovery calendar: Household budget (Question 2(6), %)

almost all elements of "Recovery calendar" when compared to these of Barangay 90 representing a high income class (Figs. 20, 21, 22, 23, 24, 25, 26 and 27).

These difference imply a tendency that the governmental intervention into the communities' safety through the construction works or dwelling bans has caused a severer effect on the life reconstruction of the affected population and the communities, which is making the alternative choice between safety and livelihood more severe, instead of mitigating such difficulties.

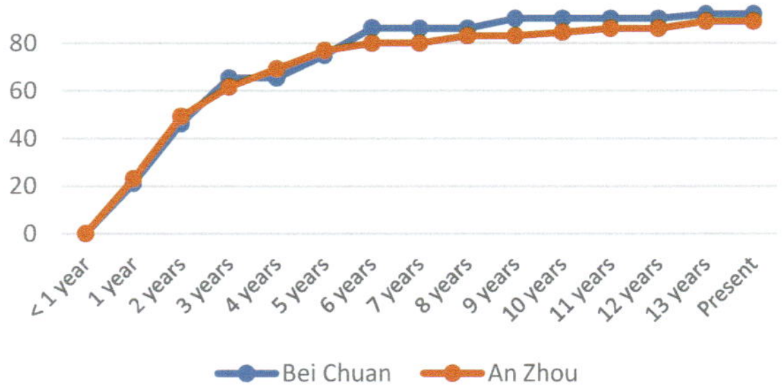

Fig. 14 Sichuan recovery calendar: Community (Question 2(8), %)

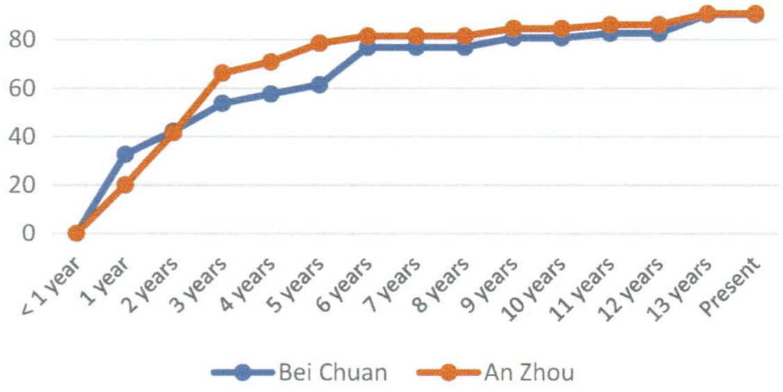

Fig. 15 Sichuan recovery calendar: Perception as a victim (Question 2(9), %)

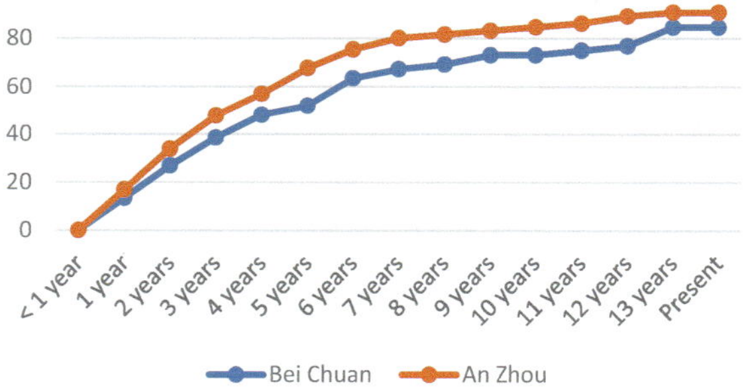

Fig. 16 Sichuan recovery calendar: Local economy (Question 2(10), %)

Further, international comparison across the disasters reveal certain similar phenomena. Comparing the "Recovery Calendars" of Lambung village in Aceh (Fig. 10) and Rikuzen-Talata in East Japan (Figs. 28 and 29), both commonly applied a Japanese style land-readjustment project, we can notice a plenty of similar trends such as the prolonged delay in the attainment of the safety (Question 2 (2)), mental

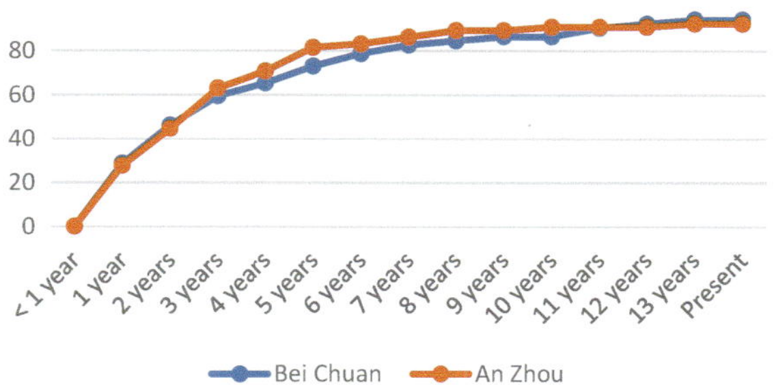

Fig. 17 Sichuan recovery calendar: Infrastructure (Question 2(11), %)

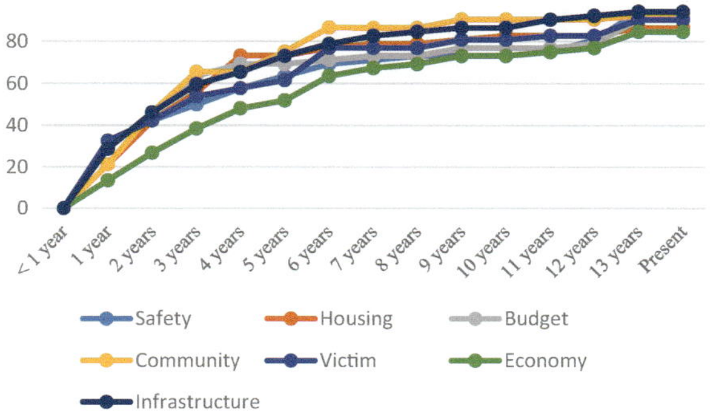

Fig. 18 Sichuan recovery calendar: Beichuan (Collective relocation) (%)

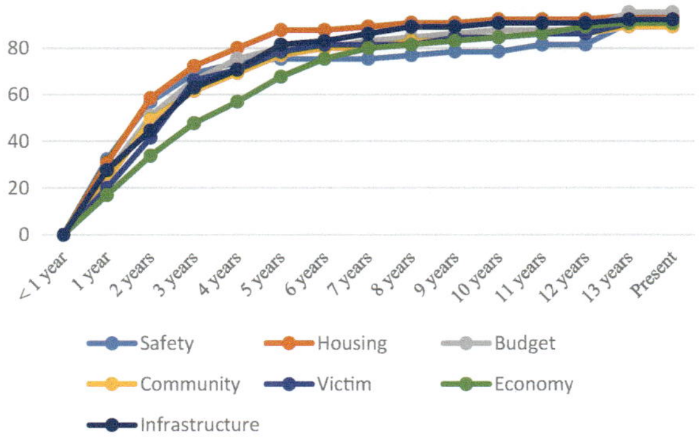

Fig. 19 Sichuan recovery calendar: An Zhou district (%)

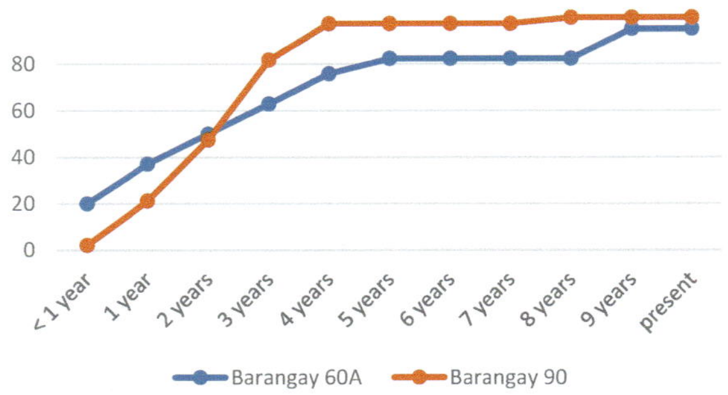

Fig. 20 Tacloban recovery calendar: "Safety" (Question 2(2), %)

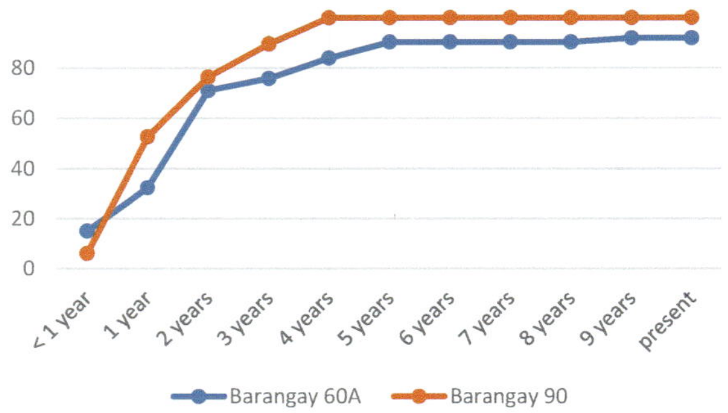

Fig. 21 Tacloban recovery calendar: Housing (Question 2(5), %)

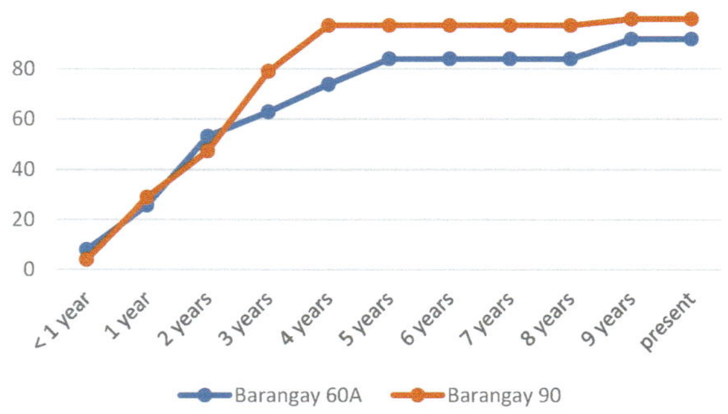

Fig. 22 Tacloban recovery calendar: Household budget (Question 2(6), %)

perception as victims (Question 2 (9)) and local economy (Question 2(10)), even after the attainment of the long awaited reconstruction of housing (Question 2(5)) following the completion of public construction works (Question 2(11)).

Differences are seen between the areas which applied the relocation meant for the choice of safety, reflecting the length of construction works which compelled the

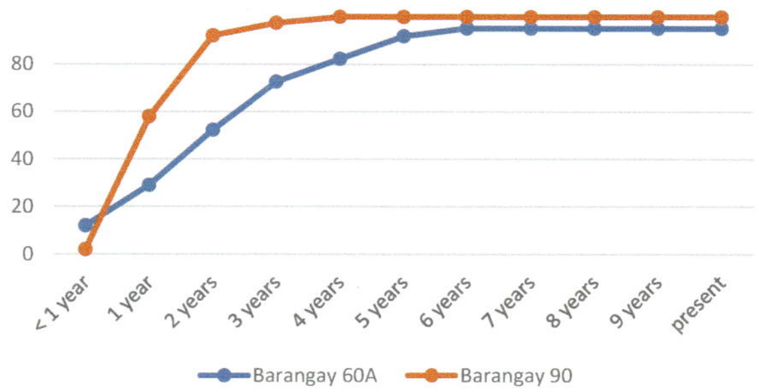

Fig. 23 Tacloban recovery calendar: Community (Question 2(8), %)

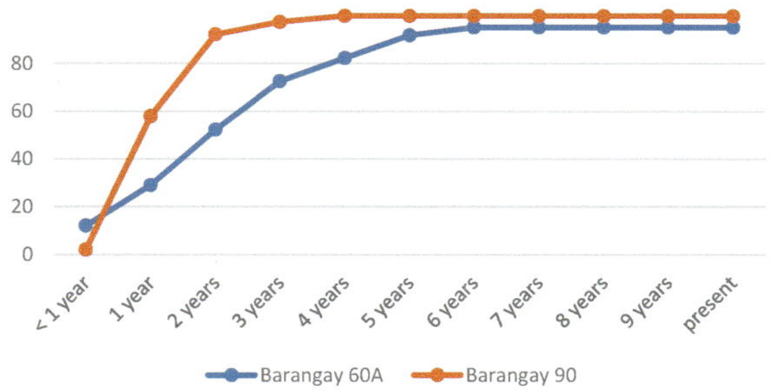

Fig. 24 Tacloban recovery calendar: Perception as a victim (Question 2(9), %)

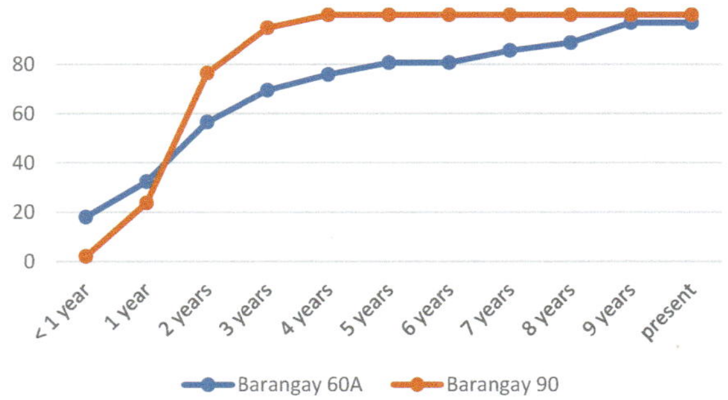

Fig. 25 Tacloban recovery calendar: Local economy (Question 2(10), %)

suspension of life reconstruction for certain period. Comparing the "Recovery Calendars" between Neuheun village in Aceh (Fig. 9) and Beichuan district in Sichuan (18), the former constantly shows speedier attainment for the elements of housing and infrastructure reconstruction such that 80% of interviewees answered to attain

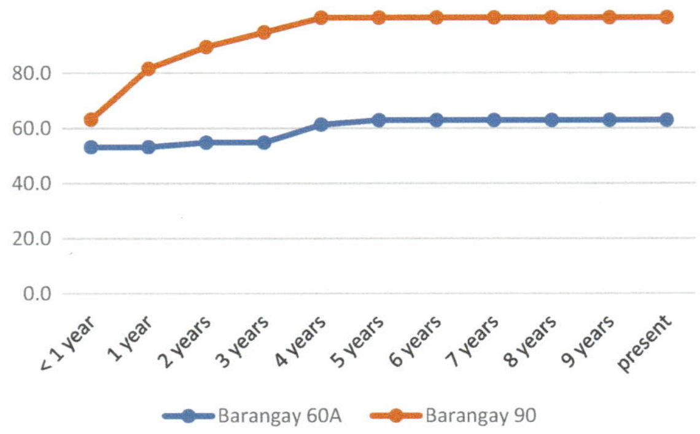

Fig. 26 Tacloban recovery calendar: Infrastructure (Question 2(11), %)

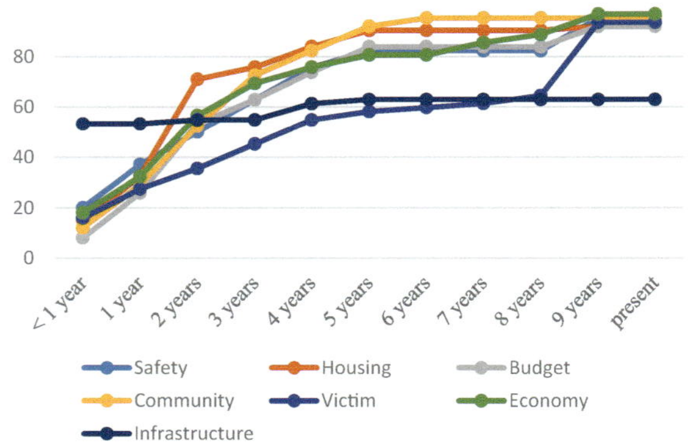

Fig. 27 Tacloban recovery calendar: Barangay 60A (%)

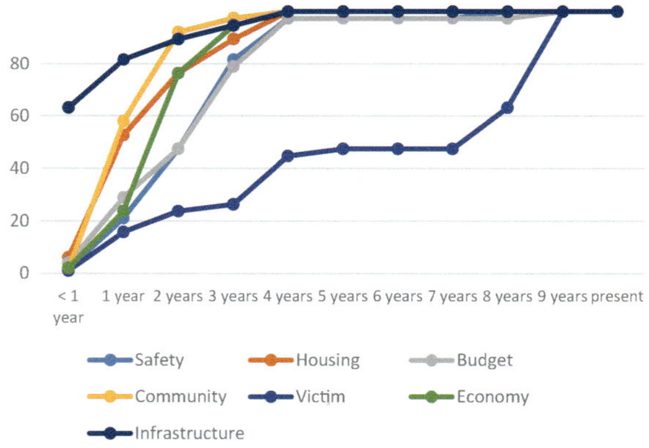

Fig. 28 Tacloban recovery calendar: Barangay 90 (%)

them within two years or three, but the latter needed six to seven year to attain the same. It even took twelve years until 80% of Beichuan interviewees felt to have attained the recovery of local economy. Similarly to this difference, the "Recovery Calendar" of Masaki area in Ofunato city in East Japan where a flexible "insertion" method of relocation was applied so as to let small number of residents to relocate in nearby vacant lots, instead of obliging them to wait for years until the completion of the construction works for building new town, showed a speedier housing recovery and also the recovery of local economy (Fig. 2 of Chap. 5), while Akahama area in Otsuchi town where the long delay of relocation works was caused by the land taking by the government for clearing new lots has showed enormous delay in all aspects of "Recovery Calendar" (Fig. 3 of Chap. 5).

These similar results teach us the common tendencies across the national borders in the evaluation by the disaster affected population on the results of governmental construction works for safety, calling for the governmental efforts for realizing a design of speedier works which enable the reconstruction of an integrated functioning of communities in both terms of dwelling and livelihood, instead of spending years for aiming at the construction of great cities (Figs. 30 and 31) .

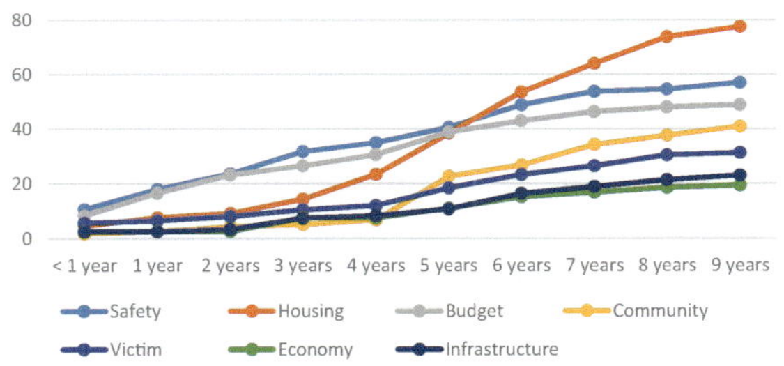

Fig. 29 East Japan earthquake recovery calendar: Rikuzentakata (Land Readjustment) (%)

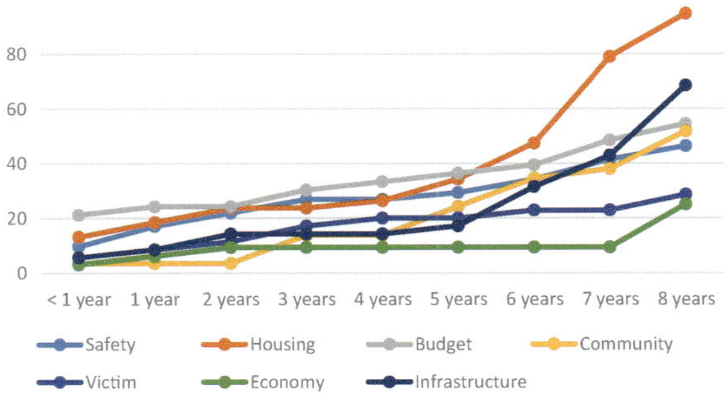

Fig. 30 East Japan earthquake recovery calendar: Ohtsuchi akahama (Relocation) (%)

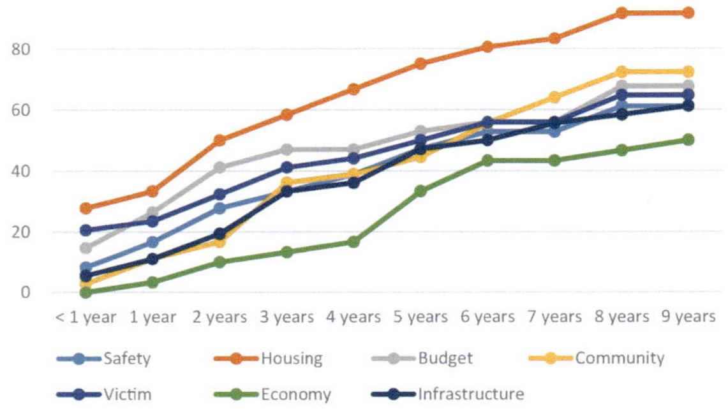

Fig. 31 East Japan earthquake recovery calendar: Ohfunato matsaki (Relocation) (%)

(3) Government Role Toward the Concurrent Attainment of Safety and Livelihood

For the purpose of realizing the build back safer spirit as emphasized in the United Nations' Sendai Framework for Disaster Risk Reduction, a concurrent achievement of safety and livelihood should be placed as a goal for future policy setting, especially for the vulnerable groups of people who tend to sacrifice their safety in order to achieve survival. Then, what is the role of the government to support the disaster-affected population toward the achievement of both safety and livelihood, instead of worsening the dilemma? The succeeding chapters in this volume will attempt to induce some hints to answer this question, particularly including the following aspects.

First, the authoritarian approach that the Asian countries' governments have been accustomed to in planning and conducting the post-disaster town building since the twentieth century modernist time should come to an end, because of its failure in attaining post-disaster recovery goals. The best policy mix cannot be reached without realizing substantive disclosure of information to local communities, with utmost effort at guidance to help people understand such information, which should be the basis of reasonable consideration by individuals and community reconstruction.

Second, in particular, such information disclosure should include the government's role to realize substantive discussion on the choices for safety, based on an established participatory procedure. This is a necessary basis for building a safer community through not only the increased awareness of the local people, but also to avoid governmental failure in setting a standard of safety which is unacceptable in the eyes of local communities and thus inviting dissatisfaction and ignorance, or a large population drain. The multiple approach applied by the government to the safety projects in East Japan, which set a second-class safety of Level-1, was meaningless for the local people who had to wait for the completion of such works for several years, as shown in the results of "Recovery Calendar"; the construction ban demarcated at 40 m has also been unreasonable for many Filipinos in the Tacloban barangays who continue their livelihood in risk areas. Elaboration of legal design should be continued, as attempted in the post- Hanshin-Awaji Earthquake recovery (Kaneko 2016).

Third, the government's role to concurrently incorporate both safety and livelihood considerations in its recovery planning. To realize this goal, this joint survey has identified a few cases of successful cooperation between the local government and communities through the inclusive participation of various institutions representing the variety of interests in each community. A further empirical approach to such cases will guide us to a new mode of disaster recovery through a genuine interaction between the government and the affected population.

References

Hayashi, Haruo. 2000. *Kobe city disaster recovery overview and validation –livelihood reconstruction topic report*, research center for disaster reduction systems technical report. Disaster Prevention Research Institute, Kyoto University

Honjo, Yuichi, Toyoda, Toshihisa, Hokugo Akihiko, Kaneko Yuka, Shiomi Yumi, Pinheiro Abel T. K., Yegane Ghezelloo. 2021. The causal factors on the degree of achievement of reconstruction based on the subjectivity of the victims—Resident questionnaire survey on the lives and livelihoods recovery in 2020. *Institute of Social Safety Science Special Edition on East Japan Earthquake* 10: 5–10

Kaneko, Yuka. 2014. Procedural requirements enabling the participatory decision-making in the disaster recovery: a comparative study of cases in Japan, Thailand and Indonesia. *Journal of International Corporation Studies (kobe University)* 21 (2–3): 1–40.

Kaneko, Yuka. 2015. Loss compensation for civil property rights and the judicial access in disaster recovery in Asia. *Journal of International Corporation Studies (kobe University)* 22 (2–3): 1–40.

Kaneko, Yuka. 2016. Lessons from post-2011 East Japan earthquake recovery: issues of participation and early recovery. In *Asian law in disasters: Toward a human-centered recovery*. eds. Kaneko Y., Matsuoka K. & Toyoda, T, pp. 15–46. Routledge

Kaneko, Yuka. 2021. Balancing of the State responsibility for safety and disaster victims' right of reconstruction: A lesson from the Great East Japan earthquake recovery. in *Build Back Better: Challenges of Asian Disaster Recovery*, ed. Toyoda T., Wang J. & Kaneko, Y. Springer

Kimura, Reo, Hayashi, Haru, Tatsuki, Shigeo, and Tamura, Keiko. 2001. Determinants and timing of housing reconstruction decisions by the victims of the 1995 Hanshin-Awaji Earthquake Disaster: A 2001 replication. *Journal of Social Safety Science* 3:23-32(in Japanese)

Recovery Agency Great East Japan Earthquake Livelihood Recovery Survey Team. 2016. *Survey on the recovery of livelihoods after 5 years from the great east japan earthquake and tsunami* (in Japanese) *Studies* 22(2). Kobe University

Taqwaddin Husin and Teuku Alvisyahrin. 2013. Role of community and communal law of Aceh in the Great Sumatra earthquake and Tsunami recovery: A case study in Lambada in the Lhok Village, Aceh Besar District, Aceh, Indonesia. *Journal of International Cooperation Studies,* 22(2). Kobe University

Taqwaddin, Husin and Teuku, Alvisyahrin. 2016. The legal framework of community-based land administration in Tsunami-Impacted areas of aceh: a case study in Baitussalam Sub-District, Aceh Besar District, Indonesia. In *Asian law in disasters: Toward a human-centered recovery*, eds. Kaneko Y., Matsuoka K. and Toyoda, T. Routledge

Tatsuki, Shigeo. 2013. What is important for reconstructing livelihoods? a comparison of the results of livelihood recovery surveys after the hanshin-awaji earthquake and the great East Japan earthquake, *Toshi Seisaku*, (161): 86-103 (in Japanese)

Wang, Jinping. 2021. A major legal issues ub the post-wenchuan earthqauke restration and reconstruction: From the perspective of 'property donation' in Beichuan Old County. In *Build back better: Challenges of Asian disaster recovery,* eds. Toyoda T., Wang J. & Kaneko, Y. Springer

Resident Questionnaire Survey on the Lives and Livelihoods Recovery in the Devastated Area After Ten Years from the Great East Japan Earthquake and Tsunami: Overall Results Review

Akihiko Hokugo, Yuka Kaneko, Yuichi Honjo, Toshihisa Toyoda, Yumi Shiomi, Abel Táiti Konno Pinheiro, and Yegane Ghezelloo

1 Introduction

(1) Objective of this paper

This paper is a summary of the result of simple tabulation of the responses to the resident questionnaire survey on livelihood recovery conducted by the author group (in March, July, and October 2020) in the coastal disaster areas of Iwate and Miyagi prefectures, leading up to the 10-year anniversary of the Great East Japan Earthquake.

A feature of this survey is that it was intended to evaluate recovery from the perspective of the residents who directly suffered damage in the coastal areas of

A. Hokugo
Graduate School of International Cooperation Studies, Graduate School of Engineering, Research Center for Urban Safety and Security, Kobe University, Kobe, Japan

Y. Kaneko (✉)
Kobe University Center for Social System Innovation, Kobe, Japan
e-mail: ykaneko@kobe-u.ac.jp

Y. Honjo · T. Toyoda
Graduate School of Disaster Resilience and Governance, University of Hyogo, Kobe, Japan

T. Toyoda
Kobe University, Kobe, Japan

Y. Shiomi
Asian Disaster Reduction Center, Kobe, Japan

A. T. K. Pinheiro
Disaster Reduction and Human Renovation Institution, Kobe, Japan

Y. Ghezelloo
Architecture and Urbanism, Graduate School of Engineering, Kobe University, Kobe, Japan

Y. Kaneko et al. (eds.), *Recovery of Disaster Victims*, Kobe University Monograph Series in Social Science Research, https://doi.org/10.1007/978-981-99-2957-3_2

Iwate and Miyagi prefectures that were inundated by the tsunami after the Great East Japan Earthquake. Recovery evaluations have been carried out by the Reconstruction Agency and the affected prefectures each year since the earthquake, but they are mainly an evaluation regarding the progress of public reconstruction works projects, and although an awareness survey of the prefectures' residents is also taken into consideration, residents of the entire prefecture are requested to respond, which means it cannot necessarily be called a recovery evaluation by the victims in the impacted areas.[1] By distributing the questionnaire for this survey around the areas along the coast of Iwate and Miyagi prefectures that were designated as disaster risk areas and the subject of disaster-prevention group relocation projects or land-filling readjustment projects, it is intended to get closer to the actual situation of the ten years of recovery from the perspective of the victims who were directly affected by the earthquake. This survey does not cover Fukushima Prefecture, because it was considered difficult to compare the status of recovery with the two aforementioned prefectures due to the establishment of evacuation zones (difficult-to-return zones, restricted residence zones, evacuation order lifting preparation zones) arising from the accident at the Fukushima Daiichi Nuclear Power Plant.

As the implementation of this survey was delayed in some areas due to the effects of the COVID-19 pandemic, the preliminary results of the portion conducted in March 2020 (four districts in three municipalities, 1,554 questionnaires distributed) have already been reported (Hokugo et al. 2021). In this paper, we will integrate the results of the entire survey (16 districts in 13 municipalities, 7,895 questionnaires distributed), including the previously reported results, and add some consideration.

(2) Survey method

The method of this survey was a paper-based questionnaire. A total of 7,895 questionnaires were distributed using the drop-off/pick-up method to all households in the 16 districts listed in Table 1 that are in 13 municipalities in the coastal areas of Iwate and Miyagi prefectures. 1,273 responses were received (16.1% response rate). The number of valid responses is shown in the tables for each of the tabulated items that follow.

(3) Surveyed districts

The target districts of this survey are the 16 districts listed in Table 1 that are in 13 municipalities in the coastal areas of Iwate and Miyagi prefectures. The target districts were selected in accordance with the intention of the survey for an evaluation of the recovery by the people who directly suffered damage in the areas inundated by

---

[1] The recovery evaluation by Iwate Prefecture in the "Iwate Reconstruction Report 2019" (Iwate Prefecture 2019) incorporates the idea of recovery evaluation by the victims by including a "Iwate Recovery Watcher Survey" of about 150 people who live and work in the disaster area, in addition to an objective index (the "Iwate Reconstruction Index") of measurements such as the progress rate of public reconstruction works projects, population changes, and mining and industrial production indices, as well as a random "recovery awareness survey" of 5,000 people throughout the entire prefecture. However, the questions of the "Iwate Recovery Watcher Survey" mainly relate to the level of progress of the public reconstruction works projects.

Table 1 Overview of the survey

District name	Distribution period	Number distributed	Number of responses	Response rate	Remarks: outline of the reconstruction development plan, etc.
Kuwagasaki District, Miyako City, Iwate Prefecture (Kuwagasaki, Miyako)	October 2020	286	43	15.0	*Damage*: 9 m inundation height, 39 ha inundated, 57 deaths and 8 missing from the district, 800 buildings damaged, 88% completely destroyed or swept away *Reconstruction development plan*: 10.4 m seawall for Level 1 tsunamis, land readjustment project (23.8 ha). It is located outside of the floodgate construction project to protect the center of Miyako City. Construction period: FY 2012–2018. In the readjusted area there are several blocks with only a few buildings on them (as of October 2020 (Google Earth))
Central area of Yamada, Yamada Town, Iwate Prefecture (Yamada, Yamada)	October 2020	610	76	12.5	*Damage*: 7 m inundation height, 284 deaths and 5 missing from the district, 1,593 buildings damaged, 81% completely destroyed or swept away *Reconstruction development plan*: 10.4 m seawall for Level 1 tsunamis, land readjustment project (56 ha) that combines a "living town" base development project in cooperation with the chamber of commerce and industry, and public disaster housing. Construction period: FY 2012–2018. In the readjusted area there are several blocks with only a few buildings on them (as of October 2020 (Google Earth))

(continued)

Table 1 (continued)

District name	Distribution period	Number distributed	Number of responses	Response rate	Remarks: outline of the reconstruction development plan, etc.
Machikata, Otsuchi Town, Iwate Prefecture, and adjacent public disaster housing areas (Machikata, Otsuchi)	March 2020	451 (Machikata)	58	12.9	*Damage*: 10.7 m inundation height, 660 deaths and 271 missing from the district, 1,421 buildings damaged *Reconstruction development plan*: 14.5 m seawall for Level 1 tsunamis, land readjustment project (23.8 ha). Construction period: FY 2012–2018. In the readjusted area there are several blocks with only a few buildings on them (as of October 2020 (Google Earth))
	July 2020	242 (Public housing)	29	12.0	
	Subtotal	693	87	12.6	
Akahama district, Otsuchi Town, Iwate Prefecture (Akahama, Otsuchi)	March 2020	233	23	9.9	*Damage*: 12.9 m inundation height, 39 ha inundated, 90 deaths and 35 missing from the district, 230 buildings completely destroyed *Reconstruction development plan*: Maintained existing 6.4 m seawall height, land-filling readjustment project and group relocation project for Level 2 tsunamis. Construction period: FY 2012–2018. In the readjusted area there are several blocks with only a few buildings on them (as of October 2020 (Google Earth))
	July 2020	Redistribution (reminder)	25	8.7	
	Subtotal	233	48	20.6	
Hirata district, Kamaishi City, Iwate Prefecture (Hirata, Kamaishi)	October 2020	288	41	14.2	*Damage*: 10.0 m inundation height, 29 deaths from the district, 170 buildings completely destroyed *Reconstruction development plan*: 6.1 m seawall for Level 1 tsunamis (plus the seawall at the entrance to Kamaishi Bay), land-filling readjustment project. Construction period: FY 2012–2020. In the readjusted area there are several blocks with only a few buildings on them (as of October 2020 (Google Earth))

(continued)

Table 1 (continued)

District name	Distribution period	Number distributed	Number of responses	Response rate	Remarks: outline of the reconstruction development plan, etc.
Reconstruction development project district in the center of Takata-cho, Rikuzentakata City, Iwate Prefecture (Central Rikuzentakata)	October 2020	693	146	21.1	*Damage*: 17.6 m inundation height, 1,173 deaths from the district, 2,047 buildings completely destroyed *Reconstruction development plan*: 12.5 m seawall for Level 1 tsunamis, land readjustment project (186 ha in the Takata district) that integrated the raising of elevation to 16 m and created hills. Construction period: FY 2012–2020. In the readjusted area there are several blocks with no buildings on them (as of October 2020 (Google Earth))
Voluntary relocation district north of Takata-cho, Rikuzentakata City, Iwate Prefecture (Takata-kita, Rikuzentakata)	October 2020	539	95	17.6	Affected households that chose to relocate voluntarily to higher ground inland, instead of waiting for the completion of the reconstruction development project, gathered at the periphery of an existing village
Suezaki district, Ofunato City, Iwate Prefecture (Suezaki, Ofunato)	October 2020	500	41	8.2	*Damage*: 11 m inundation height, 42 deaths and 22 missing from the district, 505 buildings completely destroyed *Reconstruction development plan*: 7.2 m seawall for Level 1 tsunamis (plus seawall at the entrance to the bay), a speedy disaster-prevention group relocation project in the form of infilling vacant land. Construction period: FY 2012–2013

(continued)

Table 1 (continued)

District name	Distribution period	Number distributed	Number of responses	Response rate	Remarks: outline of the reconstruction development plan, etc.
Shishiori district, Kesennuma City, Miyagi Prefecture (Shishiori, Kesennuma)	March 2020	516	79	15.3	*Damage*: 7 m inundation height, 206 deaths from the district, 1,055 buildings completely destroyed *Reconstruction development plan*: 5.0 m seawall for Level 1 tsunamis, land-filling readjustment project (41.8 ha), disaster public housing (200 apartments). Construction period: FY 2013–2020. In the readjusted area there are several blocks with only a few buildings on them (as of October 2020 (Google Earth))
Shizugawa-higashi, Shizugawa-chuo and Shizugawa-nishi districts, Minamisanriku Town, Miyagi Prefecture (Shizugawa, Minamisanriku)	October 2020	758	132	17.4	*Damage*: 15.5 m inundation height, 254.5 ha inundated, 2,044 houses damaged, damage rate of 73.8%, 600 deaths and 211 missing from Minamisanriku Town *Reconstruction development plan*: 8.7 m seawall for Level 1 tsunamis, base development project on higher ground that links to the Sanriku Expressway, land-filling readjustment project (60.2 ha), disaster prevention group relocation project, linked to disaster public housing area. Construction period: FY 2012–2018
Shinkadonowaki district, Minato-kita district and surrounding area, Ishinomaki City, Miyagi Prefecture (Shinkadonowaki and Minato, Ishinomaki)	October 2020	520	92	17.7	*Damage*: Almost all of the central urban area of Ishinomaki city was inundated, 3,703 people deceased or missing and 20,039 buildings completely in Ishinomaki city overall *Reconstruction development plan*: 7.2 m seawall for Level 1 tsunamis, land-filling and disaster public housing complexes established via an urban reconstruction readjustment project (23.7.8 ha). Construction period: FY 2013–2019. In the readjusted area there are several blocks with only a few buildings on them (as of October 2020 (Google Earth))

(continued)

Table 1 (continued)

District name	Distribution period	Number distributed	Number of responses	Response rate	Remarks: outline of the reconstruction development plan, etc.
Shinhebita-minami district, Ishinomaki City, Miyagi Prefecture (Ayumino, Ishinomaki)	October 2020	683	98	14.3	A land readjustment project (376 households) and recovery public housing (389 households) were built as an inland relocation complex (27.4 ha). Construction period: FY 2013–2018
Higashiyamoto Station North district, Higashimatsushima City, Miyagi Prefecture (Aoi, Higashimatsushima)	July 2020	542	97	17.9	*Damage*: 36% of the city area (65% of the urban area) was inundated, 1,133 deaths and 5,513 buildings completely destroyed *Reconstruction development plan*: A group relocation site was developed via a land readjustment project for victims, who mainly relocated from the coastal Omagarihama district that suffered catastrophic damage. 307 units were constructed under a disaster public housing project. Construction period: FY 2012–2015
Arai-higashi district, Wakabayashi Ward, Sendai City, Miyagi Prefecture (Arai-higashi, Sendai)	October 2020	542	63	11.6	*Damage*: 56% of Wakabayashi Ward was inundated, 339 deaths and 6,427 buildings completely destroyed *Reconstruction development plan*: Group relocation of coastal villages from the Arahama area to the urban area, and land readjustment projects were implemented. 313 units were constructed by a public disaster housing development project. Construction period: FY 2012–2015

(continued)

Table 1 (continued)

District name	Distribution period	Number distributed	Number of responses	Response rate	Remarks: outline of the reconstruction development plan, etc.
Tamaura-nishi district, Iwanuma City, Miyagi Prefecture (Tamaura-nishi, Iwanuma)	March 2020	354	103	29.1	*Damage*: 48% of the city area (almost all of the former Tamaura Village) was inundated, 181 deaths and 736 buildings completely destroyed *Reconstruction development plan*: Group relocation of all of the coastal villages in the city area to Tamaura-nishi. The land was acquired through the purchase of agricultural and residential land, and the collective relocation site was created. 111 units were constructed in the relocation complex and 67 units in other public disaster housing. Construction period: FY 2011–2013
Shin-Sakamoto Station district, Yamamoto Town, Miyagi Prefecture (Shin-Sakamoto, Yamamoto)	July 2020	138	32	23.2	*Damage*: 40% of the entire town (60% of inhabitable land) was inundated, 637 deaths and 2,217 buildings completely destroyed *Reconstruction Development Plan*: A compact new urban area was constructed via a tsunami reconstruction base project and disaster prevention group relocation promotion project at one of the group relocation sites for the coastal villages of Yamamoto Town. Construction of 31 public disaster housing units in the relocation complex. Construction period: FY 2013–2015
Total		7,895	1,273	16.1	

Note In the tables below, the district names will be described using the abbreviations in the parentheses

the tsunami; accordingly, the districts selected were centered around those districts in tsunami-inundated coastal municipalities that were the subject of public reconstruction works projects such as disaster-prevention group relocation projects, land-filling readjustment projects and disaster public housing construction projects, due to being designated as disaster risk areas.

As shown in the Remarks column of Table 1, in the selection of the target districts, attention was given to the differences in the conditions in the recovery plan of each district, such as the reconstruction development project methods. The recovery plans for each district were based on the "multiple disaster prevention" safety measures outlined in the national government's basic reconstruction policy (published in July 2011) and centered around the construction of Level 1 tsunami (Meiji Sanriku tsunami class) seawalls and land-filling readjustment projects. However, some differences are seen in the combination of measures used, such as the establishment of disaster risk areas and disaster prevention group relocation projects, reflecting the topographical factors in each area, which resulted in differences in the safety outcomes and the length of the construction periods. Therefore, in this survey, the target districts were selected so that a comparison could be made based on the differences in the recovery plans and regional characteristics. For example, the differences between the Hirata district of Kamaishi City and the Suezaki district of Ofunato City that are both fishing villages and underwent Level 1 measures based upon "multiple disaster prevention", and the Akahama district of Otsuchi Town that pursued both Level 2 safety without relying on seawalls and the continuation of its fishery industry; the Kuwagasaki district of Miyako city and Machikata district of Otsuchi town, which was affected in regards to the industrial recovery of their fishing and seafood processing industries due to the acceptance of "multiple disaster prevention" measures; the Yamada district of Yamada town and Shizugawa district of Minamisanriku town, which committed to the recovery of their shopping streets which were connected to the location of residential areas; the central district of Rikuzentakata city that underwent wide-ranging land-filling projects that were not completed until Mach 2021; the Shishiori district of Kesennuma city, which built a large-scale disaster public housing project on land that was inundated by the tsunami; and the Ayumino district of Ishinomaki city, the Arai-higashi district of Sendai city, and the Tamaura-nishi district of Iwanuma City, which are part of new compact-city urban areas developed inland. There are some areas where several districts within the same municipality were separated and subject to different project methods; in Otsuchi town, the Machikata district was subject to a land-filling readjustment project as a measure against Level 1 tsunamis, while the Akahama district was subjected to safety measures against a Level 2 tsunami; in Rikuzentakata city, the central district was subjected to a land-filling readjustment project which reached a maximum of 16 m in height, while individual households in the Takata-kita district voluntarily relocated without waiting for the completion of the project; in Ishinomaki city, the Shinkadonowaki and Minato-kita districts had river levees, coastal levees, and high embankment roads constructed as multiple disaster protection facilities in the tsunami inundation area, while the Ayumino district is a group relocation complex established in a new urban area in the Shinhebita area, a safe inland zone.

(4) Questions asked in the survey

In this survey, the questions were extracted with a focus on the three aspects of rebuilding livelihoods, recovering local economies, and building safe local communities for the future, which are listed as the basic principles of recovery in Article 3 of the 2013 Act on Recovery from Large-Scale Disaster Recovery. Specifically, Question 1 explored the status of rebuilding livelihoods, including housing and household budgets, and the background factors, Question 3 asked about the status of recovery of the local economy, and Question 4 explored issues related to community revitalization. In this report, we the results of Question 4 have been omitted due to tabulation reasons.

In addition to the above, we inserted the so-called "recovery calendar" in Question 2. Since the Great Hanshin-Awaji Earthquake, various recovery evaluation methods have been attempted,[2] and the "Recovery Calendar" is a method arising from ethnographic surveys that emphasize the narratives of individual victims and focuses on changes in the victims' subjective sense of recovery over time. Initially, the survey consisted of six items: external factors (damage, work/school, and housing) and internal factors (inconvenient life, safety, and self-perception as a disaster victims) (Kimura et al. 2004); subsequently, items such as regional activity and the regional economy were added and it has settled as a survey of twelve items (1) grasped an overall image of the damage, (2) thought it is now safe, (3) resolved that an inconvenient life will continue for a while, (4) work has returned to normal, (5) problems with housing have been finally resolved, (6) the disaster's effect on the household budget has ended, (7) daily life has settled down, (8) local activities have returned to normal, self-perception as a disaster victim has disappeared, (10) the local economy has recovered from the effects of the disaster, (11) local roads have returned to normal, and (12) local schools have returned to normal. This method was also used in the five-year survey conducted after the Great East Japan Earthquake in cooperation with the Reconstruction Agency and the affected prefectures (Great East Japan Earthquake Livelihood Recovery Survey Team 2016).

The "recovery calendar" is a meaningful method of measuring the achievement of recovery goals based on the subjective view of the disaster victims, and although very

---

[2] In Kobe City's 5-year recovery assessment, the "7 elements of life recovery" (housing, connections, town, preparation, mind and body, lifestyle, and relationship with the government) obtained from residents' workshops were used as outcome indices (Hayashi 2000), and further indexing subsequently progressed (Kimura et al. 2001). In the 10-year assessment of the Great Hanshin-Awaji Earthquake by Hyogo Prefecture, the "3 scales of sense of life recovery" (degree of completeness of life, degree of satisfaction with life, and future prospects) were adopted, and their correlation with the above "7 elements of life recovery" was verified (Tamura et al. 2001). Recovery research based on these existing studies was also seen after the Great East Japan Earthquake. This includes Tatsuki (2013) and Matsukawa et al. (2015) which measured the differences in the "7 elements of life recovery" and "sense of livelihood recovery" by focusing on the housing reconstruction status of disaster victims, and Kawawaki (2014) that focused on community revitalization (connection and town) among the "7 elements of life recovery".

interesting results have been obtained on the differences in the timing of achievement of the 12 items by individuals and regions, it cannot be said that there has been sufficient analysis of the background factors. In this study, while relying on the 12 items used in the prior research, unique questions have been added in order to conduct a more in-depth analysis of the background factors, regarding the regional economy and regional activities in particular, and clarify the issues that remain outstanding regarding recovery.

In the portion of this survey conducted in October, some questions are slightly different from those in the March and July portions. The respondents were asked not only about their pre-earthquake employment and position, but also about their current employment and position, and in the question about the "livelihood recovery calendar" the most recent date was set to 2020.

(5) Analysis methods

The analysis methods used in this study are simple tabulation, cross tabulation and chi-square test.

(6) Structure of this paper

This paper will follow the structure of the questions in the survey; first, Sect. 2 will confirm the demographics of the respondents. Section 3 will present the results regarding the status of reconstruction of the respondents' housing. Section 4 will present the results regarding the status of recovery of the respondents' household finances. Section 5 will present the results regarding the respondents' perceptions of the reconstruction of the regional economy. Section 6 will present the results regarding the respondents' perceptions of the status of regional population recovery. Section 7 will present the results of the recovery calendar. Section 8 contains a summary with some discussion.

2 Demography of the Respondents

This section describes the attributes of the respondents. Throughout this survey, in the "Invalid responses" row of the tables that tally the responses of single-answer questions, "No response" indicates that no answer was given for the question, "Not applicable" indicates the number of respondents to whom the question did not apply, and "Unclear" indicates that blanks were entered in the raw data, such that coding was not possible.

(1) District of residence

Regarding the district the respondents currently reside in (Q1 (2)), as shown in Table 2, a total of 1,273 valid responses were obtained in the 16 target districts.

Table 2 Respondents' current area of residence (Q1 (2))

	Number	Percentage
Kuwagasaki, Miyako (land-filling readjustment, seawall)	43	3.4
Yamada, Yamada (land-filling readjustment, seawall)	76	6.0
Machikata, Otsuchi (land-filling readjustment, seawall)	87	6.8
Akahama, Otsuchi (land-filling readjustment, group relocation to higher ground)	48	3.8
Hirata, Kamaishi (land-filling readjustment, seawall)	41	3.2
Central Rikuzentakata (land-filling readjustment, group relocation to higher ground)	146	11.5
Takata-kita, Rikuzentakata (voluntary relocation near an existing village)	95	7.5
Suezaki, Ofunato (in-filling of vacant land)	41	3.2
Shishiori, Kesennuma (land-filling readjustment, seawall)	79	6.2
Shizugawa, Minamisanriku (group relocation to higher ground)	132	10.4
Shinkadonowaki and Minato, Ishinomaki (multiple disaster prevention, land readjustment)	92	7.2
Ayumino, Ishinomaki (group relocation inland)	98	7.7
Aoi, Higashimatsushima (multiple disaster prevention, group relocation)	97	7.6
Arai-higashi, Sendai (group relocation inland)	63	4.9
Tamaura-nishi, Iwanuma (multiple disaster prevention, group relocation)	103	8.1
Shin-Sakamoto, Yamamoto (multiple disaster prevention, group relocation)	32	2.5
Total	1,273	100.0

The characteristics of the reconstruction project method of each district are described in the parenthesis

(2) Age composition

Regarding the age composition of the respondents (Q1 (1)), as shown in Table 3, many of the respondents were in their 1970s, accounting for 30.7% of the valid responses. Looking at the age composition by district, while many of the respondents were in their 1970s overall, some differences appeared, such as there being relatively more respondents in their 1930s or younger and in their 1950s in the Takata-kita, Rikuzentakata district where the working-age population voluntarily relocated, and in the Ayumino, Ishinomaki district and Aoi, Higashimatsushima district, which were created as inland relocation complexes, as well as there being relatively more respondents in their 1930s or younger and 1940s in the Arai-higashi, Sendai district, which is a commuter town of a major metropolitan area; these differences were significant in the cross tabulation (P value < 0.01 in the chi-square test).

Table 3 Age composition of respondents (Q1 (1))

		Number	Percentage	Percentage of valid responses	Cumulative percentage
Valid responses	39 or under	59	4.6	4.7	4.7
	40–49	129	10.1	10.3	15.0
	50–59	208	16.3	16.5	31.5
	60–69	310	24.4	24.7	56.2
	70–79	386	30.3	30.7	86.9
	80 or older	165	13.0	13.1	100.0
	Total	1,257	98.7	100.0	
Invalid responses	No response	4	0.3		
	Unclear	12	0.9		
	Total	16	1.3		
Total		1,273	100.0		

Table 4 Gender of respondents (Q1 (1)(ii))

		Number	Percentage	Percentage of valid responses	Cumulative percentage
Valid responses	Male	621	48.8	49.2	49.2
	Female	642	50.4	50.8	100.0
	Total	1,263	99.2	100.0	
Invalid responses	No response	9	0.7		
	Unclear	1	0.1		
	Total	10	0.8		
Total			100.0		

(3) Gender

Regarding the gender of the respondents (Q1 (1)(ii)), as shown in Table 4, the ratio of male to female respondents was 49.2–50.8%

3 Housing Reconstruction Status

(1) Respondents' pre-earthquake housing type

Regarding the type of their residence before the earthquake (Q1 (3)), as shown in Table 5, the majority of respondents (66.9%) owned their own house on their own land, followed by 13.3% who lived in privately leased housing, 9.4% in public housing, 6.7% in owner-occupied houses on land subject to a registered lease, and 1.3% in owner-occupied houses on land subject to an unregistered lease. There were

Table 5 Respondents' pre-earthquake residence type (Q1 (3))

		Number	Percentage	Percentage of valid responses	Cumulative percentage
Valid responses	Own land/house	843	66.2	66.9	66.9
	Leased land/own house (registered)	84	6.6	6.7	73.6
	Leased land/own house (unregistered)	17	1.3	1.3	74.9
	Privately leased house or apartment	167	13.1	13.3	88.2
	Public housing	118	9.3	9.4	97.5
	Other	31	2.4	2.5	100.0
	Total	1,260	99.0	100.0	
Invalid responses	No response	13	1.0		
Total		1,273	100.0		

Table 6 Housing damage status based on respondents' disaster victim certification (Q1 (4))

		Number	Percentage	Percentage of valid responses	Cumulative percentage
Valid responses	Swept away	191	15.0	16.0	16.0
	Completely destroyed	705	55.4	59.0	75.0
	Mostly damaged	74	5.8	6.2	81.2
	Half-damaged	31	2.4	2.6	83.8
	Partially damaged	42	3.3	3.5	87.3
	No disaster victim certification (No response about damage)	125	9.8	10.5	97.7
	No disaster victim certification (Had damage)	9	0.7	0.8	98.5
	No disaster victim certification (No damage)	18	1.4	1.5	100.0
	Total	1,195	93.9	100.0	
Invalid responses	No response	78	6.1		
Total		1,273	100.0		

significant differences in the cross-tabulation of the type of residence by area, such as the large number of responses of "owner-occupied houses on leased land (registered)" in the Kuwagasaki, Miyako district, and the large number of responses of "privately leased house/apartment" or "other" in the Arai-Higashi, Sendai district (P values < 0.05 in the chi-square test).

(2) Respondents' housing damage status in disaster certification

Regarding the damage to houses caused by the earthquake (Q1 (4)), as shown in Table 6, if the classification under the "disaster victim certificate" issued by the government is relied upon, the majority of responses was complete destruction, at 59.0% of valid responses, followed by 16.0% that were swept away, 6.2% that were mostly damaged, 3.5% that were partially damaged, 2.6% that were half damaged, and 1.5% that were not damaged. The percentage of respondents who did not receive a "disaster victim certificate" was 12.8% in total.

Housing damage due to the earthquake by district (cross tabulation of Q1 (2) and Q1 (4)), as shown in Table 7, displays a significant difference (P value < 0.01 in the chi-square test), which appears to reflect the difference in the damage caused by inundation, tsunami fires, etc. in each district.

Also, as shown in Table 8, significant differences were found in the housing damage based on the disaster victim certification in relation to the type of residence before the earthquake (cross tabulation of Q1 (3) and Q1 (4)), such as the large number of owner-occupied houses on their own land that were swept away and the large number of owner-occupied houses on leased land that were completely destroyed (P value < 0.01 in the chi-square test).

(3) Post-earthquake housing reconstruction status

Regarding the status of post-earthquake housing reconstruction (Q1 (5)), as shown in Table 9, 43.8% of the respondents moved into public disaster housing, 15.2% rebuilt their houses in a group relocation site, 14.3% rebuilt their houses on land that was exchanged in a land readjustment project, 7.4% repaired their houses on the original site, 5.5% built new houses on the original site, and 4.9% rebuilt at a voluntary relocation site.

Looking at the housing reconstruction status by the type of residence before the earthquake (cross tabulation of Q1 (3) and Q1 (5), significant P value < 0.01 in the chi-square test), as shown in Table 10, more than 30% of households that owned their own house on their own land before the earthquake are living in disaster public housing after the earthquake. 50% of households that owned their own house on leased land before the earthquake are living in disaster public housing after the earthquake. 60% of households living in privately rented housing and almost 80% of households living in public housing before the earthquake are living in disaster public housing after the earthquake. Thus, in terms of the form of housing reconstruction 10 years after the earthquake, disaster public housing has a remarkable weighting in areas where 60% of households were completely destroyed, washed away or otherwise suffered direct damage, such as the districts where the survey was conducted.

Table 7 Housing damage by district (cross tabulation of Q1 (2) and Q1 (4))

	Swept away	Completely destroyed	Mostly damaged	Half-damaged	Partially damaged	Uncertified (Unknown)	Uncertified (Undamaged)	Uncertified (Damaged)	Total
Kuwagasaki, Miyako	2	17	5	1	0	17	0	0	42
	4.8%	40.5%	11.9%	2.4%	0.0%	40.5%	0.0%	0.0%	100.0%
Yamada, Yamada	8	50	2	2	1	11	0	0	74
	10.8%	67.6%	2.7%	2.7%	1.4%	14.9%	0.0%	0.0%	100.0%
Machikata, Otsuchi	5	69	6	2	0	0	2	0	84
	6.0%	82.1%	7.1%	2.4%	0.0%	0.0%	2.4%	0.0%	100.0%
Akahama, Otsuchi	5	26	1	1	0	0	2	8	43
	11.6%	60.5%	2.3%	2.3%	0.0%	0.0%	4.7%	18.6%	100.0%
Hirata, Kamaishi	0	13	4	2	0	15	0	0	34
	0.0%	38.2%	11.8%	5.9%	0.0%	44.1%	0.0%	0.0%	100.0%
Central Rikuzentakata	29	98	0	2	2	7	0	0	138
	21.0%	71.0%	0.0%	1.4%	1.4%	5.1%	0.0%	0.0%	100.0%
Takata-kita, Rikuzentakata	6	19	0	0	19	47	0	0	91
	6.6%	20.9%	0.0%	0.0%	20.9%	51.6%	0.0%	0.0%	100.0%
Suezaki, Ofunato	1	19	1	3	7	9	0	0	40
	2.5%	47.5%	2.5%	7.5%	17.5%	22.5%	0.0%	0.0%	100.0%
Shishiori, Kesennuma	5	46	0	3	1	0	4	9	68
	7.4%	67.6%	0.0%	4.4%	1.5%	0.0%	5.9%	13.2%	100.0%

(continued)

Table 7 (continued)

	Swept away	Completely destroyed	Mostly damaged	Half-damaged	Partially damaged	Uncertified (Unknown)	Uncertified (Undamaged)	Uncertified (Damaged)	Total
Shizugawa, Minamisanriku	50	65	3	0	0	5	0	0	123
	40.7%	52.8%	2.4%	0.0%	0.0%	4.1%	0.0%	0.0%	100.0%
Shinkadonowaki and Minato, Ishinomaki	9	65	8	1	3	4	0	0	90
	10.0%	72.2%	8.9	1.1%	3.3%	4.4%	0.0%	0.0%	100.0%
Ayumino, Ishinomaki	12	67	14	0	2	0	0	0	95
	12.6%	70.5%	14.7%	0.0%	2.1%	0.0%	0.0%	0.0%	100.0%
Aoi, Higashimatsushima	26	54	9	4	1	1	0	0	95
	27.4%	56.8%	9.5%	4.2%	1.1%	1.1%	0.0%	0.0%	100.0%
Arai-higashi, Sendai	10	27	9	3	2	9	0	0	60
	16.7%	45.0%	15.0%	5.0%	3.3%	15.0%	0.0%	0.0%	100.0%
Tamaura-nishi, Iwanuma	14	62	8	1	0	0	1	0	86
	16.3%	72.1%	9.3%	1.2%	0.0%	0.0%	1.2%	0.0%	100.0%
Shin-Sakamoto, Yamamoto	9	8	4	6	4	0	0	1	32
	28.1%	25.0%	12.5%	18.8%	12.5%	0.0%	0.0%	3.1%	100.0%
Total	191	705	74	31	42	125	9	18	1,195
	16.0%	59.0%	6.2%	2.6%	3.5%	10.5%	0.8%	1.5%	100.0%

Table 8 Housing damage by pre-earthquake residence type (cross tabulation of Q1 (3) and Q1 (4))

	Swept away	Completely destroyed	Mostly damaged	Half-damaged	Partially damaged	Uncertified (Unknown)	Uncertified (Undamaged)	Uncertified (Damaged)	Total
Own land/house	153	474	30	18	32	71	6	13	797
	19.2%	59.5%	3.8%	2.3%	4.0%	8.9%	0.8%	1.6%	100.0%
Leased land/own house (registered)	9	51	3	2	1	12	0	0	78
	11.5%	65.4%	3.8%	2.6%	1.3%	15.4%	0.0%	0.0%	100.0%
Leased land/own house (unregistered)	1	9	2	0	1	3	0	1	17
	5.9%	52.9%	11.8%	0.0%	5.9%	17.6%	0.0%	5.9%	100.0%
Privately leased house or apartment	13	91	26	8	3	16	2	2	161
	8.1%	56.5%	16.1%	5.0%	1.9%	9.9%	1.2%	1.2%	100.0%
Public housing	14	58	11	3	3	16	1	1	107
	13.1%	54.2%	10.3%	2.8%	2.8%	15.0%	0.9%	0.9%	100.0%
Other	1	14	2	0	2	7	0	1	27
	3.7%	51.9%	7.4%	0.0%	7.4%	25.9%	0.0%	3.7%	100.0%
Total	191	697	74	31	42	125	9	18	1,187
	16.1%	58.7%	6.2%	2.6%	3.5%	10.5%	0.8%	1.5%	100.0%

Table 9 Respondents' post-earthquake housing reconstruction status (Q1 (5))

		Number	Percentage	Percentage of valid responses	Cumulative percentage
Valid responses	Rebuild on original site	66	5.2	5.5	5.5
	Repair on original site	88	6.9	7.4	12.9
	Construct on readjusted land	170	13.4	14.3	27.2
	Construct at group relocation site	181	14.2	15.2	42.4
	Construct at voluntary relocation site	58	4.6	4.9	47.2
	Disaster public housing	522	41.0	43.8	91.0
	Private lease	14	1.1	1.2	92.2
	Living in temporary housing	14	1.1	1.2	93.4
	Other	79	6.2	6.6	100.0
	Total	1,192	93.6	100.0	
Invalid	No response	81	6.4		
Total		1,273	100.0		

In addition, the results seen in the housing reconstruction status by district are in Table 11 (cross tabulation of Q1 (2) and Q1 (5)) and there were significant differences by district (P value < 0.01 in the chi-square test). Respondents in the Yamada, Yamada district, Machikata, Otsuchi district, Central Rikuzentakata district, Shishiori, Kesennuma district, and the Shinkadonowaki and Minato, Ishinomaki district mainly responded that they reconstructed in public disaster housing and land readjustment project land. On the other hand, the number of disaster prevention group relocation projects in the Shizugawa, Minamisanriku district, Ayumino, Ishinomaki district, Aoi, Higashimatsushima district, and Tamaura-nishi, Iwanuma district stood out. In the Takata-kita, Rikuzentakata and Suezaki, Ofunato districts the ratio of voluntary relocation projects is conspicuous. In the Akahama, Otsuchi district reconstruction was carried out on raised land, while in the Arai-higashi, Sendai district reconstruction was centered around public disaster housing, reflecting the characteristics of the reconstruction projects in each district.

It should be noted that in the districts where the responses regarding reconstruction were centered around public disaster housing and land readjustment projects, the percentage of land that was subject to land readjustment projects was high, but as shown in Table 1, there are large areas where there have been no buildings or

Table 10 Housing reconstruction status by pre-earthquake residence type (cross tabulation of Q1 (3) and Q1 (5))

		Housing reconstruction status									Total
		Rebuild on original site	Repair on original site	Construct on readjusted land	Construct at group relocation site	Construct at voluntary relocation site	Disaster public housing	Private lease	Living in temporary housing	Other	
Pre-earthquake residence type	Own land/ house	57	77	139	149	47	270	3	4	44	790
		7.2%	9.7%	17.6%	18.9%	5.9%	34.2%	0.4%	0.5%	5.6%	100.0%
	Leased land/ own house (registered)	5	4	7	12	3	40	2	1	6	80
		6.3%	5.0%	8.8%	15.0%	3.8%	50.0%	2.5%	1.3%	7.5%	100.0%
	Leased land/ own house (unregistered)	1	1	4	0	0	8	0	1	1	16
		6.3%	6.3%	25.0%	0.0%	0.0%	50.0%	0.0%	6.3%	6.3%	100.0%
	Privately leased house or apartment	1	4	14	16	6	99	7	4	9	160
		0.6%	2.5%	8.8%	10.0%	3.8%	61.9%	4.4%	2.5%	5.6%	100.0%
	Public housing	1	0	4	3	1	84	1	2	12	108
		1%	0%	4%	3%	1%	78%	1%	2%	11%	100.0%
	Other	1	2	2	0	1	14	1	1	7	29
		3.4%	6.9%	6.9%	0.0%	3.4%	48.3	3.4%	3.4%	24.1%	100.0%
Total		66	88	170	180	58	515	14	13	79	1,183
		5.6%	7.4%	14.4	15.2%	4.9%	43.5	1.2%	1.1%	6.7%	100.0%

Table 11 Housing reconstruction status by district (cross tabulation of Q1 (2) and Q1 (5))

	Rebuild on original site	Repair on original site	Construct on readjusted land	Construct at group relocation site	Construct at voluntary relocation site	Disaster public housing	Private lease	Living in temporary housing	Other	Total
Kuwagasaki, Miyako	3	8	7	0	1	5	2	0	8	34
	8.8%	23.5%	20.6%	0.0%	2.9%	14.7%	5.9%	0.0%	23.5	100.0%
Yamada, Yamada	6	0	12	5	2	38	1	0	7	71
	8.5%	0.0%	16.9%	7.0%	2.8%	53.5%	1.4%	0.0%	9.9%	100.0%
Machikata, Otsuchi	15	0	16	1	2	49	0	1	2	86
	17.4%	0.0%	18.6%	1.2%	2.3%	57.0%	0.0%	1.2%	2.3%	100.0%
Akahama, Otsuchi	9	4	10	5	5	4	0	1	3	41
	22.0%	9.8%	24.4%	12.2%	12.2%	9.8%	0.0%	2.4%	7.3%	100.0%
Hirata, Kamaishi	1	7	9	1	3	12	0	0	3	36
	2.8%	19.4%	25.0%	2.8%	8.3%	33.3%	0.0%	0.0%	8.3%	100.0%
Central Rikuzentakata	4	0	35	8	2	88	2	0	5	144
	2.8%	0.0%	24.3%	5.6%	1.4%	61.1%	1.4%	0.0%	3.5%	100.0%
Takata-kita, Rikuzentakata	3	21	0	1	20	1	1	1	25	73
	4.1%	28.8%	0.0%	1.4%	27.4%	1.4%	1.4%	1.4%	34.2%	100.0%
Suezaki, Ofunato	2	9	1	4	8	7	0	0	6	37
	5.4%	24.3%	2.7%	10.8%	21.6%	18.9%	0.0%	0.0%	16.2%	100.0%
Shishiori, Kesennuma	5	5	15	0	2	37	1	1	6	72
	6.9%	6.9%	20.8%	0.0%	2.8%	51.4%	1.4%	1.4%	8.3	100.0%

(continued)

Table 11 (continued)

	Rebuild on original site	Repair on original site	Construct on readjusted land	Construct at group relocation site	Construct at voluntary relocation site	Disaster public housing	Private lease	Living in temporary housing	Other	Total
Shizugawa, Minamisanriku	3	1	10	35	3	70	1	1	2	126
	2.4%	0.8%	7.9%	27.8%	2.4%	55.6%	0.8%	0.8%	1.6%	100.0%
Shinkadonowaki and Minato, Ishinomaki	7	15	9	0	1	48	3	1	6	90
	7.8%	16.7%	10.0%	0.0%	1.1%	53.3%	3.3%	1.1%	6.7%	100.0%
Ayumino, Ishinomaki	3	1	26	16	4	43	0	3	1	97
	3.1%	1.0%	26.8%	16.5%	4.1%	44.3%	0.0%	3.1%	1.0%	100.0%
Aoi, Higashimatsushima	0	1	8	47	2	36	1	2	0	97
	0.0%	1.0%	8.2%	48.5%	2.1%	37.1%	1.0%	2.1%	0.0%	100.0%
Arai-higashi, Sendai	2	5	2	4	3	36	2	2	3	59
	3.4%	8.5%	3.4%	6.8%	5.1%	61.0%	3.4%	3.4%	5.1%	100.0%
Tamaura-nishi, Iwanuma	2	1	4	50	0	38	0	1	2	98
	2.0%	1.0%	4.1%	51.0%	0.0%	38.8%	0.0%	1.0%	2.0%	100.0%
Shin-Sakamoto, Yamamoto	1	10	6	4	0	10	0	0	0	31
	3.2%	32.3%	19.4%	12.9%	0.0%	32.3%	0.0%	0.0%	0.0%	100.0%
Total	66	88	170	181	58	522	14	14	79	1,192
	5.5%	7.4%	14.3%	15.2%	4.9%	43.8%	1.2%	1.2%	6.6%	100.0%

only a few buildings built on the land readjustment project land; this has resulted in the percentage of "disaster public housing" being as high as 50–60%, while the percentage of respondents who answered "construct on readjusted land" being only 10–30%.

On the other hand, in districts where disaster prevention group relocation projects were used, even if the relocation sites were secured via land readjustment projects, buildings were already built on most of the residential lots in the readjusted area, resulting in responses that 30–50% of the respondents had "constructed at a group relocation site", 10–30% had "constructed on readjusted land" and 30–50% responded with "disaster public housing".

4 Livelihood Reconstruction Status

(1) Respondents' pre-earthquake workplace industry and title

When asked about the status of their occupation before the earthquake (Q1 (6)), as shown in Table 12, the most common response was unemployed (22.5% of valid responses), followed by 12.5% in the manufacturing industry, 10.8% in the wholesale/retail industry, 8.1% in the construction industry, 7.9% in the health, welfare and medical industry, 5.8% in the hospitality service industry, 4.7% in the fishing industry, and 3.8% in the transportation industry.

Regarding the pre-earthquake employment status of the respondents, as shown in Table 13, 36.7% of the respondents were permanent employees, 16.4% were part-time/casual employees, 14.2% were receiving a pension, 8.6% were self-employed without any employees, 6.5% were self-employed with employees, and 6.4% were housewives.

(2) Respondents' current workplace industry and status (October survey results only)

When asked about the status of their current employment (Q1 (8) of the October survey), as shown in Table 14, the most common response was unemployed (45.0% of valid responses), followed by 8.4% in the health, welfare and medical industry, 6.3% in the construction industry, 6.0% in the manufacturing industry, 5.6% in the wholesale/retail industry, 4.6% in the hospitality service industry, 3.3% in the fishing industry, and 2.7% in the public service.

Further, regarding the respondents' current employment status (Q1 (9) of the October survey), as shown in Table 15, 30.5% were receiving a pension, 24.8% were permanent employees, 13.3% were part-time/casual employees, 7.1% were self-employed without any employees, 6.3% were housewives, 3.6% were seeking employment, and 3.0% were self-employed with employees.

Table 12 Respondents' pre-earthquake employment industry (Q1 (6))

		Number	Percentage	Percentage of valid responses	Cumulative percentage
Valid responses	Agriculture/forestry	35	2.7	2.9	2.9
	Fishing	56	4.4	4.7	7.6
	Manufacturing	149	11.7	12.5	20.1
	Construction	97	7.6	8.1	28.2
	Wholesale/retail	129	10.1	10.8	39.0
	Banking/insurance	19	1.5	1.6	40.6
	Real estate/product leasing	2	0.2	0.2	40.8
	Transportation	45	3.5	3.8	44.6
	Telecommunications	11	0.9	0.9	45.5
	Hospitality services	69	5.4	5.8	51.3
	Health, welfare, medical	94	7.4	7.9	59.1
	Education	34	2.7	2.8	62.0
	Public servant	34	2.7	2.8	64.8
	Unemployed	269	21.1	22.5	87.4
	Other	151	11.9	12.6	100.0
	Total	1,194	93.8	100.0	
Invalid	No response	79	6.2		
Total		1,273	100.0		

(3) Post-earthquake changes to respondents' occupation

When asked about changes to their occupation after the earthquake (Q1 (10)), as shown in Table 16, 32.4% of the valid responses said they continued to work in the same occupation, and 6.3% resumed the same occupation after a temporary suspension. On the other hand, 11.5% of the respondents had closed their business or were unemployed, and 9.3% had closed their former business and changed occupations. In addition, 5.3% of the respondents had changed their occupation and 4.6% had closed their business due to personal reasons not affected by the earthquake. Further, 23.4% of the respondents were unemployed both before and after the earthquake.

Looking at the post-earthquake changes to occupation by the pre-earthquake industry (cross tabulation of Q1 (6) and Q1 (10), significant P value < 0.01 in the chi-square test), as shown in Table 17, 60% of the respondents in the construction, education, and public sectors resumed the same occupation, while many in the agriculture/forestry and other industries closed their business or changed occupations, and in the manufacturing and hospitality service industries there was a contrasting

Table 13 Respondents' pre-earthquake employment status (Q1 (7))

		Number	Percentage	Percentage of valid responses	Cumulative percentage
Valid responses	Permanent employee	426	33.5	36.7	36.7
	Dispatch employee	12	0.9	1.0	37.7
	Part-time/casual employee	190	14.9	16.4	54.0
	Family business, etc.	4	0.3	0.3	54.4
	Company director	37	2.9	3.2	57.6
	Self-employed with employees	75	5.9	6.5	64.0
	Self-employed with no employees	100	7.9	8.6	72.6
	Pensioner	165	13.0	14.2	86.8
	Housewife	74	5.8	6.4	93.2
	Student	9	0.7	0.8	94.0
	Not working (self-employed)	7	0.5	0.6	94.6
	Looking for work	15	1.2	1.3	95.9
	Other	48	3.8	4.1	100.0
	Total	1,162	91.3	100.0	
Invalid	No response	111	8.7		
Total		1,273	100.0		

division between those that resumed the same occupation and those that had changed occupations.

(4) Changes to respondents' workplace's business performance

The questions then proceeded with the intention of asking further about the business performance status of the respondents' workplace, by first asking whether the earthquake had an impact (Q1 (11)(i)), to which 73.0% of the valid responses indicated that the earthquake had an impact, as shown in Table 18.

The respondents who answered that there was an impact in the above question were then asked to compare the pre- and post-earthquake business performance (Q1 (11)(ii)), and as shown in Table 19, 35.2% of the valid responses were that their business performance had recovered to the pre-earthquake level, while 37.9% answered that it had not recovered to the pre-earthquake level, and 9.7% answered that it was continuing to deteriorate.

Table 14 Respondents' current workplace industry (Question 1 (8) of the October survey)

		Number	Percentage	Percentage of valid responses	Cumulative percentage
Valid responses	Agriculture/forestry	5	0.6	0.7	0.7
	Fishing	25	3.0	3.3	3.9
	Manufacturing	46	5.6	6.0	9.9
	Construction	48	5.8	6.3	16.2
	Wholesale/retail	43	5.2	5.6	21.8
	Banking/insurance	9	1.1	1.2	23.0
	Real estate/product leasing	3	0.4	0.4	23.4
	Transportation	12	1.5	1.6	25.0
	Telecommunications	5	0.6	0.7	25.6
	Hospitality services	35	4.2	4.6	30.2
	Health, welfare, medical	64	7.7	8.4	38.6
	Education	13	1.6	1.7	40.3
	Public servant	21	2.5	2.7	43.0
	Unemployed	344	41.6	45.0	88.0
	Other	92	11.1	12.0	100.0
	Total	765	92.5	100.0	
Invalid	No response	62	7.5		
Total		827	100.0		

Looking at business performance before and after the earthquake by industry (cross-verification of Q1 (6) and Q1 (11)(ii)), as shown in Table 20, only about 30% of the respondents in the agriculture, fishery, hospitality services, and wholesale/retail industries have "recovered to the pre-earthquake level", while about 50% "haven't returned to the pre-earthquake level" or "business performance has continued to deteriorate since before the earthquake". On the other hand, in the construction and transportation sectors, about 50% of the respondents said that their business has "recovered to the pre-earthquake level", while about 40% said that their business "haven't returned to the pre-earthquake level" or "business performance has continued to deteriorate since before the earthquake". The manufacturing industry was between these, and significant differences appeared between industries (P value $= 0.027 < 0.05$ in the chi-square test). However, there was no significant difference in the cross tabulation by district (P value $= 0.055 > 0.05$ in the chi-square test).

(5) Reasons for post-earthquake deterioration of business performance

When those who responded that the earthquake had an effect on their workplace (response to Q1 (11)(i)) were asked about the reasons in a multiple response format (Q1 (11)(iii)), as shown in Table 21, the most common responses were "destruction

Table 15 Respondents' current employment status (Q1 (9))

		Number	Percentage	Percentage of valid responses	Cumulative percentage
Valid responses	Permanent employee	181	21.9	24.8	24.8
	Dispatch employee	6	0.7	0.8	25.7
	Part-time/casual employee	97	11.7	13.3	39.0
	Family business, etc.	17	2.1	2.3	41.3
	Company director	22	2.7	3.0	44.3
	Self-employed with employees	52	6.3	7.1	51.4
	Self-employed with no employees	222	26.8	30.5	81.9
	Pensioner	46	5.6	6.3	88.2
	Housewife	6	0.7	0.8	89.0
	Student	26	3.1	3.6	92.6
	Not working (self-employed)	181	21.9	24.8	24.8
	Looking for work	6	0.7	0.8	25.7
	Other	54	6.5	7.4	100.0
	Total	729	88.1	100.0	
Invalid	No response	98	11.9		
Total		827	100.0		

of buildings and equipment" at 32.8% and "loss of customers" at 28.9%, followed by "insufficient staff" at 14.9% and "Japan's nationwide recession" at 14.0%.

Looking at these responses by district (cross analysis of Q1 (2) and Q1 (11)(iii)), there was a significant difference in the cross tabulation for "loss of customers" (P value < 0.05 in the chi-square test), and in particular, the majority of respondents in the Shishiori, Kesennuma district cited "loss of customers". There were no significant differences by district for the other responses.

Looking at the responses by industry (cross analysis of Q1 (6) and Q1 (11)(iii)), as shown in Table 22, there were significant differences in the responses for "destruction of buildings and equipment," "loss of customers," "insufficient staff" and "cannot obtain stock" (P value < 0.01 in the chi-square test). In particular, "destruction of buildings and equipment" was frequently cited in the manufacturing and wholesale/

Table 16 Post-earthquake changes to respondents' occupation (Q1 (10))

		Number	Percentage	Percentage of valid responses	Cumulative percentage
Valid responses	Same employment	376	29.5	32.4	32.4
	Employment suspended then resumed	73	5.7	6.3	38.7
	Changed employer/ industry due to earthquake	108	8.5	9.3	48.0
	Lost job/ceased business due to earthquake	133	10.4	11.5	59.5
	Commenced business after the earthquake	7	0.5	0.6	60.1
	Changed employer/ industry due to personal circumstances	62	4.9	5.3	65.4
	Resigned/ceased business due to personal circumstances	53	4.2	4.6	70.0
	Commenced business due to personal circumstances	7	0.5	0.6	70.6
	Was unemployed before and after	271	21.3	23.4	94.0
	Other	70	5.5	6.0	100.0
	Total	1,160	91.1	100.0	
Invalid	No response	113	8.9		
Total		1,273	100.0		

retail industries, and "loss of customers" was the most cited reason by the wholesale/retail, banking, and hospitality services industries. There were no significant differences by industry (P value > 0.05 in the chi-square test) for the other reasons.

(6) Timing and reasons that workplaces' business performance started to recover

Table 17 Post-earthquake occupation changes by respondents' pre-earthquake industry (cross tabulation of Q1 (6) and Q1 (10))

		Same employment	Employment suspended then resumed	Changed employer/ industry due to earthquake	Lost job/ ceased business due to earthquake	Commenced business after the earthquake	Changed due to personal circumstances	Resigned/ ceased due to personal circumstances	Commenced business due to personal circumstances	Unemployed before and after	Other	Total
Pre-earthquake industry	Agriculture/forestry	9	0	3	6	1	2	1	1	8	0	31
		29.0%	0.0%	9.7%	19.4%	3.2%	6.5%	3.2%	3.2%	25.8%	0.0%	100.0%
	Fishing	18	3	4	15	0	4	4	0	4	1	53
		34.0%	5.7%	7.5%	28.3%	0.0%	7.5%	7.5%	0.0%	7.5%	1.9%	100.0%
	Manufacturing	53	11	29	17	1	10	8	0	9	4	142
		37.3%	7.7%	20.4%	12.0%	0.7%	7.0%	5.6%	0.0%	6.3%	2.8%	100.0%
	Construction	55	6	5	9	2	2	2	0	11	2	94
		58.5%	6.4%	5.3%	9.6%	2.1%	2.1%	2.1%	0.0%	11.7%	2.1%	100.0%
	Wholesale/retail	48	13	19	27	0	6	4	0	3	6	126
		38.1%	10.3%	15.1%	21.4%	0.0%	4.8%	3.2%	0.0%	2.4%	4.8%	100.0%
	Banking/insurance	9	1	0	0	0	1	6	1	0	1	19
		47.4%	5.3%	0.0%	0.0%	0.0%	5.3%	31.6%	5.3%	0.0%	5.3%	100.0%
	Real estate/product leasing	2	0	0	0	0	0	0	0	0	0	2
		100.0%	0.0%	0.0%	0.0%	0.0%	0.0%	0.0%	0.0%	0.0%	0.0%	100.0%
	Transportation	19	3	5	3	1	7	4	0	1	2	45
		42.2%	6.7%	11.1%	6.7%	2.2%	15.6%	8.9%	0.0%	2.2%	4.4%	100.0%
	Telecommunications	5	1	1	0	1	0	1	0	1	0	10
		50.0%	10.0%	10.0%	0.0%	10.0%	0.0%	10.0%	0.0%	10.0%	0.0%	100.0%
	Hospitality services	15	10	13	14	1	5	1	1	3	3	66
		22.7%	15.2%	19.7%	21.2%	1.5%	7.6%	1.5%	1.5%	4.5%	4.5%	100.0%
	Health, welfare, medical	38	8	9	12	0	10	6	1	1	8	93

(continued)

Table 17 (continued)

		Same employment	Employment suspended then resumed	Changed employer/ industry due to earthquake	Lost job/ ceased business due to earthquake	Commenced business after the earthquake	Changed due to personal circumstances	Resigned/ ceased due to personal circumstances	Commenced business due to personal circumstances	Unemployed before and after	Other	Total
		40.9%	8.6%	9.7%	12.9%	0.0%	10.8%	6.5%	1.1%	1.1%	8.6%	100.0%
	Education	20	0	2	1	0	5	1	0	1	4	34
		58.8%	0.0%	5.9%	2.9%	0.0%	14.7%	2.9%	0.0%	2.9%	11.8%	100.0%
	Public servant	21	0	0	1	0	0	2	0	4	4	32
		65.6%	0.0%	0.0%	3.1%	0.0%	0.0%	6.3%	0.0%	12.5%	12.5%	100.0%
	Unemployed	2	1	1	3	0	6	3	2	206	11	235
		0.9%	0.4%	0.4%	1.3%	0.0%	2.6%	1.3%	0.9%	87.7%	4.7%	100.0%
	Other	52	13	12	19	0	3	10	1	12	21	143
		36.4%	9.1%	8.4%	13.3%	0.0%	2.1%	7.0%	0.7%	8.4%	14.7%	100.0%
Total		366	70	103	127	7	61	53	7	264	67	1,125
		32.5%	6.2%	9.2%	11.3%	0.6%	5.4%	4.7%	0.6%	23.5%	6.0%	100.0%

Table 18 Impact of the earthquake on the respondents' workplace's business performance (Q1 (11)(i))

		Number	Percentage	Percentage of valid responses	Cumulative percentage
Valid responses	Impacted by the earthquake	626	49.2	73.0	73.0
	Earthquake had little impact	141	11.1	16.4	89.4
	Other	91	7.1	10.6	100.0
	Total	858	67.4	100.0	
Invalid	No response	415	32.6		
Total		1,273	100.0		

Table 19 Business performance recovery status of workplaces that were affected by the earthquake (Q1 (11)(ii))

		Number	Percentage	Percentage of valid responses	Cumulative percentage
Valid responses	Recovered to pre-earthquake level	229	18.0	35.2	35.2
	Haven't returned to pre-earthquake level	247	19.4	37.9	73.1
	Pre-earthquake deterioration is continuing	63	4.9	9.7	82.8
	Other	112	8.8	17.2	100.0
	Total	651	51.1	100.0	
Invalid responses	Not applicable	142	11.2		
	No response	480	37.7		
Total		1,273	100.0		

When those who responded that the "earthquake had an effect" on business performance or "other" to Q1 (11)(i) were asked about when business performance subsequently recovered (Q1 (11)(iv)), as shown in Table 23, the largest percentage of valid responses at 16.2% was that business performance had not yet recovered. Of those who answered that they had already seen a recovery, the most common result at 13.3% was that recovery was "during 2020″. Further, when the respondents who answered to Q1 (11)(iv) that business performance had recovered were asked about the reasons in a multiple response format (Q1 (11)(v)), as shown in Table 24, "increase in earthquake reconstruction-related work" was the most common at 40.7%, followed by "functional restoration of facilities and machinery" at 24.3%, "marketing efforts" at 18.8%, "return of customers" at 16.4% and "government support" at 16.2%.

Looking further at the reasons for the recovery by industry (cross-verification of Q1 (6) and Q1 (11)(iv)), as shown in Table 25, there were significant differences in the

Table 20 Post-earthquake business performance recovery status by industry (cross tabulation of Q1 (6) and Q1 (11)(ii))

	Recovered to pre-earthquake level	Haven't returned to pre-earthquake level	Pre-earthquake deterioration is continuing	Other	Total
Agriculture/forestry	6	10	3	4	23
	26.1%	43.5	13.0%	17.4	100.0%
Fishing	13	15	7	8	43
	30.2%	34.9%	16.3	18.6%	100.0%
Manufacturing	39	35	11	18	103
	37.9%	34.0%	10.7%	17.5%	100.0%
Construction	31	19	6	10	66
	47.0	28.8%	9.1%	15.2%	100.0%
Wholesale/retail	35	41	8	13	97
	36.1%	42.3%	8.2%	13.4%	100.0%
Banking/insurance	3	8	1	0	12
	25.0%	66.7%	8.3	0.0%	100.0%
Real estate/product leasing	0	1	0	0	1
	0.0%	100.0%	0.0%	0.0%	100.0%
Transportation	13	13	0	2	28
	46.4%	46.4%	0.0%	7.1%	100.0%
Telecommunications	3	2	1	1	7
	42.9%	28.6%	14.3	14.3	100.0%
Hospitality services	13	24	4	7	48
	27.1	50.0%	8.3	14.6%	100.0%
Health, welfare, medical	20	22	3	5	50
	40.0%	44.0%	6.0%	10.0%	100.0%
Education	4	7	0	4	15
	26.7%	46.7%	0.0%	26.7%	100.0%
Public servant	7	5	1	2	15
	46.7%	33.3%	6.7%	13.3%	100.0%
Unemployed	5	8	8	16	37
	13.5%	21.6%	21.6%	43.2%	100.0%
Other	29	30	8	18	85
	34.1%	35.3%	9.4	21.2	100.0%
Total	221	240	61	108	630
	35.1%	38.1%	9.7%	17.1%	100.0%

Table 21 Causes of poor post-earthquake business performance of respondents' workplaces (Q1 (11)(iii), multiple answers, n = 591)

		Number of responses		Percentage of cases
		Number	Percentage	
Causes of post-earthquake deterioration	Destruction of buildings, etc.	194	23.7	32.8
	Loss of customers	171	20.9	28.9
	Insufficient staff	88	10.8	14.9
	Insufficient funds	38	4.7	6.4
	Cannot obtain stock	29	3.5	4.9
	Japan's nationwide recession	83	10.2	14.0
	Other	41	5.0	6.9
	Turnover has not decreased	36	4.4	6.1
	I don't know	137	16.8	23.2
Total		817	100.0	138.2

cross tabulation for "increase in earthquake reconstruction-related work", "functional restoration of facilities and machinery", "return of customers" and "other" (P value < 0.01 in the chi-square test). In particular, the effect of reconstruction demand on the construction industry and the recovery of facilities and machinery on the manufacturing industry was visible. On the other hand, there was no significant difference between industries regarding "economic recovery," "marketing efforts," "support from customers and head office" and "government support" (P value > 0.05 in the chi-square test).

(7) Receipt, type, and effectiveness of public support for workplace

Regarding whether or not the respondents' workplaces received public support payments (Q3 (4), multiple responses), as shown in Table 26, over 70% did not receive any public support. Of those who responded that support was received, the most common was the SME group subsidy.

When the receipt of public support and its type was cross tabulated with the pre-earthquake industry (cross tabulation of Q1 (6) and Q3 (4)), as shown in Table 27, there was a significant difference for all types of support (P value < 0.01 in the chi-square test).

When those who responded that they had received public support were further asked about its effect (Q3 (5)), as shown in Table 28, about 70% answered that it was either "very" or "somewhat" effective, while less than 10% answered negatively. When looking at the effect of support by each type of subsidy, there was no significant

Table 22 Causes of poor business performance by industry (cross tabulation of Q1 (6) and Q1 (11)(iii))

	Destruction of buildings, etc.	Loss of customers	Insufficient staff	Cannot obtain stock	Total
Agriculture/forestry	7	1	0	0	8
	87.5%	12.5%	0.0%	0.0%	100.0%
Fishing	13	6	5	1	25
	52.0%	24.0%	20.0%	4.0%	100.0%
Manufacturing	44	19	17	15	95
	46.3%	20.0%	17.9%	15.8%	100.0%
Construction	12	11	10	3	36
	33.3%	30.6%	27.8%	8.3	100.0%
Wholesale/retail	39	52	10	3	104
	37.5%	50.0%	9.6%	2.9%	100.0%
Banking/insurance	4	8	0	0	12
	33.3%	66.7%	0.0%	0.0%	100.0%
Real estate/product leasing	1	0	0	0	1
	100.0%	0.0%	0.0%	0.0%	100.0%
Transportation	10	5	6	0	21
	45.5%	22.7%	27.3%	0.0%	100.0%
Telecommunications	2	2	0	0	4
	40.0%	40.0%	0.0%	0.0%	100.0%
Hospitality services	12	19	8	1	40
	26.7%	42.2%	17.8%	2.2%	100.0%
Health, welfare, medical	10	16	16	3	45
	19.6%	31.4%	31.4%	5.9%	100.0%
Education	7	3	2	1	13
	50.0%	21.4%	14.3%	7.1%	100.0%
Public servant	5	2	5	0	12
	41.7%	16.7%	41.7%	0.0%	100.0%
Unemployed	2	4	1	0	7
	5.3%	10.5%	2.6%	0.0%	100.0%
Other	19	21	5	2	47
	22.9%	25.3%	6.0%	2.4%	100.0%
Total	187	169	85	29	470
	32.5%	29.4%	14.8%	5.0%	100.0%

Table 23 Timing of business performance of respondents' workplace beginning to recover (Q1 (11)(iv))

		Number	Percentage	Percentage of valid responses	Cumulative percentage
Valid responses	By March 2012	34	2.7	6.7	6.7
	During 2012	64	5.0	12.5	19.2
	During 2013	53	4.2	10.4	29.5
	During 2014	38	3.0	7.4	37.0
	During 2015	32	2.5	6.3	43.2
	During 2016	56	4.4	11.0	54.2
	During 2017	27	2.1	5.3	59.5
	During 2018	22	1.7	4.3	63.8
	During 2019	34	2.7	6.7	70.5
	During 2020	68	5.3	13.3	83.8
	Hasn't recovered	83	6.5	16.2	100.0
	Total	511	40.1	100.0	
Invalid responses	Not applicable	141	11.1		
	No response	621	48.8		
	Total	762	59.9		
Total		1,273	100.0		

Table 24 Reasons for recovery of business performance of respondents' workplaces (Q1 (11)(v), multiple answers, n = 383)

		Number of responses		Percentage of cases
		Number	Percentage	
Reasons that business performance recovered	Earthquake reconstruction related	156	27.4	40.7
	Economic recovery	41	7.2	10.7
	Marketing efforts	72	12.6	18.8
	Functional restoration of facilities, etc.	93	16.3	24.3
	Support was received	30	5.3	7.8
	Customers returned	63	11.1	16.4
	Government support	62	10.9	16.2
	Other	53	9.3	13.8
Total		570	100.0	148.8

Table 25 Reasons for recovery of business performance by industry (cross tabulation of Q1 (6) and Q1 (11)(iv))

	Earthquake reconstruction related	Functional restoration of facilities, etc.	Customers returned	Total
Agriculture/forestry	2	3	0	5
	40.0%	60.0%	0.0%	100.0%
Fishing	2	9	2	13
	15.4%	69.2%	15.4%	100.0%
Manufacturing	25	25	8	58
	43.1%	43.1%	13.8%	100.0%
Construction	49	6	5	60
	81.7%	10.0%	8.3%	100.0%
Wholesale/retail	27	11	10	48
	56.3%	22.9%	20.8%	100.0%
Banking/insurance	3	2	3	8
	37.5%	25.0%	37.5%	100.0%
Real estate/product leasing	1	1	0	2
	50.0%	50.0%	0.0%	100.0%
Transportation	5	7	3	15
	33.3%	46.7%	20.0%	100.0%
Telecommunications	2	3	0	5
	40.0%	60.0%	0.0%	100.0%
Hospitality services	13	2	11	26
	50.0%	7.7%	42.3%	100.0%
Health, welfare, medical	4	4	7	15
	26.7%	26.7%	46.7%	100.0%
Education	0	3	0	3
	0.0%	100.0%	0.0%	100.0%
Public servant	0	4	2	6
	0.0%	66.7%	33.3%	100.0%
Unemployed	1	1	0	2
	50.0%	50.0%	0.0%	100.0%
Other	18	11	11	40
	45.0%	27.5%	27.5%	100.0%
Total	152	92	62	306
	49.7%	30.1%	20.3%	100.0%

Table 26 Receipt and type of public support for respondents' workplaces (Q3 (4), multiple answers, n = 984)

		Number of responses		Percentage of cases
		Number	Percentage	
Support for business/ workplace	Various support for agriculture	22	2.2	2.2
	Various support for fishing	33	3.3	3.4
	SME group subsidy	119	11.8	12.1
	Other support measures for SMEs	62	6.1	6.3
	Other	57	5.6	5.8
	Not received	717	71.0	72.9
Total		1,010	100.0	102.6

difference in the cross tabulation. In other words, all subsidies were seen as generally effective.

Looking at the effect of public support by pre-earthquake industry (cross tabulation of Q1 (6) and Q3 (5)), there was a significant difference in the cross tabulation as shown in Table 29 (P value < 0.05 in the chi-square test).

(8) Status of respondents' household finances: income, expenses, savings, and loan balances

As a series of questions on the post-earthquake status of household finances, the first question was about income (Q1 (12)(i)); as shown in Table 30, 53.2% of the respondents answered that their income had decreased from before the earthquake and 36.8% responded that it had remained the same.

On the expenditure side (Q1 (12)(ii)), as shown in Table 31, more than 50% of the respondents answered that it had increased from before the earthquake, while less than 40% responded that it had remained the same.

Regarding the balance of deposits and savings (Q1 (12)(iii)), more than 60% of the respondents answered that they had decreased from before the earthquake, as shown in Table 32.

Concerning loan balances (Q1 (12)(iv)), as shown in Table 33, 45.3% of the respondents answered that they had remained the same from before the earthquake and 41.2% answered that they had increased from before the earthquake.

Table 27 Receipt and type of public support by industry (cross tabulation of Q1 (6) and Q3 (4))

		Receipt of public support by respondents (multiple responses)						Total
		Agriculture	Fishing	Group subsidy	Other SME support	Other	Not received	
Pre-earthquake industry	Agriculture/forestry	10	1	2	0	1	14	26
		38.5%	3.8%	7.7%	0.0%	3.8%	53.8%	100.0%
	Fishing	0	16	6	0	2	23	45
		0.0%	35.6%	13.3%	0.0%	4.4%	51.1%	100.0%
	Manufacturing	3	5	23	11	3	87	131
		2.3%	3.8%	17.6%	8.4%	2.3%	66.4%	100.0%
	Construction	2	0	10	6	3	61	79
		2.5%	0.0%	12.7%	7.6%	3.8%	77.2%	100.0%
	Wholesale/retail	1	0	23	17	7	70	109
		0.9%	0.0%	21.1%	15.6%	6.4%	64.2%	100.0%
	Banking/insurance	0	0	2	0	0	14	16
		0.0%	0.0%	12.5%	0.0%	0.0%	87.5%	100.0%
	Real estate/product leasing	0	0	0	1	0	1	2
		0.0%	0.0%	0.0%	50.0%	0.0%	50.0%	100.0%
	Transportation	2	0	5	1	0	29	37
		5.4%	0.0%	13.5%	2.7%	0.0%	78.4%	100.0%
	Telecommunications	0	1	1	1	0	8	11
		0.0%	9.1%	9.1%	9.1%	0.0%	72.7%	100.0%
	Hospitality services	1	3	11	3	4	35	55
		1.8%	5.5%	20.0%	5.5%	7.3%	63.6%	100.0%

(continued)

Table 27 (continued)

		Receipt of public support by respondents (multiple responses)						Total
		Agriculture	Fishing	Group subsidy	Other SME support	Other	Not received	
	Health, welfare, medical	0	0	11	6	6	60	83
		0.0%	0.0%	13.3%	7.2%	7.2%	72.3%	100.0%
	Education	0	0	1	0	5	28	34
		0.0%	0.0%	2.9%	0.0%	14.7%	82.4%	100.0%
	Public servant	0	1	0	0	1	27	29
		0.0%	3.4%	0.0%	0.0%	3.4%	93.1%	100.0%
	Unemployed	1	1	3	2	5	142	152
		0.7%	0.7%	2.0%	1.3%	3.3%	93.4%	100.0%
	Other	2	2	13	10	14	84	123
		1.6%	1.6%	10.6%	8.1%	11.4	68.3%	100.0%
Total		22	30	111	58	51	683	932
		2.4%	3.2%	11.9%	6.2%	5.5%	73.3%	100.0%

Table 28 Effect of public support (Q3 (5))

		Number	Percentage	Percentage of valid responses	Cumulative percentage
Valid responses	Very effective	109	8.6	34.4	34.4
	Somewhat effective	111	8.7	35.0	69.4
	Not very effective	22	1.7	6.9	76.3
	Not effective at all	5	0.4	1.6	77.9
	Don't know	70	5.5	22.1	100.0
	Total	317	24.9	100.0	
Invalid responses	Not applicable	716	56.2		
	No response	240	18.9		
	Total	956	75.1		
Total		1,273	100.0		

5 Recovery Status of the Local Economy

(1) Respondents' perspective of the characteristics of the pre-earthquake local economy

When asked about the characteristics of their local economy before the earthquake (Q3 (1)), as shown in Table 34, overall a large percentage of respondents (19.2% of valid responses) answered that it was a "fishery processing" town, followed by 17.9% who answered that it was a "fishing village," 15.6% who answered that it was a "residential area," 11.0% who answered that it was a "shopping district," and 25.8% who answered that they did not know.

Table 35 (cross tabulation of Q1 (2) and Q3 (1)) shows the characteristics of the local economies by district (P value < 0.01 is significant in the chi-square test).

The districts where the fishing town response was large were the Akahama, Otsuchi district, Hirata, Kamaishi district, Suezaki, Ofunato district and Shin-Sakamoto, Yamamoto district.

The districts where the fishing and fish processing town responses were large were the Kuwagasaki, Miyako district, Yamada, Yamada district, Shizugawa, Minamisanriku district and Ayumino, Ishinomaki district.

In Machikata, Otsuchi district the responses as a fish processing town and shopping district were both large. In the Takata-kita, Rikuzentakata district, the largest response was that it is a shopping district, followed by a fish processing town.

In Central Rikuzentakata district, the responses of shopping district and residential area who answered that it was a shopping and residential area were followed by those who answered that it was a fishing town.

Table 29 Effect of public support by industry (cross tabulation of Q1 (6) and Q3 (5))

	Very effective	Somewhat effective	Not very effective	Not effective at all	Don't know	Total
Agriculture/forestry	6	4	3	0	1	14
	42.9%	28.6%	21.4%	0.0%	7.1%	100.0%
Fishing	10	7	3	1	3	24
	41.7%	29.2%	12.5%	4.2%	12.5%	100.0%
Manufacturing	23	17	1	0	7	48
	47.9%	35.4%	2.1%	0.0%	14.6%	100.0%
Construction	6	9	1	0	8	24
	25.0%	37.5%	4.2%	0.0%	33.3%	100.0%
Wholesale/retail	16	16	1	0	8	41
	39.0%	39.0%	2.4%	0.0%	19.5%	100.0%
Banking/insurance	2	0	0	0	1	3
	66.7%	0.0%	0.0%	0.0%	33.3%	100.0%
Real estate/product leasing	0	0	1	0	0	1
	0.0%	0.0%	100.0%	0.0%	0.0%	100.0%
Transportation	5	3	2	0	1	11
	45.5%	27.3%	18.2%	0.0%	9.1%	100.0%
Telecommunications	1	1	1	0	1	3
	33.3%	0.0%	33.3%	0.0%	33.3%	100.0%
Hospitality services	8	6	3	0	5	22
	36.4%	27.3%	13.6%	0.0%	22.7%	100.0%
Health, welfare, medical	5	12	0	0	7	24
	20.8%	50.0%	0.0%	0.0%	29.2%	100.0%
Education	2	2	0	0	1	5
	40.0%	40.0%	0.0%	0.0%	20.0%	100.0%
Public servant	1	2	0	0	1	4
	25.0%	50.0%	0.0%	0.0%	25.0%	100.0%
Unemployed	3	6	1	3	12	25
	12.0%	24.0%	4.0%	12.0%	48.0%	100.0%
Other	16	17	3	1	5	42
	38.1%	40.5%	7.1%	2.4%	11.9%	100.0%
Total	104	101	20	5	61	291
	35.7%	34.7%	6.9%	1.7%	21.0%	100.0%

Table 30 Status of respondents' post-earthquake household finances—Income (Q1 (12)(i))

		Number	Percentage	Percentage of valid responses	Cumulative percentage
Valid responses	Increased	110	8.6	10.0	10.0
	Remained the same	403	31.7	36.8	46.8
	Decreased	583	45.8	53.2	100.0
	Total	1,096	86.1	100.0	
Invalid responses	No response	177	13.9		
Total		1,273	100.0		

Table 31 Status of respondents' post-earthquake household finances—expenses (Q1 (12)(ii))

		Number	Percentage	Percentage of valid responses	Cumulative percentage
Valid responses	Increased	530	41.6	51.6	51.6
	Remained the same	368	28.9	35.8	87.4
	Decreased	129	10.1	12.6	100.0
	Total	1,027	80.7	100.0	
Invalid responses	No response	246	19.3		
Total		1,273	100.0		

Table 32 Status of respondents' post-earthquake household finances—deposits and savings (Q1 (12)(iii))

		Number	Percentage	Percentage of valid responses	Cumulative percentage
Valid responses	Increased	86	6.8	8.3	8.3
	Remained the same	303	23.8	29.1	37.4
	Decreased	651	51.1	62.6	100.0
	Total	1,040	81.7	100.0	
Invalid responses	No response	233	18.3		
Total		1,273	100.0		

In Aoi, Higashimatsushima district the responses of residential area and fishing town were most common, and it can be said that Shin-Sakamoto, Yamamoto district is also an example of this. The districts where residential area along with fishery

Table 33 Status of respondents' post-earthquake household finances—loan balances (Q1 (12)(iv))

		Number	Percentage	Percentage of valid responses	Cumulative percentage
Valid responses	Increased	331	26.0	41.2	41.2
	Remained the same	364	28.6	45.3	86.4
	Decreased	109	8.6	13.6	100.0
	Total	804	63.2	100.0	
Invalid responses	No response	469	36.8		
Total		1,273	100.0		

Table 34 Characteristics of pre-earthquake local economy: all responses (Q3 (1))

		Number	Percentage	Percentage of valid responses	Cumulative percentage
Valid responses	Fishing village	177	13.9	17.9	17.9
	Shopping district	109	8.6	11.0	28.9
	Fishery processing	190	14.9	19.2	48.2
	Industrial area	22	1.7	2.2	50.4
	Residential area	154	12.1	15.6	66.0
	Other	81	6.4	8.2	72.1
	Do not know	255	20.0	25.8	97.9
	Total	988	77.6	100.0	
Invalid responses	No response	285	22.4		
Total		1,273	100.0		

processing town were the most common responses were the Shishiori, Kesennuma district and Shinkadonowaki and Minato, Ishinomaki district.

The districts where residential area was the overwhelming majority of responses were the Arai-higashi, Sendai district and the Tamaura-nishi, Iwanuma district.

(2) Respondents' perspective of the recovery status of the local economy

When the respondents were asked about the recovery status of the local economy (Q3 (2)), as shown in Table 36, "do not know" was the most common response at 34.5% of valid responses, followed by 21.2% who responded that the economy had recovered 60–80%, 17.4% who responded that it had recovered 40–50%, 11.3% who

Table 35 Characteristics of pre-earthquake local economy by district: all responses (cross tabulation of Q1 (2) and Q3 (1))

	Fishing village	Shopping district	Fishery processing	Industrial area	Residential area	Other	Do not know	Total
Kuwagasaki, Miyako	13	1	13	0	1	0	4	32
	40.6%	3.1%	40.6%	0.0%	3.1%	0.0%	12.5%	100.0%
Yamada, Yamada	24	3	11	1	1	1	11	52
	46.2%	5.8%	21.2%	1.9%	1.9%	1.9%	21.2%	100.0%
Machikata, Otsuchi	7	12	18	0	9	0	19	65
	10.8%	18.5%	27.7%	0.0%	13.8%	0.0%	29.2%	100.0%
Akahama, Otsuchi	17	2	5	0	1	0	10	35
	48.6%	5.7%	14.3%	0.0%	2.9%	0.0%	28.6%	100.0%
Hirata, Kamaishi	12	0	3	2	2	0	7	26
	46.2%	0.0%	11.5%	7.7%	7.7%	0.0%	26.9%	100.0%
Central Rikuzentakata	11	32	6	0	21	4	39	113
	9.7%	28.3%	5.3%	0.0%	18.6%	3.5%	34.5%	100.0%
Takata-kita, Rikuzentakata	5	21	10	0	9	3	32	80
	6.3%	26.3%	12.5%	0.0%	11.3%	3.8%	40.0%	100.0%
Suezaki, Ofunato	10	2	5	0	6	1	7	31
	32.3%	6.5%	16.1%	0.0%	19.4%	3.2%	22.6%	100.0%
Shishiori, Kesennuma	7	5	35	1	9	1	5	63

(continued)

Table 35 (continued)

	Fishing village	Shopping district	Fishery processing	Industrial area	Residential area	Other	Do not know	Total
	11.1%	7.9%	55.6%	1.6%	14.3%	1.6%	7.9%	100.0%
Shizugawa, Minamisanriku	22	15	22	1	7	7	21	95
	23.2%	15.8%	23.2%	1.1%	7.4%	7.4%	22.1%	100.0%
Shinkadonowaki and Minato, Ishinomaki	5	4	33	2	14	4	13	75
	6.7%	5.3%	44.0%	2.7%	18.7%	5.3%	17.3%	100.0%
Ayumino, Ishinomaki	12	3	22	3	12	2	17	71
	16.9%	4.2%	31.0%	4.2%	16.9%	2.8%	23.9%	100.0%
Aoi, Higashimatsushima	23	2	4	1	23	10	22	85
	27.1%	2.4%	4.7%	1.2%	27.1%	11.8%	25.9%	100.0%
Arai-higashi, Sendai	3	3	1	3	21	3	17	51
	5.9%	5.9%	2.0%	5.9%	41.2%	5.9%	33.3%	100.0%
Tamaura-nishi, Iwanuma	3	2	2	8	16	35	21	87
	3.4%	2.3%	2.3%	9.2%	18.4%	40.2%	24.1%	100.0%
Shin-Sakamoto, Yamamoto	3	2	0	0	2	10	10	27
	11.1%	7.4%	0.0%	0.0%	7.4%	37.0%	37.0%	100.0%
Total	177	109	190	22	154	81	255	988
	17.9%	11.0%	19.2%	2.2%	15.6%	8.2%	25.8%	100.0%

answered that it had recovered 20–30%, and 9.7% who responded that it had almost completely recovered.

Looking further at the trends by district in the above responses (cross tabulation of Q1 (2) and Q3 (2)), there was a significant difference (P value < 0.01 in the chi-square test) as shown in Table 37. If the characteristics of the local economy as shown in Table 35 above are taken into account when looking at these trends, in districts that have the characteristics of a "residential area", such as the Arai-higashi, Sendai district and the Tamaura-nishi, Iwanuma district, the response that the local economy had almost completely recovered was the most common. In contrast, in regions where the number of responses that consider the district to be a residential area were similar to the number of responses for fishing village or fishery processing town, such as the Shishiori, Kesennuma district, the Shinkadonowaki and Minato, Ishinomaki district, the Aoi, Higashimatsushima district and the Shin-Sakamoto, Yamamoto district, the response that the local economy had recovered to 60–80% of the pre-earthquake level was the most common. In districts where the number of responses considering the local economy to be a shopping district were similar to the number of responses for fishing village or fishery processing town, such as the Machikata, Otsuchi district and the Central Rikuzentakata district, the response that the local economy had recovered to 20–30% of the pre-earthquake level was the most common.

(3) Recovery status of local shopping streets

Table 36 Respondents' perspective of the recovery status of the local economy (Q3 (2))

		Number	Percentage	Percentage of valid responses	Cumulative percentage
Valid responses	Less than 10% of pre-earthquake level	49	3.8	4.1	4.1
	20–30% of pre-earthquake level	134	10.5	11.3	15.4
	40–50% of pre-earthquake level	207	16.3	17.4	32.9
	60–80% of pre-earthquake level	252	19.8	21.2	54.1
	Almost completely recovered	115	9.0	9.7	63.8
	Above pre-earthquake level	20	1.6	1.7	65.5
	Do not know	410	32.2	34.5	100.0
	Total	1,187	93.2	100.0	
Invalid responses	No response	86	6.8		
Total		1,273	100.0		

Table 37 Recovery status of the local economy by district (cross tabulation of Q1 (2) and Q3 (1))

	Less than 10% of pre-earthquake level	20–30% of pre-earthquake level	40–50% of pre-earthquake level	60–80% of pre-earthquake level	Almost complete recovery	Above pre-earthquake level	Do not know	Total
Kuwagasaki, Miyako	3	3	7	16	1	0	11	41
	7.3%	7.3%	17.1%	39.0%	2.4%	0.0%	26.8%	100.0%
Yamada, Yamada	2	7	19	10	1	2	29	70
	2.9%	10.0%	27.1%	14.3%	1.4%	2.9%	41.4%	100.0%
Machikata, Otsuchi	8	16	14	6	1	0	35	80
	10.0%	20.0%	17.5%	7.5%	1.3%	0.0%	43.8%	100.0%
Akahama, Otsuchi	3	8	10	3	2	0	16	42
	7.1%	19.0%	23.8%	7.1%	4.8%	0.0%	38.1%	100.0%
Hirata, Kamaishi	1	4	2	10	4	0	14	35
	2.9%	11.4%	5.7%	28.6%	11.4%	0.0%	40.0%	100.0%
Central Rikuzentakata	4	33	31	22	1	0	48	139
	2.9%	23.7%	22.3%	15.8%	0.7%	0.0%	34.5%	100.0%
Takata-kita, Rikuzentakata	4	16	29	17	1	1	24	92
	4.3%	17.4%	31.5%	18.5%	1.1%	1.1%	26.1%	100.0%
Suezaki, Ofunato	1	0	10	8	8	0	11	38
	2.6%	0.0%	26.3%	21.1%	21.1%	0.0%	28.9%	100.0%
Shishiori, Kesennuma	2	6	18	22	3	0	26	77

(continued)

Table 37 (continued)

	Less than 10% of pre-earthquake level	20–30% of pre-earthquake level	40–50% of pre-earthquake level	60–80% of pre-earthquake level	Almost complete recovery	Above pre-earthquake level	Do not know	Total
	2.6%	7.8%	23.4%	28.6%	3.9%	0.0%	33.8%	100.0%
Shizugawa, Minamisanriku	1	4	19	34	15	5	43	121
	0.8%	3.3%	15.7%	28.1%	12.4%	4.1%	35.5%	100.0%
Shinkadonowaki and Minato, Ishinomaki	11	14	12	22	4	1	24	88
	12.5%	15.9%	13.6%	25.0%	4.5%	1.1%	27.3%	100.0%
Ayumino, Ishinomaki	2	10	17	28	7	0	25	89
	2.2%	11.2%	19.1%	31.5%	7.9%	0.0%	28.1%	100.0%
Aoi, Higashimatsushima	1	4	8	21	17	3	36	90
	1.1%	4.4%	8.9%	23.3%	18.9%	3.3%	40.0%	100.0%
Arai-higashi, Sendai	0	1	4	7	13	5	28	58
	0.0%	1.7%	6.9%	12.1%	22.4%	8.6%	48.3%	100.0%
Tamaura-nishi, Iwanuma	3	6	4	18	31	3	31	96
	3.1%	6.3%	4.2%	18.8%	32.3%	3.1%	32.3%	100.0%
Shin-Sakamoto, Yamamoto	3	2	3	8	6	0	9	31
	9.7%	6.5%	9.7%	25.8%	19.4%	0.0%	29.0%	100.0%
Total	49	134	207	252	115	20	410	1,187
	4.1%	11.3%	17.4%	21.2%	9.7%	1.7%	34.5%	100.0%

In order to enquire about the conditions of the local economy in the area closest to the respondents' daily lives, they were asked about the recovery status of their local shopping streets (Q3 (3)). As shown in Table 38, the largest percentage of valid responses was "do not know" at 25.6%, followed by 18.2% who answered "40–50% of pre-earthquake level", 17.4% who answered "20–30% of pre-earthquake level", 16.5% who answered "60–80% of pre-earthquake level", and 9.7% for each of "less than 10% of pre-earthquake level" and "almost completely recovered".

Looking at the responses to the question about the recovery status of the local shopping streets by district (cross tabulation of Q1 (2) and Q3 (3)), there was a significant difference (P value < 0.01 in the chi-square test) as shown in Table 39. If the characteristics of the local economy are taken into account when looking at these trends, in the Machikata, Otsuchi district and the Central Rikuzentakata district where the responses centered on the characteristic of the local economy being a shopping district, the response that the shopping streets had recovered to 20–30% of their pre-earthquake level was the most common. In contrast, in the Arai-higashi, Sendai district and the Tamaura-nishi, Iwanuma district, where many respondents indicated that the local economy had the characteristics of a "residential area," the number of respondents who responded that the local shopping streets had almost completely recovered were remarkably large. On the other hand, it is noteworthy that in districts where the number of responses that consider the region to be a residential area were similar to the number of responses for fishing village or fishery processing town, such as the Shishiori, Kesennuma district, the Shinkadonowaki

Table 38 Recovery status of local shopping streets (Q3 (3))

		Number	Percentage	Percentage of valid responses	Cumulative percentage
Valid responses	Less than 10% of pre-earthquake level	115	9.0	9.7	9.7
	20–30% of pre-earthquake level	207	16.3	17.4	27.0
	40–50% of pre-earthquake level	217	17.0	18.2	45.3
	60–80% of pre-earthquake level	196	15.4	16.5	61.7
	Almost completely recovered	115	9.0	9.7	71.4
	Above pre-earthquake level	36	2.8	3.0	74.4
	Do not know	305	24.0	25.6	100.0
	Total	1,191	93.6	100.0	
Invalid responses	No response	82	6.4		
Total		1,273	100.0		

Table 39 Recovery status of local shopping streets by district (cross tabulation of Q1 (2) and Q3 (3))

	Less than 10% of pre-earthquake level	20–30% of pre-earthquake level	40–50% of pre-earthquake level	60–80% of pre-earthquake level	Almost complete recovery	Above pre-earthquake level	Do not know	Total
Kuwagasaki, Miyako	14	3	5	10	1	0	9	42
	33.3%	7.1%	11.9%	23.8%	2.4%	0.0%	21.4%	100.0%
Yamada, Yamada	4	13	17	13	3	1	22	73
	5.5%	17.8%	23.3%	17.8%	4.1%	1.4%	30.1%	100.0%
Machikata, Otsuchi	16	22	14	10	3	1	17	83
	19.3%	26.5%	16.9%	12.0%	3.6%	1.2%	20.5%	100.0%
Akahama, Otsuchi	8	14	6	2	1	1	12	44
	18.2%	31.8%	13.6%	4.5%	2.3%	2.3%	27.3%	100.0%
Hirata, Kamaishi	2	2	7	7	6	0	11	35
	5.7%	5.7%	20.0%	20.0%	17.1%	0.0%	31.4%	100.0%
Central Rikuzentakata	8	49	29	13	0	0	42	141
	5.7%	34.8%	20.6%	9.2%	0.0%	0.0%	29.8%	100.0%
Takata-kita, Rikuzentakata	5	29	30	13	1	0	13	91
	5.5%	31.9%	33.0%	14.3%	1.1%	0.0%	14.3%	100.0%
Suezaki, Ofunato	6	3	7	7	5	0	10	38
	15.8%	7.9%	18.4%	18.4%	13.2%	0.0%	26.3	100.0%
Shishiori, Kesennuma	5	18	17	18	1	0	15	74

(continued)

Table 39 (continued)

	Less than 10% of pre-earthquake level	20–30% of pre-earthquake level	40–50% of pre-earthquake level	60–80% of pre-earthquake level	Almost complete recovery	Above pre-earthquake level	Do not know	Total
	6.8%	24.3%	23.0%	24.3%	1.4%	0.0%	20.3%	100.0%
Shizugawa, Minamisanriku	3	10	29	25	10	14	33	124
	2.4%	8.1%	23.4%	20.2%	8.1%	11.3%	26.6%	100.0%
Shinkadonowaki and Minato, Ishinomaki	20	16	11	18	4	2	17	88
	22.7%	18.2%	12.5%	20.5%	4.5%	2.3%	19.3%	100.0%
Ayumino, Ishinomaki	9	9	21	20	10	1	18	88
	10.2%	10.2%	23.9%	22.7%	11.4%	1.1%	20.5%	100.0%
Aoi, Higashimatsushima	1	6	10	18	18	6	30	89
	1.1%	6.7%	11.2%	20.2%	20.2%	6.7%	33.7%	100.0%
Arai-higashi, Sendai	2	4	4	4	16	4	22	56
	3.6%	7.1%	7.1%	7.1%	28.6%	7.1%	39.3%	100.0%
Tamaura-nishi, Iwanuma	5	4	7	13	32	6	28	95
	5.3%	4.2%	7.4%	13.7%	33.7%	6.3%	29.5%	100.0%
Shin-Sakamoto, Yamamoto	7	5	3	5	4	0	6	30
	23.3%	16.7%	10.0%	16.7%	13.3%	0.0%	20.0%	100.0%
Total	115	207	217	196	115	36	305	1,191
	9.7%	17.4%	18.2%	16.5%	9.7%	3.0%	25.6%	100.0%

and Minato, Ishinomaki district, and the Shin-Sakamoto, Yamamoto district, the responses regarding the recovery of the local shopping streets were divided from 10% recovery up to 60–80% recovery in terms of their pre-earthquake level. This was also the case in the Kuwagasaki, Miyako district. On the other hand, in districts such as the Yamada, Yamada district, the Shizugawa, Minamisanriku district and the Ayumino, Ishinomaki district where the characteristic of the local economy is a fishing village or fishery processing town, the response that the local shopping streets had recovered 40–50% was the most common.

In Table 40, the correlation between the recovery status of the local economy and the recovery status of the local shopping streets was looked at (cross tabulation of Q3 (2) and Q3 (3)) and a strong correlation was found (Spearman's rank correlation coefficient is 0.653 and Kendall's rank correlation coefficient is 0.590). This would suggest that the scope of the respondents' subjective view of the "local economy" tends to almost overlap with the trading area of the local shopping street.

(4) Drivers and factors of local economic recovery

When asked about the private sector organizations that led the recovery of the local economy (Q3 (6)), as shown in Table 41, 60% of respondents answered, "do not know", while the most common organization was the "community-building association", followed by the "chamber of commerce and industry" and the "fishery cooperative".

Looking at the private sector organizations that led the recovery of the local economy by district (cross-verification of Q1 (2) and Q3 (6)), there was variation as shown in Table 42, with some being led by the chamber of commerce and industry and others by organizations such as a community-building association; it is assumed that the differences are due to the differences in the reconstruction development project methods and the differences in local characteristics, such as whether the area is mainly a shopping district or a residential area.

When asked about the decisive factor in the recovery of the local economy (Q3 (7)), as shown in Table 43, the answer was "do not know" in 45.5% of the cases, with the most common factors given being support from the government, followed by new places to work.

6 Local Population Recovery Status

(1) Respondents' perspective of local population recovery status

When asked about the district's population recovery status from the respondents' perspective (Q3 (8)), as shown in Table 44, the largest number of valid responses was "do not know" at 33.4%, followed by 29.5% who answered "70% of pre-earthquake level", 15.4% who answered "50% of pre-earthquake level", and 10.4% who answered "30% of pre-earthquake level".

Table 40 Correlation between recovery status of the local economy and the reconstruction status of local shopping streets (cross tabulation of Q3 (2) and Q3 (3))

		Reconstruction of local shopping streets							Total
		Less than 10% of pre-earthquake level	20–30% of pre-earthquake level	40–50% of pre-earthquake level	60–80% of pre-earthquake level	Almost complete recovery	Above pre-earthquake level	Do not know	
Recovery Status of the Local Economy	Less than 10% of pre-earthquake level	40	4	0	1	1	0	2	48
		83.3%	8.3%	0.0%	2.1%	2.1%	0.0%	4.2%	100.0%
	20–30% of pre-earthquake level	25	83	19	2	0	2	3	134
		18.7%	61.9%	14.2%	1.5%	0.0%	1.5%	2.2%	100.0%
	40–50% of pre-earthquake level	18	54	91	26	5	1	10	205
		8.8%	26.3%	44.4%	12.7%	2.4%	0.5%	4.9%	100.0%
	60–80% of pre-earthquake level	10	22	58	117	21	4	15	247
		4.0%	8.9%	23.5%	47.4%	8.5%	1.6%	6.1%	100.0%
	Almost completely recovered	1	5	7	18	64	8	9	112
		0.9%	4.5%	6.3%	16.1%	57.1%	7.1%	8.0%	100.0%

(continued)

Table 40 (continued)

		Reconstruction of local shopping streets							Total
		Less than 10% of pre-earthquake level	20–30% of pre-earthquake level	40–50% of pre-earthquake level	60–80% of pre-earthquake level	Almost complete recovery	Above pre-earthquake level	Do not know	
	Above pre-earthquake level	0	0	1	0	1	14	3	19
		0.0%	0.0%	5.3%	0.0%	5.3%	73.7%	15.8%	100.0%
	Do not know	17	34	36	27	21	5	257	397
		4.3%	8.6%	9.1%	6.8%	5.3%	1.3%	64.7%	100.0%
Total		111	202	212	191	113	34	299	1,162
		9.6%	17.4%	18.2%	16.4%	9.7%	2.9%	25.7%	100.0%

Table 41 Private and civic organizations that led the recovery of the local economy (Q3 (6), multiple answers, n = 1055)

		Number of responses		Percentage of cases
		Number	Percentage	
Private and civic organizations that participated in local economic recovery	Chamber of commerce and industry	174	12.2	16.5
	Shopping street association	91	6.4	8.6
	Agricultural cooperative	82	5.7	7.8
	Fishery cooperative	95	6.7	9.0
	Community-building association	241	16.9	22.8
	NGO	63	4.4	6.0
	Other	43	3.0	4.1
	Do not know	639	44.7	60.6
Total		1,428	100.0	135.4

Looking at this by district (cross tabulation of Q1 (2) and Q3 (8)), there was a significant difference (P value < 0.01 in the chi-square test) as shown in Table 45. While overall the most common response in most of the districts was that the population is 70% of the pre-earthquake level, in the Kuwagasaki, Miyako district the most common response was that the population is 30% of the pre-earthquake level, and in the Arai-higashi, Sendai district the most common response was that the population had increased compared to before the earthquake.

(2) Respondents' perspective on causes of population outflow

When asked about the causes of population flow (Q3 (9), multiple answers), as shown in Table 46, 65.2% of the valid responses cited "lack of work opportunities and places" as the reason, followed by "being made to wait for public reconstruction works" at 51.8% and "inconvenience of transportation" at 37.4%.

Looking at the responses regarding the causes of population outflow by district (cross tabulation of Q1 (2) and Q3 (9)), there was no significant difference in the cross table for "being made to wait for public reconstruction works" (P value $= 0.053 > 0.05$ in the chi-square test), and it can be considered to be a common factor in many districts. Regarding the other causes, there was a significant difference in the cross tabulation (P value < 0.01 in the chi-square test). As shown in Table 47, the results were that the most common responses were "being made to wait for public reconstruction works" in Tamaura-nishi, Iwanuma district and Shinkadonowaki and Minato, Ishinomaki district, and "inconvenience of transportation" in Shin-Sakamoto, Yamamoto district and Arai-higashi, Sendai district. In the other 12 districts, "lack of work opportunities and places" was the most common response.

Table 42 Regional economic recovery leaders by district

	Private and civic organizations that participated in regional economic recovery								Total
	Chamber of commerce and industry	Shopping street association	Agricultural cooperative	Fishery cooperative	Community-building association	NGO	Other	Do not know	
Kuwagasaki, Miyako	5	3	3	5	8	1	1	27	39
	12.8%	7.7%	7.7%	12.8%	20.5%	2.6%	2.6%	69.2%	100.0%
Yamada, Yamada	15	7	5	6	7	2	5	37	65
	23.1%	10.8%	7.7%	9.2%	10.8%	3.1%	7.7%	56.9%	100.0%
Machikata, Otsuchi	13	10	4	8	14	7	3	36	68
	19.1%	14.7%	5.9%	11.8%	20.6%	10.3%	4.4%	52.9%	100.0%
Akahama, Otsuchi	0	0	0	3	5	1	0	26	33
	0.0%	0.0%	0.0%	9.1%	15.2%	3.0%	0.0%	78.8%	100.0%
Hirata, Kamaishi	2	1	2	4	4	1	3	20	31
	6.5%	3.2%	6.5%	12.9%	12.9%	3.2%	9.7%	64.5%	100.0%
Central Rikuzentakata	26	17	14	12	23	17	2	77	125
	20.8%	13.6%	11.2%	9.6%	18.4%	13.6%	1.6%	61.6%	100.0%
Takata-kita, Rikuzentakata	16	10	6	6	9	3	2	63	85
	18.8%	11.8%	7.1%	7.1%	10.6%	3.5%	2.4%	74.1%	100.0%
Suezaki, Ofunato	9	4	6	5	10	2	2	17	33
	27.3%	12.1%	18.2%	15.2%	30.3%	6.1%	6.1%	51.5%	100.0%

(continued)

Table 42 (continued)

	Private and civic organizations that participated in regional economic recovery								Total
	Chamber of commerce and industry	Shopping street association	Agricultural cooperative	Fishery cooperative	Community-building association	NGO	Other	Do not know	
Shishiori, Kesennuma	14	11	2	5	22	4	1	35	66
	21.2%	16.7%	3.0%	7.6%	33.3%	6.1%	1.5%	53.0%	100.0%
Shizugawa, Minamisanriku	31	14	11	17	23	5	8	63	109
	28.4%	12.8%	10.1%	15.6%	21.1%	4.6%	7.3%	57.8%	100.0%
Shinkadonowaki and Minato, Ishinomaki	9	4	2	5	16	5	6	49	77
	11.7%	5.2%	2.6%	6.5%	20.8%	6.5%	7.8%	63.6%	100.0%
Ayumino, Ishinomaki	12	3	2	8	12	4	1	56	83
	14.5%	3.6%	2.4%	9.6%	14.5%	4.8%	1.2%	67.5%	100.0%
Aoi, Higashimatsushima	12	3	8	8	33	3	1	41	79
	15.2%	3.8%	10.1%	10.1%	41.8%	3.8%	1.3%	51.9%	100.0%
Arai-higashi, Sendai	1	0	2	0	7	1	2	44	53
	1.9%	0.0%	3.8%	0.0%	13.2%	1.9%	3.8%	83.0%	100.0%
Tamaura-nishi, Iwanuma	5	3	9	2	39	5	2	39	86
	5.8%	3.5%	10.5%	2.3%	45.3%	5.8%	2.3%	45.3%	100.0%
Shin-Sakamoto, Yamamoto	4	1	6	1	9	2	4	9	23
	17.4%	4.3%	26.1%	4.3%	39.1%	8.7%	17.4%	39.1%	100.0%
Total	174	91	82	95	241	63	43	639	1,055
	16.5%	8.6%	7.8%	9.0%	22.8%	6.0%	4.1%	60.6%	100.0%

Table 43 Decisive factors in the recovery of the local economy (Q3 (7), multiple answers, n = 1,084)

		Number of responses		Percentage of cases
		Number	Percentage	
Decisive factor in local economy	Government	407	28.3	37.5
	Chamber of commerce and industry	138	9.6	12.7
	Shopping street association	90	6.3	8.3
	New places to work	271	18.8	25.0
	Other	40	2.8	3.7
	Do not know	493	34.3	45.5
Total		1,439	100.0	132.7

Table 44 Status of the local population recovery (Q3 (8))

		Number	Percentage	Percentage of valid responses	Cumulative percentage
Valid responses	10% of pre-earthquake level	51	4.0	4.5	4.5
	30% of pre-earthquake level	117	9.2	10.4	14.9
	50% of pre-earthquake level	174	13.7	15.4	30.3
	70% of pre-earthquake level	333	26.2	29.5	59.7
	Almost completely recovered	43	3.4	3.8	63.5
	Greater than pre-earthquake level	35	2.7	3.1	66.6
	Do not know	377	29.6	33.4	100.0
	Total	1,130	88.8	100.0	
Invalid responses	No response	143	11.2		
Total		1,273	100.0		

Furthermore, when looking at respondents' perception of population recovery in relation to their perception of the recovery status of the local economy as described above (cross tabulation of Q3 (8) and Q3 (2)), a correlation was confirmed as displayed in Table 48 (Kendall's rank correlation coefficient is 0.367 and Spearman's rank correlation coefficient is 0.425).

Similarly, when looking at the responses regarding population recovery in relation to the responses regarding the recovery status of local shopping streets (cross

Table 45 Respondents perspective of population recovery by district (cross tabulation of Q1 (2) and Q3 (8))

	10% of pre-earthquake level	30% of pre-earthquake level	50% of pre-earthquake level	70% of pre-earthquake level	Almost completely recovered	Greater than pre-earthquake level	Do not know	Total
Kuwagasaki, Miyako	5	11	7	7	0	0	9	39
	12.8%	28.2%	17.9%	17.9%	0.0%	0.0%	23.1%	100.0%
Yamada, Yamada	1	5	5	26	0	0	27	64
	1.6%	7.8%	7.8%	40.6%	0.0%	0.0%	42.2%	100.0%
Machikata, Otsuchi	6	12	14	22	0	1	22	77
	7.8%	15.6%	18.2%	28.6%	0.0%	1.3%	28.6%	100.0%
Akahama, Otsuchi	2	9	12	7	0	0	12	42
	4.8%	21.4%	28.6%	16.7%	0.0%	0.0%	28.6%	100.0%
Hirata, Kamaishi	1	2	9	6	1	1	15	35
	2.9%	5.7%	25.7%	17.1%	2.9%	2.9%	42.9%	100.0%
Central Rikuzentakata	6	14	19	39	1	2	45	126
	4.8%	11.1%	15.1%	31.0%	0.8%	1.6%	35.7%	100.0%
Takata-kita, Rikuzentakata	1	5	15	45	1	1	22	90
	1.1%	5.6%	16.7%	50.0%	1.1%	1.1%	24.4%	100.0%
Suezaki, Ofunato	0	3	6	11	1	1	15	37
	0.0%	8.1%	16.2%	29.7%	2.7%	2.7%	40.5%	100.0%
Shishiori, Kesennuma	4	9	18	23	0	0	19	73

(continued)

Table 45 (continued)

	10% of pre-earthquake level	30% of pre-earthquake level	50% of pre-earthquake level	70% of pre-earthquake level	Almost completely recovered	Greater than pre-earthquake level	Do not know	Total
	5.5%	12.3%	24.7%	31.5%	0.0%	0.0%	26.0%	100.0%
Shizugawa, Minamisanriku	2	10	23	52	0	1	25	113
	1.8%	8.8%	20.4%	46.0%	0.0%	0.9%	22.1%	100.0%
Shinkadonowaki and Minato, Ishinomaki	17	13	6	17	1	1	31	86
	19.8%	15.1%	7.0%	19.8%	1.2%	1.2%	36.0%	100.0%
Ayumino, Ishinomaki	2	8	10	22	4	3	39	88
	2.3%	9.1%	11.4%	25.0%	4.5%	3.4%	44.3%	100.0%
Aoi, Higashimatsushima	2	4	2	21	15	4	35	83
	2.4%	4.8%	2.4%	25.3%	18.1%	4.8%	42.2%	100.0%
Arai-higashi, Sendai	0	4	3	3	8	13	26	57
	0.0%	7.0%	5.3%	5.3%	14.0%	22.8%	45.6%	100.0%
Tamaura-nishi, Iwanuma	1	5	19	18	10	7	31	91
	1.1%	5.5%	20.9%	19.8%	11.0%	7.7%	34.1%	100.0%
Shin-Sakamoto, Yamamoto	1	3	6	14	1	0	4	29
	3.4%	10.3%	20.7%	48.3	3.4%	0.0%	13.8%	100.0%
Total	51	117	174	333	43	35	377	1,130
	4.5%	10.4%	15.4%	29.5%	3.8%	3.1%	33.4%	100.0%

Table 46 Respondents' perspective on causes of population outflow (Q3 (9), multiple answers, n = 768)

		Number of responses		Percentage of cases
		Number	Percentage	
Population outflow causes	Being made to wait for public reconstruction works	398	24.0	51.8
	Lack of safety measures	121	7.3	15.8
	Lack of work opportunities and places	501	30.2	65.2
	Lack of living-related facilities	245	14.8	31.9
	Inconvenience of transportation	287	17.3	37.4
	Other	60	3.6	7.8
	Do not know	47	2.8	6.1
Total		1,659	100.0	216.0

tabulation of Q3 (8) and Q3 (3)), a correlation was confirmed as displayed in Table 49 (Kendall's rank correlation coefficient is 0.360 and Spearman's rank correlation coefficient is 0.423).

7 Results and Consideration of Responses Regarding the Recovery Calendar

(1) Overall results of responses regarding the recovery calendar

As mentioned at the beginning of this chapter, the "Recovery Calendar" is a method of assessing recovery since the Great Hanshin-Awaji Earthquake and is a survey which relies on the subjectivity of disaster-affected people regarding when each of 12 items are achieved: (1) grasped the overall damage, (2) thought it is now safe, (3) resolved to live an inconvenient life for a while, (4) work has returned to normal, (5) have resolved finally their housing problems, (6) the impact of the disaster on their household budget had disappeared, (7) their daily life had settled down, (8) local activities had returned to normal, (9) their self-perception as a disaster victim has disappeared, (10) the local economy had recovered from the impact of the disaster, (11) local roads had returned to normal, and (12) local schools had returned to normal.

Figure 1 shows the results of the "Recovery Calendar" for all districts in the survey. Looking at the items that show a similar recovery curve shape over time, the items that were quickly achieved within one to two years of the earthquake included "(1) grasped the overall damage", "(3) resolved to live an inconvenient life for a while", and "(4) work has returned to normal". On the other hand, the group of items which

Table 47 Causes of local population outflow by district (cross tabulation of Q1 (2) and Q3 (9))

		Population outflow causes							Total
		Being made to wait for public reconstruction works	Lack of safety measures	Lack of work opportunities and places	Lack of living-related facilities	Inconvenience of transportation	Other	Do not know	
District	Kuwagasaki, Miyako	17	12	18	10	7	4	6	32
		53.1%	37.5%	56.3%	31.3%	21.9%	12.5%	18.8%	100.0%
	Yamada, Yamada	17	6	33	12	13	3	3	41
		41.5%	14.6%	80.5%	29.3%	31.7%	7.3%	7.3%	100.0%
	Machikata, Otsuchi	34	11	41	18	18	0	1	57
		59.6%	19.3%	71.9%	31.6%	31.6%	0.0%	1.8%	100.0%
	Akahama, Otsuchi	18	7	22	16	14	3	0	80
		22.5%	8.8%	27.5%	20.0%	17.5%	3.8%	0.0%	100.0%
	Hirata, Kamaishi	8	3	10	4	7	3	1	19
		42.1%	15.8%	52.6%	21.1%	36.8%	15.8%	5.3%	100.0%
	Central Rikuzentakata	56	13	77	31	51	5	1	92
		60.9%	14.1%	83.7%	33.7%	55.4%	5.4%	1.1%	100.0%
	Takata-kita, Rikuzentakata	37	7	61	35	30	5	1	69
		53.6%	10.1%	88.4%	50.7%	43.5%	7.2%	1.4%	100.0%
	Suezaki, Ofunato	9	3	17	3	8	1	3	21
		42.9%	14.3%	81.0%	14.3%	38.1%	4.8%	14.3%	100.0%
	Shishiori, Kesennuma	31	6	40	18	17	0	2	57
		54.4%	10.5%	70.2%	31.6%	29.8%	0.0%	3.5%	100.0%

(continued)

Table 47 (continued)

		Population outflow causes							Total
		Being made to wait for public reconstruction works	Lack of safety measures	Lack of work opportunities and places	Lack of living-related facilities	Inconvenience of transportation	Other	Do not know	
	Shizugawa, Minamisanriku	60	8	78	39	43	10	1	99
		60.6%	8.1%	78.8%	39.4%	43.4%	10.1%	1.0%	100.0%
	Shinkadonowaki and Minato, Ishinomaki	27	16	20	22	22	11	2	55
		49.1%	29.1%	36.4%	40.0%	40.0%	20.0%	3.6%	100.0%
	Ayumino, Ishinomaki	21	8	27	14	13	0	3	48
		43.8%	16.7%	56.3%	29.2%	27.1%	0.0%	6.3%	100.0%
	Aoi, Higashimatsushima	18	5	25	2	8	5	8	47
		38.3%	10.6%	53.2%	4.3%	17.0%	10.6%	17.0%	100.0%
	Arai-higashi, Sendai	3	4	6	4	7	4	5	18
		16.7%	22.2%	33.3%	22.2%	38.9%	22.2%	27.8%	100.0%
	Tamaura-nishi, Iwanuma	29	9	9	6	10	3	9	53
		54.7%	17.0%	17.0%	11.3%	18.9%	5.7%	17.0%	100.0%
	Shin-Sakamoto, Yamamoto	13	3	17	11	19	3	1	27
		48.1%	11.1%	63.0%	40.7%	70.4%	11.1%	3.7%	100.0%
Total		398	121	501	245	287	60	47	768
		51.8%	15.8%	65.2%	31.9%	37.4%	7.8%	6.1%	100.0%

Table 48 Relationship between population recovery status and local economic recovery status (cross tabulation of Q3 (8) and (2))

		Recovery status of local economic activity							Total
		Less than 10% of pre-earthquake level	20–30% of pre-earthquake level	40–50% of pre-earthquake level	60–80% of pre-earthquake level	Almost completely recovered	Above pre-earthquake level	Do not know	
Population recovery status	10% of pre-earthquake level	11	12	6	8	1	0	12	50
		22.0%	24.0%	12.0%	16.0%	2.0%	0.0%	24.0%	100.0%
	30% of pre-earthquake level	11	32	27	16	7	0	21	114
		9.6%	28.1%	23.7%	14.0%	6.1%	0.0%	18.4%	100.0%
	50% of pre-earthquake level	4	31	51	43	6	4	33	172
		2.3%	18.0%	29.7%	25.0%	3.5%	2.3%	19.2%	100.0%
	70% of pre-earthquake level	11	29	70	120	30	5	64	329
		3.3%	8.8%	21.3%	36.5%	9.1%	1.5%	19.5%	100.0%
	Almost completely recovered	0	1	2	8	21	1	8	41
		0.0%	2.4%	4.9%	19.5%	51.2%	2.4%	19.5%	100.0%
	Greater than pre-earthquake level	0	2	5	7	10	4	6	34
		0.0%	5.9%	14.7%	20.6%	29.4%	11.8%	17.6%	100.0%
	Do not know	8	21	32	38	32	3	231	365
		2.2%	5.8%	8.8%	10.4%	8.8%	0.8%	63.3%	100.0%
Total		45	128	193	240	107	17	375	1,105

(continued)

Table 48 (continued)

Recovery status of local economic activity						Total
Less than 10% of pre-earthquake level	20–30% of pre-earthquake level	40–50% of pre-earthquake level	60–80% of pre-earthquake level	Almost completely recovered	Above pre-earthquake level	Do not know	
4.1%	11.6%	17.5%	21.7%	9.7%	1.5%	33.9%	100.0%

Table 49 Relationship between population recovery status and local shopping street recovery status (cross tabulation of Q3 (8) and (3))

		Recovery status of local economic activity							Total
		Less than 10% of pre-earthquake level	20–30% of pre-earthquake level	40–50% of pre-earthquake level	60–80% of pre-earthquake level	Almost completely recovered	Above pre-earthquake level	Do not know	
Population recovery status	10% of pre-earthquake level	20	11	8	3	0	2	6	50
		40.0%	22.0%	16.0%	6.0%	0.0%	4.0%	12.0%	100.0%
	30% of pre-earthquake level	25	36	21	11	8	2	13	116
		21.6%	31.0%	18.1%	9.5%	6.9%	1.7%	11.2%	100.0%
	50% of pre-earthquake level	17	44	47	26	6	3	25	168
		10.1%	26.2%	28.0%	15.5%	3.6%	1.8%	14.9%	100.0%
	70% of pre-earthquake level	23	61	83	93	26	10	34	330
		7.0%	18.5%	25.2%	28.2%	7.9%	3.0%	10.3%	100.0%
	Almost completely recovered	1	1	4	7	22	3	4	42
		2.4%	2.4%	9.5%	16.7%	52.4%	7.1%	9.5%	100.0%
	Greater than pre-earthquake level	1	3	5	5	12	3	6	35
		2.9%	8.6%	14.3%	14.3%	34.3%	8.6%	17.1%	100.0%
	Do not know	20	37	38	41	35	7	190	368
		5.4%	10.1%	10.3%	11.1%	9.5%	1.9%	51.6%	100.0%
Total		107	193	206	186	109	30	278	1,109
		9.6%	17.4%	18.6%	16.8%	9.8%	2.7%	25.1%	100.0%

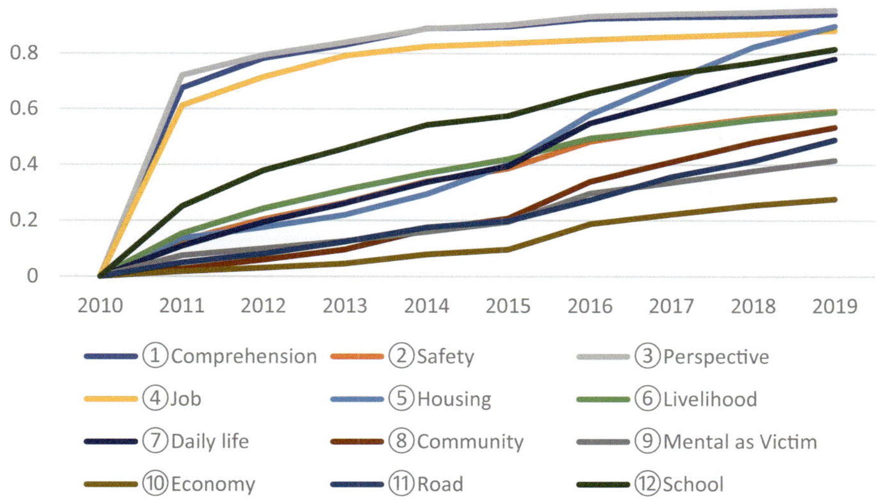

Fig. 1 Recovery calendar (combined results of responses from all districts)

followed this, such as "(5) have resolved finally their housing problems", "(12) local schools have returned to normal", and "(7) their daily life had settled down" gradually reached over 50% achievement by around 2016, 5 years after the earthquake. In 2019, eight years after the earthquake, items for which responses that it had been achieved were still around 60% were "(6) the impact of the disaster on their household budget had disappeared", "(2) thought it is now safe", and "(8) local activities had returned to normal". In addition, "(10) the local economy had recovered from the impact of the disaster", "(9) their self-perception as a disaster victim has disappeared", and "(11) Local roads had returned to normal" are items for which the responses that the item has been achieved have not yet reached 50% as of 2019. Among these, the number of responses that "(10) the local economy had recovered from the impact of the disaster" had been achieved was less than 30%, which was the lowest among the 12 items.

(2) Recovery Calendar by region

Figures 2, 3, 4, 5, 6, 7, 8, 9, 10, 11, 12, 13, 14, 15, 16, and 17 show the results of responses to the "Recovery Calendar" for each target district.

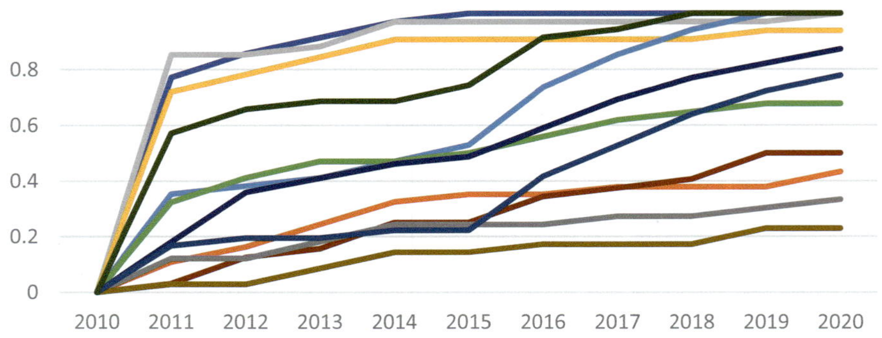

Fig. 2 Results of recovery calendar responses of Kuwagasaki, Miyako

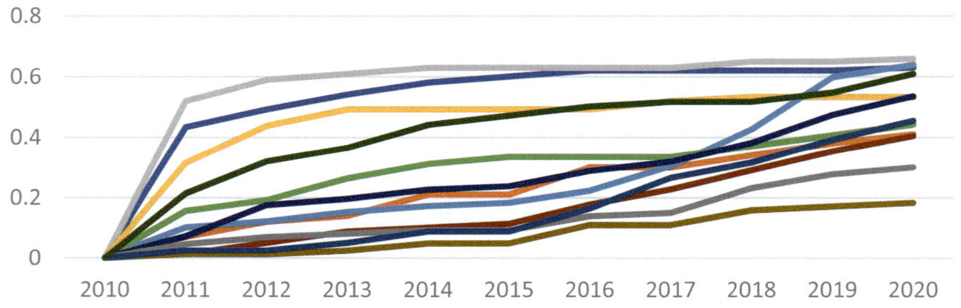

Fig. 3 Results of recovery calendar responses of Yamada, Yamada

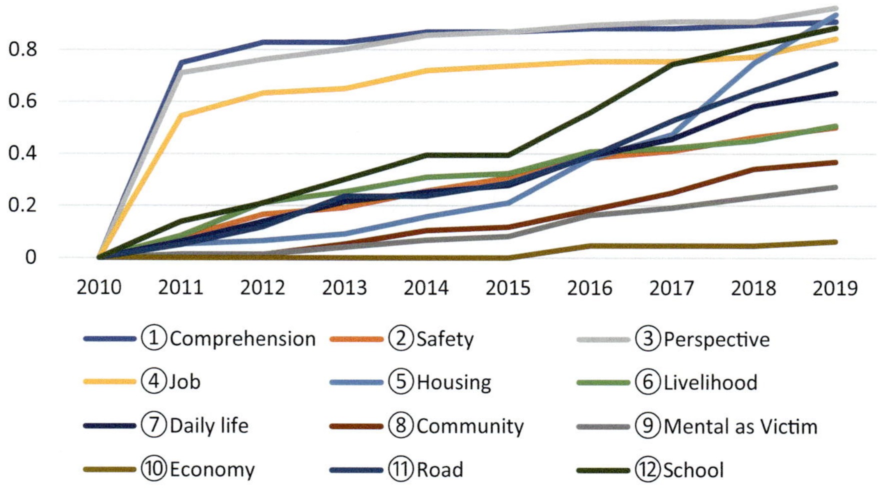

Fig. 4 Results of recovery calendar responses of Machikata, Otsuchi

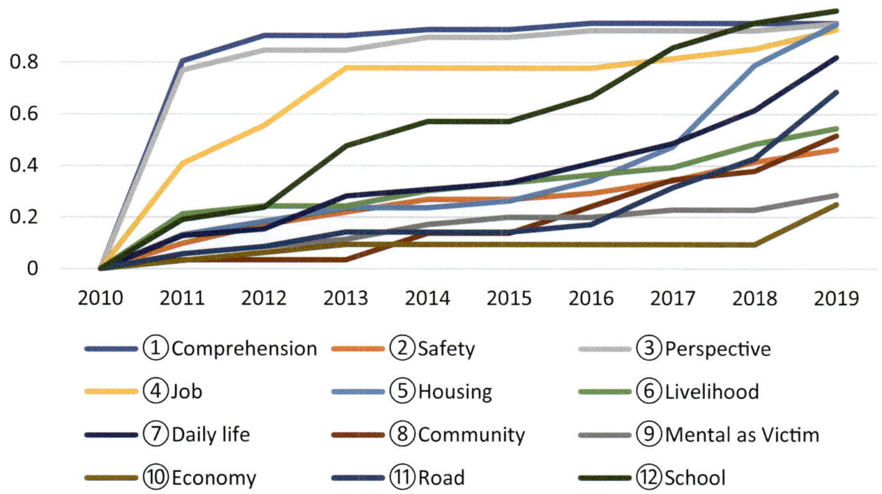

Fig. 5 Results of recovery calendar responses of Akahama, Otsuchi

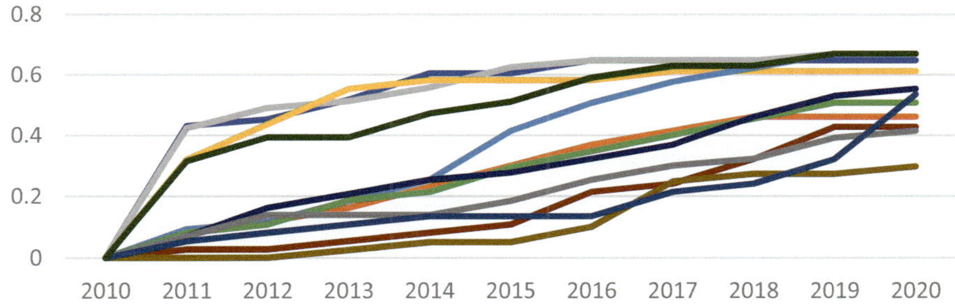

Fig. 6 Results of recovery calendar responses of Hirata, Kamaishi

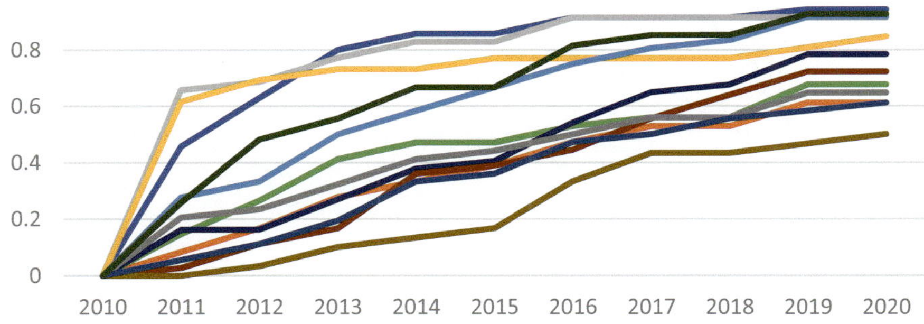

Fig. 7 Results of recovery calendar responses of Suezaki, Ofunato

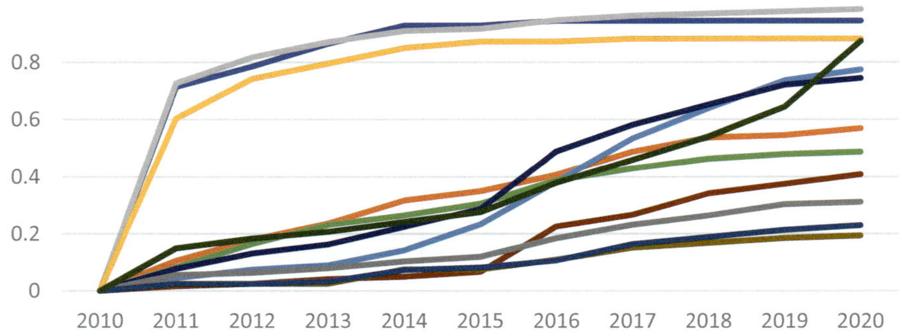

Fig. 8 Results of recovery calendar responses of Central Rikuzentakata

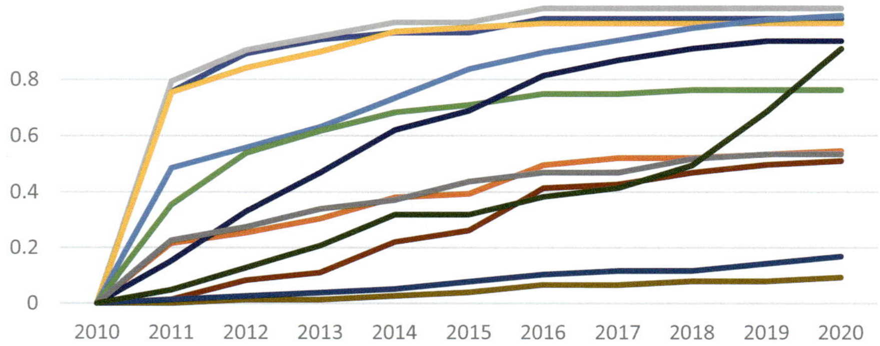

Fig. 9 Results of recovery calendar responses of Takata-kita, Rikuzentakata

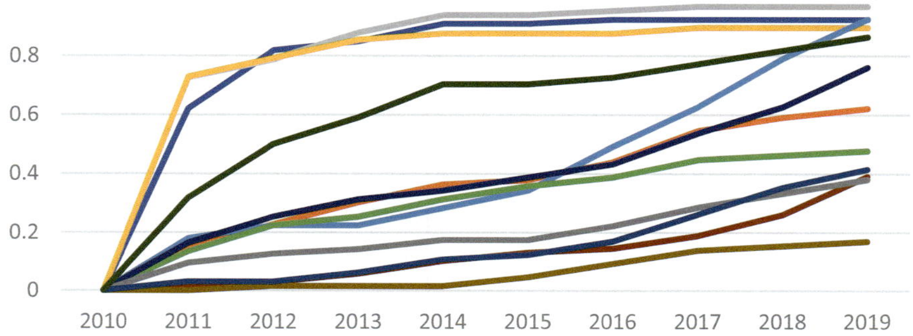

Fig. 10 Results of recovery calendar responses of Shishiori, Kesennuma

In addition, Table 50 lists the items in the "Recovery Calendar" for each district that have not yet reached achievement in 50% of the responses as of 2019 and 2020, the most recent dates of this survey.

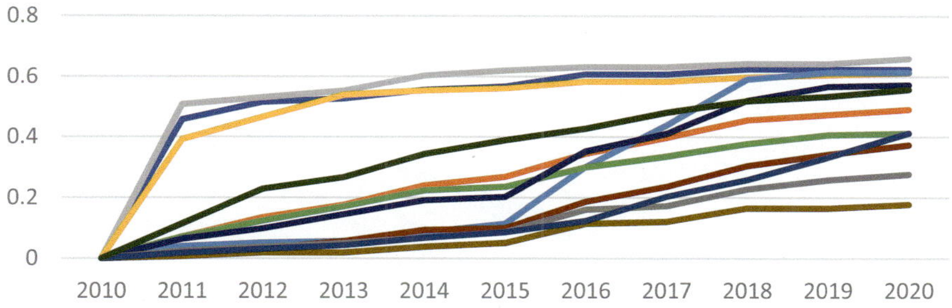

Fig. 11 Results of recovery calendar responses of Shizugawa, Minamisanriku

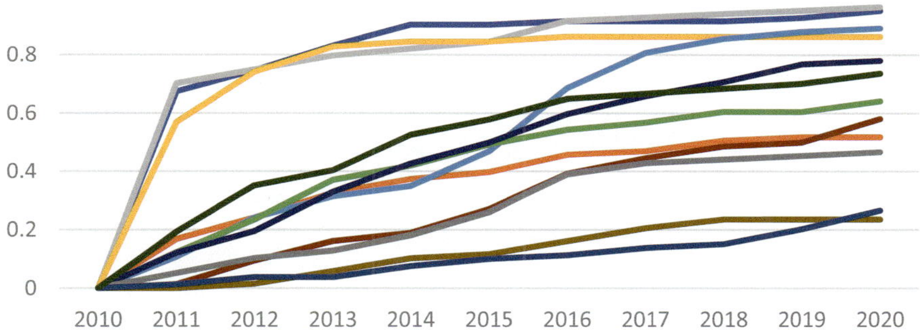

Fig. 12 Results of recovery calendar responses of Shinkadonowaki and Minato, Ishinomaki

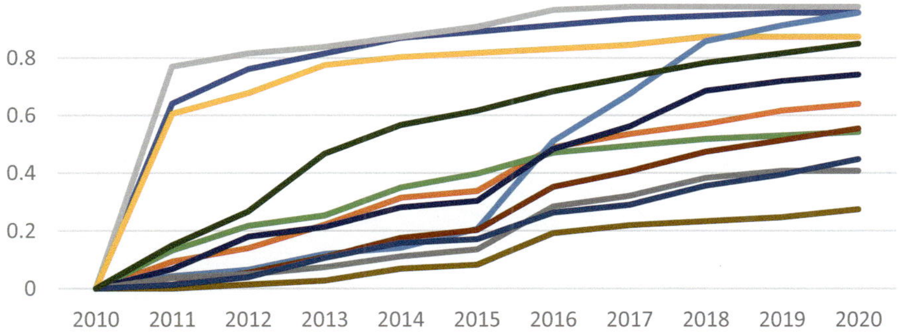

Fig. 13 Results of recovery calendar responses of Ayumino, Ishinomaki

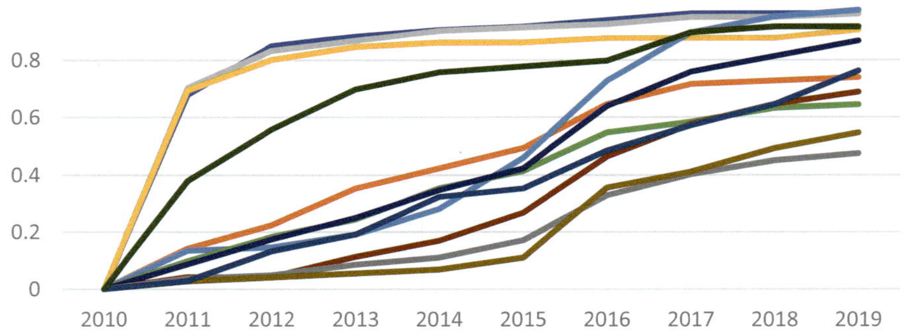

Fig. 14 Results of recovery calendar responses of Aoi, Higashimatsushima

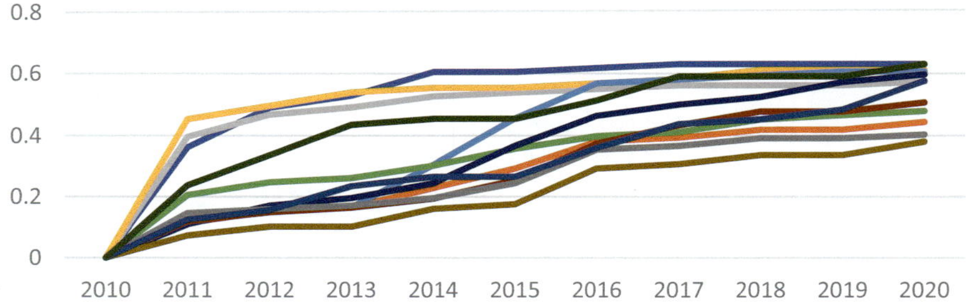

Fig. 15 Results of recovery calendar responses of Arai-higashi, Sendai

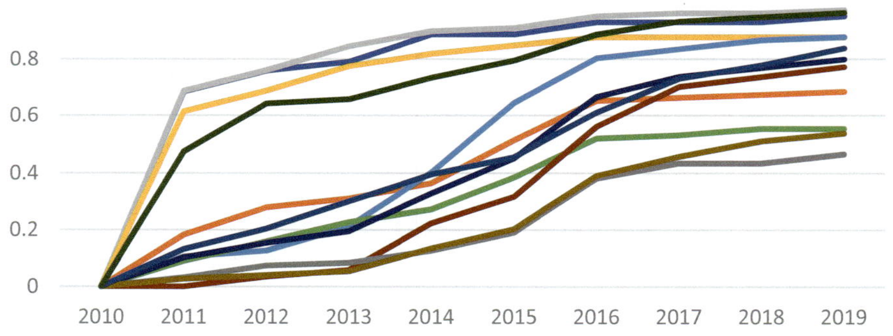

Fig. 16 Results of recovery calendar responses of Tamaura-nishi, Iwanuma

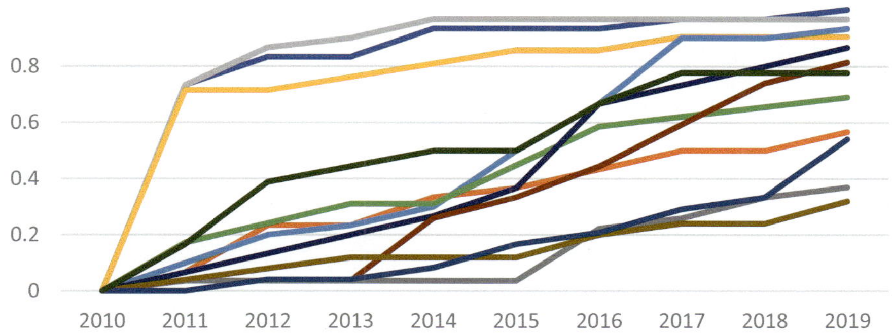

Fig. 17 Results of recovery calendar responses of Shin-Sakamoto, Yamamoto

Among them, the responses for "(10) the local economy had recovered from the impact of the disaster" were low in each district, but there was difference between districts in the extent. In particular, in the Machikata, Otsuchi district and the Takata-kita, Rikuzentakata district, less than 10% of the respondents answered that recovery of "(10) local economy" had been achieved. In addition, only 20% of the respondents in Kuwagasaki, Miyako district, Akahama, Otsuchi district, Central Rikuzentakata district, Shizugawa, Minamisanriku district, Shishiori, Kesennuma district, Shinkadonowaki and Minato, Ishinomaki district, and Ayumino, Ishinomaki district answered that it had been achieved. On the other hand, more than 50% of the respondents in the Arai-higashi, Sendai district and Tamaura-nishi, Iwanuma district answered that "(10) local economy" was achieved.

In addition, a notable trend in the responses by district was the low response rate for "(9) their self-perception as a disaster victim has disappeared". As of 2020, nine years after the disaster, the number of responses that this point had been achieved in Kuwagasaki, Miyako district, Machikata, Otsuchi district, Akahama, Otsuchi district Central Rikuzentakata district was still at only 30%. Also, in many of the districts, such as Yamada, Yamada district, Takada-kita, Rikuzentakata district, Shizugawa, Minamisanriku district, Shishiori, Kesennuma district, Shinkadonowaki and Minato, Ishinomaki district, Ayumino, Ishinomaki district, Aoi, Higashimatsushima district, Tamaura-nishi, Iwanuma district, and Shin-Sakamoto, Yamamoto district, the number of responses which indicated that this point had been achieved was 40–50%. On the other hand, in Hirata, Kamaishi district, Suezaki, Ofunato district, and Arai-higashi, Sendai district, more than 60% of respondents answered that it had been achieved.

In the Central Rikuzentakata district, the Takata-kita, Rikuzentakata district, and the Shishiori, Kesennuma district, the responses that "(8) local activities had returned to normal" were at only 40%.

On the other hand, the trends in the responses for each district to "(2) thought it is now safe" are also noteworthy. In Kuwagasaki, Miyako district, the responses that safety had been achieved were at only 40%, but the background to this may be due to the fact that Miyako City's reconstruction plan focuses on floodgate construction to

Table 50 Factors below 50% achievement on the recovery calendar by district (2019 and 2020)

Factors 50% or below as of 2019		Factors 50% or below as of 2019 and 2020 (Underlined numbers are as of 2020)	
Tamaura-nishi, Iwanuma	(9) Time that self-perception as a disaster victim disappeared (46.8%)	Kuwagasaki, Miyako	(10) Time that local economy has escaped from the impact of the disaster (22.9%, <u>22.9%</u>) (9) Time that self-perception as a disaster victim disappeared (30.3%, <u>33.3%</u>) (2) Time that thought it is now safe (39.5%, <u>44.7%</u>)
Shishiori, Kesennuma	(10) Time that local economy has escaped from the impact of the disaster (16.9%) (9) Time that self-perception as a disaster victim disappeared (38.1%) (8) Time that local activities have returned to normal (39.1%) (11) Time that local roads have been repaired (41.5%) (6) Time that household budget has recovered (47.8%)	Yamada, Yamada	(10) Time that local economy has escaped from the impact of the disaster (26.8%, <u>28.6%</u>) (9) Time that self-perception as a disaster victim disappeared (42.8%, <u>45.8%</u>)
Shin-Sakamoto, Yamamoto	(10) Time that local economy has escaped from the impact of the disaster (32.0%) (9) Time that self-perception as a disaster victim disappeared (37.0%)	Hirata, Kamaishi	(10) Time that local economy has escaped from the impact of the disaster (40.7%, <u>44.4%</u>) (11) Time that local roads have been repaired (48.0%)

(continued)

Table 50 (continued)

Factors 50% or below as of 2019		Factors 50% or below as of 2019 and 2020 (Underlined numbers are as of 2020)	
Aoi, Higashimatsushima	(9) Time that self-perception as a disaster victim disappeared (47.6%)	Central Rikuzentakata	(10) Time that local economy has escaped from the impact of the disaster (18.5%, 19.3%) (11) Time that local roads have been repaired (21.3%, 23.0%) (6) Time that household budget has recovered (47.9%, (48.8%) (9) Time that self-perception as a disaster victim disappeared (30.4%, (31.2%) (8) Time that local activities have returned to normal (37.5%, 40.8%)
Machikata, Otsuchi	(10) Time that local economy has escaped from the impact of the disaster (6.4%) (9) Time that self-perception as a disaster victim disappeared (27.4%) (8) Time that local activities have returned to normal (36.8%) (2) Time that thought it is now safe (50.0%)	Takata-kita, Rikuzentakata	(10) Time that local economy has escaped from the impact of the disaster (7.1%, 8.3%) (11) Time that local roads have been repaired (12.8%, 15.1%) (8) Time that local activities have returned to normal (44.4%, 45.7%) (9) Time that self-perception as a disaster victim disappeared (47.8%, 47.8%) (2) Time that thought it is now safe (47.7%, 48.9%)
Akahama, Otsuchi	(10) Time that local economy has escaped from the impact of the disaster (25.0%) (9) Time that self-perception as a disaster victim disappeared (28.6%) (2) Time that thought it is now safe (46.3%)	Suezaki, Ofunato	(10) Time that local economy has escaped from the impact of the disaster (46.7%, 50.0%)
		Shizugawa, Minamisanriku	(10) Time that local economy has escaped from the impact of the disaster (24.5%, 26.4%) (9) Time that self-perception as a disaster victim disappeared (38.5%, 41.3%) (11) Time that local roads have been repaired (49.5%)

(continued)

Table 50 (continued)

Factors 50% or below as of 2019		Factors 50% or below as of 2019 and 2020 (Underlined numbers are as of 2020)	
		Shinkadonowaki and Minato, Ishinomaki	(10) Time that local economy has escaped from the impact of the disaster (23.5%, <u>23.5%</u>) (11) Time that local roads have been repaired (20.3%, <u>26.6%</u>) (9) Time that self-perception as a disaster victim disappeared (45.5%, <u>46.8%</u>)
		Ayumino, Ishinomaki	(10) Time that local economy has escaped from the impact of the disaster (24.7%, <u>27.4%</u>) (11) Time that local roads have been repaired (39.5%, <u>44.7%</u>) (9) Time that self-perception as a disaster victim disappeared (40.7%, <u>40.7%</u>)
		Arai-higashi, Sendai	None

protect the city center and the Kuwagasaki district is positioned outside of it; this can also be assumed to have had an effect on the significant population outflow from the same district seen in Table 45 above. In addition, the responses in districts such as Machikata, Otsuchi district, Akahama, Otsuchi district, Takata-kita, Rikuzentakata district, Shinkadonowaki and Minato, Ishinomaki district, and the Shin-Sakamoto, Yamamoto district remained at around 50%. It is noteworthy that in other districts too, achievement of about 60% was shown from around 2016, five years after the earthquake, but the trend in the responses until 2020 has shown a flattening out.

(3) Livelihood recovery calendar and respondents' attributes

Table 51 summarizes the results of the verification to determine if there is a significant difference regarding the 11 attributes shown at the top of the table, for each of the items in the overall Recovery Calendar shown in Fig. 1.

Reading down this table vertically, first, the basic attributes of respondents' current address and age show the strongest significance for each category of recovery status (nine items are significant categories at the 1% level). Next, the livelihood-related attributes of income and savings show extremely strong significance (eight items are significant categories at the 1% level). In addition, housing reconstruction status and the details of the disaster victim certificate show strong significance (seven and six items respectively are significant categories at the 1% level). Thus, we can understand that differences in the basic attributes such as age, differences in household financial status, and differences in the status of damage to and reconstruction of houses have a strong effect on the trends in the responses to the Recovery Calendar. On the other hand, differences regarding occupation and employment status do not have such a large effect on the sense of recovery, but the difference of whether a change in occupation was experienced shows a considerable effect (four items are significant categories at the 1% level).

By looking at this table horizontally, we can see which of the attributes shown at the top of the table displayed a significant difference for each question in the Recovery Calendar. First, for many of the questions on the Recovery Calendar, we can understand that differences in housing damage status and reconstruction status and differences in household budget have a significant effect. Second, regarding the resumption of work (question (3)), it shows that differences in attributes such as pre- and post-earthquake industry, employment status, and occupational changes have a significant effect. Third, regarding the sense of recovery of the local economy (question (10)), we can see that the differences in household budget status have a strong effect.

Table 51 Factors that displayed a relationship to the recovery calendar

	Current location	Age (6 levels)	Gender	Pre-earthquake residence	Details of disaster victim certificate	Housing reconstruction status	Pre-earthquake employment industry	Pre-earthquake employment status	Current employment industry	Current employment status	Post-earthquake occupation change	Income	Expenses	Savings	Debts
(1) Grasped overall damage	○	◎												○	
(2) Thought it is now safe	◎		◎			○						◎	○	◎	
(3) Resolved to live an inconvenient life		◎		◎				○				○			○
(4) Restarted work		◎		○		◎	◎	◎	◎	◎	◎	◎	○	◎	○
(5) Have resolved housing problems	◎	◎			◎	◎	◎				◎	◎	○	◎	◎
(6) Household budget has recovered	◎	◎			◎	◎	○	○		○	◎	◎	◎	◎	◎
(7) Daily life has settled down	◎	◎	○		◎	◎		○	◎		○	◎	◎	◎	
(8) Local activities have returned to normal	◎	○			◎	◎						◎	◎	◎	
(9) Self-perception as a disaster victim has disappeared	◎	◎	◎		◎	◎		○		◎	◎	◎	◎	◎	◎

(continued)

Table 51 (continued)

	Current location	Age (6 levels)	Gender	Pre-earthquake residence	Details of disaster victim certificate	Housing reconstruction status	Pre-earthquake employment industry	Pre-earthquake employment status	Current employment industry	Current employment status	Post-earthquake occupation change	Income	Expenses	Savings	Debts
(10) Local economy has escaped from the impact of the disaster	◎	◎				○	○					◎	○	◎	◎
(11) Local roads have been repaired	◎	◎	○		◎	◎			◎		○				
(12) Local schools have recovered	◎	◎										○			

Legend: ◎ = 1% significance; ○ = 5% significance

8 Summary

This paper has reported the results of a simple tabulation of a questionnaire survey conducted in 16 districts in 13 cities and towns to mark the 10th anniversary of the Great East Japan Earthquake, with the goal of evaluating the recovery from the perspective of the disaster-affected households in tsunami-inundated areas. The fact that 75.0% of the respondents in this survey suffered severe damage, with their homes judged to have been swept away or completely destroyed in their disaster victim certification (see Table 6) reflects the intention of this survey. Although a detailed analysis of the results of this survey is a subject for future study, several implications can be drawn from the current aggregate results.

(1) Reconstruction of homes

It is noteworthy that in the responses regarding housing reconstruction status shown in Sect. 3 of this chapter, although the ratio of respondents living in detached houses before the earthquake was 74.9% (Table 5), reconstruction in disaster public housing after the earthquake accounted for 40% of the total. Amongst this, a trend was found that 30% of households that owned their own land and house before the earthquake and 50% of households that owned their own house on rented land were resigned to rebuilding in disaster public housing.

In the housing reconstruction status by district (Table 11), the impact of the differences in the reconstruction development projects in each district is found. In districts such as the Yamada, Yamada district, Machikata, Otsuchi district, Hirata, Kamaishi district, Central Rikuzentakata district, Shishiori, Kesennuma district, and Shinkadonowaki and Minato, Ishinomaki district, where the "multiple disaster prevention" policy was relied upon and land-filling readjustment projects were implemented for shopping streets and residential areas, there was a dichotomy between rebuilding detached houses on land readjustment project sites and rebuilding in disaster public housing. In the Ayumino, Ishinomaki district, Shizugawa, Minamisanriku district, Aoi, Higashimatsushima district, and Tamaura-nishi, Iwanuma district, which have become inland collective relocation areas, rebuilding via disaster-prevention collective relocation projects and disaster public housing was common. In the Takata-kita, Rikuzentakata district and Suezaki, Ofunato district, the ratio of voluntary relocation is conspicuous, and it is thought that these areas became a receptacle for young households who rebuilt by themselves on safe land within the area without waiting for the completion of reconstruction projects. As other characteristic examples, differences appeared in Akahama, Otsuchi district, which pursued Level 2 safety measures and required large-scale elevation work to secure land for higher ground, and the Arai-higashi, Sendai district, where a large-scale disaster public housing complex was developed.

These trends in the responses are thought to require further verification in view of the curve of "(5) have resolved finally their housing problems" in the "Recovery Calendar". As seen in Figs. 2, 3, 4, 5, 6, 7, 8, 9, 10, 11, 12, 13, 14, 15, 16, and 17, there are variations in the time when the responses that "(5) have resolved finally their housing problems" exceeded 50% and the current achievement levels in each district. In the Takata-kita, Rikuzentakata district, which showed a high rate of voluntary relocation in Table 11, the response rate reached 50% fastest in around 2012, and also in Suezaki, Ofunato district in around 2013. In districts such as Arai-higashi, Sendai district and Tamaura-nishi, Iwanuma district, which are inland areas that have implemented concentrated community-building including disaster public housing complexes, rapid progress is seen from around 2014, and the number of responses indicating achievement has currently reached around 90% as of 2020. However, in Central Rikuzentakata district, which was the subject of wide-scale land-filling readjustment, only about 70% of responses indicated achievement even currently as of 2020.

As described above, it is suggested that the impact that the manner of assembling reconstruction development projects which rely on "multiple disaster prevention" has on the housing reconstruction of disaster victims is significant and remains an issue for the future.

(2) Reconstruction of household finances

In the status of rebuilding household finances seen in Sect. 4 of this Chapter, first, as for the overall trend of changes in work before and after the earthquake, it is noteworthy that the proportion of respondents in the manufacturing and wholesale/retail industries decreased by half, and the number of respondents engaged in the fishing industry also decreased, while the number of respondents who said they were unemployed doubled from 20 to 40% (Tables 12 and 14). In terms of employment status too, the number of regular workers decreased by 12 points and the number of pensioners doubled (Tables 13 and 15). In light of the fact that the majority of the responses to the question about the characteristics of the local economy of each district indicated that it was a fishing town or a fishery processing industry town, as seen in Table 35 above, it can be inferred that the decrease in the number of people working in these main industries of the region has had a damaging effect on the local economy.

Regarding the status of work reconstruction, only 40% of the respondents said that their job continued or resumed, while more than 20% said that they were closed their business or changed jobs (Table 16); by industry, there was a clear division between the construction industry, which was buoyed by special reconstruction demand, and the wholesale/retail, hospitality and other industries which suffered from population outflow (Table 17). 70% of the respondents indicated that their work was affected by the earthquake (Table 18), of which 30% indicated that their business had recovered and 50% indicated that their business had not recovered or was deteriorating (Table 19). As the causes for the delay in recovery, the delay in rebuilding facilities as well as the loss of customers was identified (Table 21), and the opening of the gap in recovery can be identified in the cross-analysis by industry (Table 22).

On the other hand, the timing of recovery for those who answered that their work had recovered was very recent, such as in 2020 (Table 23), and the special reconstruction demand was the most common response for the main reason for the recovery (Table 24). Regarding the receipt of public support, 70% responded that they did not receive any (Table 26). From the above, it can be seen that many industries are facing difficulties in the recovery, and on the other hand, the industries that have been supported by the special reconstruction demand during this period are expected to turn negative upon the end of the reconstruction-related projects.

The fact that maintaining the livelihoods of the affected households during this period was not an easy task is evident from the results of the responses on household financial conditions shown in Tables 30, 31, 32, and 33 of this Chapter. Compared to pre-earthquake levels, household incomes and savings have reduced significantly by 50% and more than 60% respectively, while on the other hand, household expenditures and loan balances greatly increased by 50% and 40% respectively.

The above response trends can be thought to require further verification in view of items of the "Recovery Calendar" such as "(4) work has returned to normal" and "(6) the impact of the disaster on their household budget had disappeared". As shown in Figs. 2, 3, 4, 5, 6, 7, 8, 9, 10, 11, 12, 13, 14, 15, 16, and 17 of this Chapter, there is a characteristic gap in the recovery curves of each district, between the commencement of the recovery of "(4) work has returned to normal" which was relatively early, from immediately after the earthquake to around one year later, and "(5) housing problems" which was delayed by several years, but this difference highlights the fact that disaster-affected households were struggling to maintain their livelihoods while tolerating the delay in housing reconstruction. In addition, the recovery curve for the timing of "(6) the impact of the disaster on their household budget had disappeared" shows a delay in recovery greater than that for "(5) housing problems" in each district, and particularly in the Machikata, Otsuchi district, Akahama, Otsuchi district, Central Rikuzentakata district, Shishiori, Kesennuma district and Tamaura-nishi, Iwanuma district, only about 50% of the respondents had achieved the goal as of 2020, nine years after the earthquake.

(3) Actual feeling of economic and population recovery

The responses to this survey regarding the recovery status of the local economy and population are valuable data as they reflect the actual feelings of the affected areas and people, which are different from general statistical indicators such as the Economic Census.

The response trends regarding the recovery of the local economy shown in Table 37 correlate well with the response trends regarding the recovery of the local shopping streets shown in Table 39 (Table 40), strongly suggesting that the "local economy" the respondents envisioned when responding was the local economy around their own residence. Also, responses regarding population recovery correlated with response trends regarding the recovery status of the local economy (Table 48), and also showed a correlation with the response trends regarding the recovery status of the local shopping streets (Table 49).

Therefore, it is thought to be effective to analyze the trends in responses regarding the local economy (Table 37), local shopping streets (Table 39) and population recovery (Table 45), based on the respondents' opinion of the characteristics of the local economy for each district, as shown in Table 35. For example, in districts that have the characteristic of a "residential area" on the periphery of a metropolitan area, such as Arai-higashi, Sendai district and Tamaura-nishi, Iwanuma district, it is felt that the local economy has almost completely recovered. At the polar opposite to this, in Machikata, Otsuchi district and Central Rikuzentakata district, where the character of the area was emphasized as being a commercial center in a region with the fishing and fishery processing industry at its core, the pessimistic feeling that the recovery of the local economy was 20–30% stood out. It is thought that this is the effect of the fact that in these commercial centers in regional areas, large-scale land-filling readjustment projects with a construction period of several years were selected in the reconstruction plans, and the full-scale reconstruction of housing and shopping streets had to wait for a long time. On the other hand, in the middle of these two extremes are districts such as Shishiori, Kesennuma district, Shinkadonowaki and Minato, Ishinomaki district, Aoi, Higashimatsushima district, and Shin-Sakamoto, Yamamoto district, which were positioned as having responses split between being a "residential area" and a fishing town or fishery processing town, and the most common response was that the recovery of the local economy nine years after the earthquake was 60–80%. If we consider that the responses that the local economy is characterized as a "residential area" reflects the character of the area as a commuter town for office workers, it is likely that the respondents will feel that the economy has grown due to being within an area with access to employment in the neighboring urban area, even if the recovery of local industries such as fishing and fishery processing is delayed.

Furthermore, a combined analysis of the above response trends with the results of "(10) the local economy had recovered from the impact of the disaster" and other items in the "Recovery Calendar" is thought to be effective. In Arai-higashi, Sendai district and Tamaura-nishi, Iwanuma district, which responded as "residential areas" on the periphery of major cities, the recovery of "(10) local economy" in the "Recovery Calendar" was more than 50% as of 2020, nine years after the earthquake, as was the case in Aoi, Higashimatsushima district, which is within the employment access area of a neighboring urban area. On the other hand, in regional areas where fishing and fishery processing industries are the core, differences in the trends of the responses in the "Recovery Calendar" were seen. Even between shopping street districts where land-filling readjustment projects were implemented over many years, for example, in Yamada, Yamada district where the "life town" concept of connecting the shopping district and the disaster public housing was placed at the core of the reconstruction community building, 30% of the respondents answered "(10) local economy" had been achieved, while in Machikata, Otsuchi district the achievement level was only 10%. Yamada, Yamada district's strenuous efforts stand out among the many districts that implemented land-filling readjustment projects, such as Kuwagasaki, Miyako district, Central Rikuzentakata district, Shizugawa, Minamisanriku district, Shishiori, Kesennuma district, Shinkadonowaki and Minato, Ishinomaki district, and Ayumino, Ishinomaki district, which all had achievement levels around only 20%, but it is presumed that this is the result of the involvement of the Chamber of Commerce and Industry in the process of planning the reconstruction community-building of Yamada Town, rather than leaving it to the government (Table 42).

One of the implications that can be gained from the above may be the lesson that while it is possible for a recovery community-building plan on the periphery of a metropolitan area to prioritize the rapid construction of housing in a compact city format and leave the livelihoods of the affected households and the local economy to the economic power of the urban area, a recovery plan for a regional area with the fishing or fishery processing industry at its core cannot prioritize the reconstruction of housing only; it is essential to have a recovery plan that incorporates the recovery of the foundation of the livelihoods of the disaster victims and the local economy at the same time. Many of the recovery plans established under the lead of the government in various regions were far too lacking in their consideration of the recovery of regional industries, such as the application of a reconstruction model for the metropolitan periphery that focused on constructing residential areas and prevented businesses in the region from rebuilding for several years due to land-filling readjustment projects, as well as the disaster prevention group relocation projects in disaster risk areas that were only applied to housing and prevented house-and-business integrated reconstruction. The negative feelings regarding economic and population recovery that appeared in the results of this survey are considered to be something that urges a strict reconsideration of the conventional notion of recovery community-building administration.

(4) Self-perception as a victim

The low level of achievement in the responses to the question "(9) their self-perception as a disaster victim has disappeared" has been identified as one characteristic trend drawn from the "Recovery Calendar" of this survey (Fig. 1). Further, when attention is paid to the shape of the recovery curve of the "Recovery Calendar" over time, items such as "(1) grasped the overall damage", "(3) resolved to live an inconvenient life for a while", and "(4) work has returned to normal" showed improvement at an early stage, while for the group of questions including "(5) have resolved finally their housing problems" and "(6) the impact of the disaster on their household budget had disappeared" a gentle recovery is drawn that is delayed several years. In between, the recovery curve for the item "(9) their self-perception as a disaster victim has disappeared" shows a shape that follows the latter. This infers that "(9) self-perception as a disaster victim" was largely dependent on the normalization of the foundation of livelihoods, especially "(5) housing problems".

In addition, if the recovery curves for "(9) self-perception as a disaster victim" by district are compared, certain differences are seen, which is thought to require further consideration. The recovery curve of "(9) self-perception as a disaster victim" shows improvement that appears to follow the recovery curve of "(5) housing problems" in districts including Hirata, Kamaishi district, Suezaki, Ofunato district, Takata-kita, Rikuzentakata district, Shinkadonowaki and Minato, Ishinomaki district, and Arai-higashi, Sendai district. Conversely, there are districts where the recovery curve for "(9) self-perception as a disaster victim" remains stagnant, even though the recovery curve for "(5) housing problems" is improving. For example, in Kuwagasaki, Miyako district, although 50% achievement of "(5) housing problems" is being shown relatively early around 2015, the achievement of "(9) self-perception as a disaster victim" remains stagnant at 30% even in 2020, 9 years after the earthquake. This trend is shown other districts too, including Yamada, Yamada district, Machikata, Otsuchi district, Akahama Otsuchi district, Central Rikuzentakata district, Shishiori, Kesennuma district, Shizugawa, Minamisanriku district, Ayumino, Ishinomaki district, Tamaura-nishi, Iwanuma district, and Shin-Sakamoto, Yamamoto district; in most districts, the recovery curve for "(9) self-perception as a disaster victim" remains stagnant at around 40%. Further scrutiny of the causes of these differences is required.

(5) Safety

In the results of the "Recovery Calendar" of this survey, the tendency to answer "(2) thought it is now safe" was unique in relation to previous studies. The Recovery Calendar by the Great East Japan Earthquake Livelihood Recovery Survey Team (2016), in which the Reconstruction Agency and others were involved, indicated that 84.0% of the respondents achieved the item "(2) thought it is now safe" in 2016, five years after the earthquake. However, in this survey, the achievement result of "(2) safety" was only 60.6% overall (Fig. 1).

Furthermore, when looked at by district, there was variation in the trends in responses for "(2) safety" as described above (Figs. 2, 3, 4, 5, 6, 7, 8, 9, 10, 11, 12, 13, 14, 15, 16, and 17); in Kuwagasaki, Miyako district the responses that said safety had been achieved were only 40%, and it was around 50% in Machikata, Otsuchi district, Akahama, Otsuchi district, Takata-kita, Rikuzentakata district, Shinkadonowaki and Minato, Ishinomaki district, and Shin-Sakamoto, Yamamoto district. Further, it is noteworthy that in all districts the curve of "(2) safety" reaches its peak by around 2016, five years after the earthquake, and the responses thereafter show a sideways trend until 2020. As a result of a decade of reconstruction being spent on safety measures reliant upon the national government's "multiple disaster prevention," it does not appear that "safety" has been completed yet in the affected areas.

"Safety" is one of the most important issues to be achieved in disaster recovery, such that, as discussed at the beginning of this chapter, the 2013 Act on Recovery from Large-Scale Disaster Recovery (Article 3) places the building of safe communities as one of its basic principles. The reality that the awareness of disaster victims regarding this item has remained stagnant after a decade of recovery is worth facing up to. In addition, as seen in the remarkable delay in population recovery in Kuwagasaki, Miyako district that was shown in Table 45 above, there is a possibility that the issue of "safety" predetermined other aspects of the recovery, such as population outflow and delayed economic recovery, which is an issue for further verification in the future.

Supplementary Note

This survey is the result of research support by the Kobe University Center for Social Systems Innovation (part of July survey), and Hyogo Earthquake Memorial 21st Century Research Institute (part of October survey).

References

Hayashi, Haruo (ed.). 2000. *Kobe City Disaster Recovery Overview and Validation—Livelihood Reconstruction Topic Report*. Research Center for Disaster Reduction Systems Technical Report, Disaster Prevention Research Institute, Kyoto University (in Japanese)

Hokugo, Akihiko, Yuka Kaneko, Yuichi Honjo, Toshihisa Toyoda, Yumi Shiomi, Abel Táiti Konno Pinheiro, and Yegane Ghezelloo. 2021. Resident Questionnaire Survey on the Lives and Livelihoods Recovery in the Devastated Area After Ten Years from the Great East Japan Earthquake and Tsunami; Overall Results Review. *Journal of International Cooperation Studies* 28 (2): 23–63 (in Japanese)

Iwate Prefecture. 2019. *Report on the 2019 Status of Initiatives in the Great East Japan Earthquake and Tsunami Reconstruction Plan: Iwate Reconstruction Report 2019—8 Years of Initiatives Under the Reconstruction Plan*. Iwate Prefecture (in Japanese)

Kawawaki, Yasuo. 2014. Does Social Capital in the Community Promote Residents' Mutual Aids After Disasters?: The Empirical Analysis Based on Local Residents' Survey in the Areas Affected by the Great East Japan Earthquake. *The Nonprofit Review* 14 (1 & 2): 1–13 (in Japanese)

Kimura, Reo, Haruo Hayashi, Shigeo Tatsuki, and Keiko Tamura. 2001. Determinants and Timing of Housing Reconstruction Decisions by the Victims of the 1995 Hanshin-Awaji Earthquake Disaster: A 2001 Replication. *Journal of Social Safety Science* 3: 23–32 (in Japanese)

Kimura, Reo, Haruo Hayashi, Shigeo Tatsuki, and Keiko Tamura, et al. 2004. Psychologically Defined Life Reconstruction Processes of Disaster Victims in the 1995 Hanshin-Awaji Earthquake. *Journal of Social Safety Science* 6: 241–250 (in Japanese)

Matsukawa, Anna, Aya Tsujioka, and Shigeo Tatsuki. 2015. Life Recovery Processes and the Challenges of 4 Types of Dwellers: Life Recovery Assessment Workshop in Natori City in Miyagi Prefecture. *Journal of Social Safety Science* 25: 23–33 (in Japanese)

Recovery Agency Great East Japan Earthquake Livelihood Recovery Survey Team. 2016. *Survey on the Recovery of Livelihoods After 5 Years from the Great East Japan Earthquake and Tsunami* (in Japanese)

Tamura, Keiko, Haruo Hayashi, Shigeo Tatsuki, and Reo Kimura. 2001. A Quantitative Verification of the 7 Elements Model of Socio-Economic Recovery from the Kobe Earthquake. *Journal of Social Safety Science* 3: 1–8 (in Japanese)

Tatsuki, Shigeo. 2013. What is Important for Reconstructing Livelihoods? A Comparison of the Results of Livelihood Recovery Surveys After the Hanshin-Awaji Earthquake and the Great East Japan Earthquake. *Toshi Seisaku* 161: 86–103 (in Japanese)

Survey Results on the Recovery Perception of the Commercial and Industrial Entities as of the 10th Anniversary of the East Japan Earthquake

Yuka Kaneko, Yuichi Honjo, Toshihisa Toyoda, Akihiko Hokugo, and Yumi Shiomi

1 Introduction: Purpose and Method

This chapter provides the results and some consideration of a questionnaire survey conducted on business entities' perception of recovery in the coastal area of Iwate prefecture affected by the 2011 East Japan Earthquake, as of the 10th anniversary of the disaster.

The survey method was a paper questionnaire and, as shown in Table 1 below, the cooperation of the Miyako Chamber of Commerce and Industry ("Miyako CCI"), the Yamada Town Society of Commerce and Industry ("Yamada SCI"), the Otsuchi Society of Commerce and Industry ("Otsuchi SCI"), and the Kamaishi Chamber of Commerce and Industry ("Kamaishi CCI") in Iwate Prefecture was obtained to

Y. Kaneko (✉)
Center for Social Systems Innovation and the Research Center for Urban Safety and Security, Kobe University, Kobe, Japan
e-mail: ykaneko@kobe-u.ac.jp

Y. Honjo
Graduate School of Disaster Resilience and Governance, University of Hyogo, Kobe, Japan

T. Toyoda
Kobe University, Kobe, Japan

A. Hokugo
The Research Center for Urban Safety and Security, Kobe University, Kobe, Japan

Y. Shiomi
Asian Disaster Reduction Center, Kobe, Japan

Y. Kaneko et al. (eds.), *Recovery of Disaster Victims*, Kobe University Monograph Series in Social Science Research, https://doi.org/10.1007/978-981-99-2957-3_3

Table 1 Status of conduct of business recovery perception survey

Cooperating institution	Survey date	Number distributed	Number of responses	Response rate (%)
Miyako CCI	March 2020	1,100	229	20.7
Yamada SCI	March 2020	402	83	20.6
Otsuchi SCI	October 2020	364	63	17.3
Kamaishi CCI	March 2020	900	193	21.4
Total		2,766	568	20.5

distribute the questionnaire to a total of 2,766 target business entities,[1] from which 567 responses were obtained. The response rate was 20.5%. It was initially planned for this survey to be conducted along the coast of Iwate and Miyagi prefectures, but the survey was suspended due to the proliferation of the COVID-19 virus during 2020 and became limited to the four groups mentioned above.

The contents of the survey's questions enquired about the respondent's demographic attributes in Part 1, the details of damage suffered by the business and status of reconstruction in Part 2, the perception of the status of regional economic recovery in Part 3, and the timing of achieving recovery according to the so-called "recovery calendar" method in Part 4.[2]

The survey's analysis methods are simple tabulation, cross tabulation and the chi-square test. The same research group also conducted a livelihood recovery perception survey in 2020 of regular households in the coastal areas of Iwate and Miyagi prefectures inundated by the tsunami, which obtained responses from 1,273 of the 7,895 households that the survey was distributed to (response rate 16.1%),[3] so it is thought that by comparing it with the results obtained by the subject business recovery perception survey, it will be a useful reference for knowing the status of businesses, which differs from the status of household finances.

---

[1] OF these, the Miyako Chamber of Commerce and Industry (all members), the Yamada Town Society of Commerce and Industry (all members that have completed reconstruction after the earthquake), and the Kamaishi Chamber of Commerce and Industry (all members) distributed the questionnaire by enclosing it with the March 2020 edition of their newsletter. The Otsuchi Society of Commerce and Industry (all members) distributed the questionnaire by enclosing it with the October 2020 edition of its newsletter, when the effects of the COVID-19 pandemic were temporarily relieved.

[2] The "recovery calendar" is a survey method developed from the ethnographic survey that collated the stories of the victims of the Hanshin-Awaji Earthquake and is a research method that focuses on changes in the victims' feeling of recovery with the passage of time (Tamura et al. 2001, Kimura et al. 2004). As of now the survey has become established based on 12 factors, and there is previous research following the East Japan Earthquake (Tatsuki 2013, Kawawaki 2014, etc.) and it was also used in the 5-year livelihood recovery survey conducted with the cooperation of the Reconstruction Agency and the affected prefectures (East Japan Earthquake Livelihood Recovery Survey Team 2016).

[3] See Chap. 22 of this volume.

Hereinafter, this article will follow the structure of the survey form by presenting, the details of damage suffered and status of reconstruction of the respondent businesses in Sect. 2, the respondent businesses' perception of the status of regional economic recovery in Sect. 3, responses regarding the "recovery calendar" in Sect. 4, and some consideration and summary in Sect. 5.

We would once again like to express our gratitude to the institutions and businesses that cooperated with this survey, and offer the results of this survey as a reference in view of the ten years of recovery from the East Japan Earthquake.

2 Damage Suffered and Status of Reconstruction of the Respondent Businesses

2.1 Overview of the Businesses

Regarding the distribution of industries of the businesses that provided responses (Q2 (1)), as shown in Table 2, wholesalers and retailers were the largest in number for each chamber of commerce at around 30%, followed by the construction industry at about 20% and manufacturers at 10–20%. There was no significant differences in the cross tabulation by region.

Regarding the age of the businesses that provided responses (Q2 (2)), as shown in Table 3, there was a range from several months as the youngest to 250 years for the oldest, with the average age of businesses being about 46 to 50 years for each chamber of commerce.

Regarding the employee size of the businesses that provided responses (Q2 (3)), as shown in Table 4, the most common was 1–4 employees, which was 40–50% of businesses for each chamber of commerce, followed by 10–29 employees, which was over 20%. About 15% of businesses had 5–9 employees, and the number of individual operators without employees was also 10–20%.

Regarding the pre-earthquake operating format of the businesses that provided responses (Q2 (4)), as shown in Table 5, in each chamber of commerce 40% of businesses had its own building on its own land. Next, there were many businesses that had a home and workplace in the same building, particularly in the Yamada SCI and the Otsuchi SCI, where more than 30% of responses had this form. Following that, in the responses from the Miyako CCI and Otsuchi SCI, many businesses owned their own building on leased land, and in the Yamada SCI and Kamaishi CCI, the number of businesses that leased a building was more than 10%. The above differences were statistically significant (P value of 0.034 in the chi-square test).

Table 2 Industry type of respondent businesses (Q2 (1))

	Miyako CCI		Yamada SCI		Otsuchi SCI		Kamaishi CCI		Total	
	No	%	No	%	No	%	No	%	No	%
Agriculture/Forestry	2	0.9	–	–	–	–	2	1.1	4	0.7
Fishing	9	4.0	4	4.9	2	3.4	–	–	15	2.7
Manufacturing	38	16.8	14	17.1	6	10.3	26	14.0	84	15.2
Construction	46	20.4	10	12.2	11	19.0	36	19.4	103	18.7
Wholesale/Retail	56	24.8	25	30.5	20	34.5	49	26.3	150	27.2
Banking/Insurance	3	1.3	2	2.4	1	1.7	9	4.8	15	2.7
Real estate/Leasing	3	1.3	1	1.2	1	1.7	4	2.2	9	1.6
Transportation	1	0.4	–	–	1	1.7	4	2.2	6	1.1
Telecommunications	1	0.4	–	–	–	–	1	0.5	2	0.4
Hospitality services	27	11.9	12	14.6	8	13.8	24	12.9	71	12.9
Health, welfare, medical	2	0.9	1	1.2	3	5.2	4	2.2	10	1.8
Education	2	0.9	–	–	2	3.4	1	0.5	5	0.9
Unemployed	–	–	–	–	–	–	1	0.5	1	0.2
Other	36	15.9	13	15.9	3	5.2	25	13.4	77	13.9
Total valid responses	226	100.0	82	100.0	58	100.0	186	100.0	552	100.0
Invalid/no response	3	–	1	–	5	–	7	–	16	–

Table 3 Age of respondent businesses (Q2 (2))

	Miyako CCI (225)	Yamada SCI (81)	Otsuchi SCI (61)	Kamaishi CCI (185)
	No. of years	No. of years	No. of years	No. of years
Youngest	0.25	5	1	3
Oldest	250	160	180	198
Average age	50	47	48	46

2.2 Damage Suffered by the Businesses

Regarding the damage suffered due to the earthquake by the businesses that provided responses (Q2 (5)), as shown in Table 6, in all regions the largest number of respondents answered that "both the head office and equipment were swept away or completely destroyed", which accounted for 57% of respondents in Otsuchi in particular, 36% of respondents in Yamada, and around 20% of the respondents from Miyako and Kamaishi. In each region, this was followed by the responses that "only the head office was swept away or completely destroyed" and "only equipment was swept away or completely destroyed".

Table 4 Number of employees of respondent businesses (Q2 (3))

	Miyako CCI		Yamada SCI		Otsuchi SCI		Kamaishi CCI		Total	
	No	%	No	%	No	%	No	%	No	%
Nil	26	11.6	13	15.9	13	22.8	26	13.9	78	14.2
1–4	86	38.4	43	52.4	23	40.4	74	39.6	226	41.1
5–9	41	18.3	10	12.2	4	7.0	25	13.4	80	14.5
10–29	48	21.4	12	14.6	13	22.8	44	23.5	117	21.3
30–49	15	6.7	0	0.0	2	3.5	7	3.7	24	4.4
50–99	4	1.8	1	1.2	2	3.5	7	3.7	14	2.5
100–299	4	1.8	3	3.7	0	0.0	4	2.1	11	2.0
Total valid responses	224	100.0	82	100.0	57	100.0	187	100.0	550	100.0
Invalid/no response	5	–	1	–	6	–	6	–	18	–

Table 5 Pre-earthquake operating format of respondent businesses (Q2 (4))

	Miyako CCI		Yamada SCI		Otsuchi SCI		Kamaishi CCI		Total	
	No	%	No	%	No	%	No	%	No	%
Own land & building	87	40.3	31	38.8	25	43.9	85	45.5	228	42.2
Leased land, own building	39	18.1	5	6.3	8	14.0	23	12.3	75	13.9
Leased building	10	4.6	9	11.3	2	3.5	22	11.8	43	8.0
Combined home and workplace	56	25.9	27	33.8	19	33.3	44	23.5	146	27.0
Other	24	11.1	8	10.0	3	5.3	13	7.0	48	8.9
Total valid responses	216	100.0	80	100.0	57	100.0	187	100.0	540	100.0
Invalid/no response	13	–	3	–	6	–	6	–	28	–

If the number of businesses where the head office or equipment was swept away or completely destroyed are added together, it accounts for 80% of the respondents in Otsuchi, more than 50% of the respondents in Yamada, 40% of the respondents in Kamaishi, and 30% of the respondents in Miyako.

The percentage of respondents who responded "Other" accounted for 30% of the total, but a close examination of the breakdown revealed that it includes serious damage such as "combined house and shop were swept away or completely

Table 6 Damage suffered by respondent businesses (Q2 (5))

	Miyako CCI		Yamada SCI		Otsuchi SCI		Kamaishi CCI		Total	
	No	%	No	%	No	%	No	%	No	%
Head office & equipment swept away/completely destroyed	34	17.4	28	35.9	32	57.1	35	20.5	129	25.8
Head office swept away/completely destroyed	12	6.2	6	7.7	7	12.5	22	12.9	47	9.4
Equipment swept away/completely destroyed	18	9.2	8	10.3	4	7.1	18	10.5	48	9.6
Head office & equipment partially destroyed	14	7.2	2	2.6	1	1.8	20	11.7	37	7.4
Head office partially destroyed	16	8.2	2	2.6	3	5.4	13	7.6	34	6.8
Equipment partially destroyed	23	11.8	1	1.3	3	5.4	19	11.1	46	9.2
Other	78	40	31	39.7	6	10.7	44	25.7	159	31.8
Total valid responses	195	100.0	78	100.0	56	100.0	171	100.0	500	100.0
Invalid/no response	34	–	5	–	7	–	22	–	68	–

destroyed". For example, this applied to 11 of the 31 businesses in Yamada Town Society of Commerce and Industry that responded with "Other".

In this way, the degree of damage suffered by the respondents was extremely severe in each region, but there were regional differences that were statistically significant (*P* value 0.000 in the chi-square test).

2.3 Reconstruction Status of the Businesses

Regarding the form of post-earthquake reconstruction by the respondent businesses (Q2 (6)), the option of "rebuilding at the original site" in the question assumes that among the businesses that needed to construct a new building due to severe damage such as being swept away or complete destruction, there were businesses that were able to rebuild on the original site because they were located outside the area of land elevation readjustment projects, which is considered to mainly be the reconstruction of businesses in disaster risk areas along the ocean. The "repair at the original site" option is considered to be mainly for businesses that were near the edge of the areas of tsunami flooding, and were able to complete reconstruction of the business by repairing facilities at the original site. The option of "new construction on readjusted land" is assumed to be for those businesses that were forced to wait until the completion of land readjustment projects. The options of "new construction at a voluntary relocation site" and "leasing" are assumed to be the businesses that chose the option of restarting their business as soon as possible by either building or leasing buildings in safe inland areas.

The results of the responses are as shown in Table 7 and a significant difference between the regions (*P* value 0.000 in the chi-square test) was seen. Among the respondent businesses from the MIyako CCI and Kamaishi CCI, the most common response was "repair at the original site" at around 40%. On the other hand, the responses from the Yamada SCI and Otsuchi SCI were divided among various responses including "new construction at a voluntary relocation site", "rebuilding on the original site" and "new construction on readjusted land", and the responses given as "other" included reconstructing their business in a leased property. This diversity in the forms of reconstruction is assumed to be due to the fact that in the recovery plans of Yamada Town and Otsuchi Town, the commercial and industrial districts are the subject of recovery projects such as land elevation readjustment projects, and the tendencies of business reconstruction are divided between those inside and outside of the subject areas.

Table 7 Reconstruction form of respondent businesses (Q2 (6))

	Miyako CCI		Yamada SCI		Otsuchi SCI		Kamaishi CCI		Total	
	No	%	No	%	No	%	No	%	No	%
Rebuilding on the original site	16	9.2	12	15.8	9	16.1	20	12.5	57	12.3
Repair on the original site	74	42.8	10	13.2	10	17.9	60	37.5	154	33.1
New construction on readjusted land	14	8.1	11	14.5	10	17.9	14	8.8	49	10.5
New construction at voluntary relocation site	15	8.7	15	19.7	11	19.6	15	9.4	56	12.0
Leasing	10	5.8	5	6.6	4	7.1	17	10.6	36	7.7
Other	44	25.4	23	30.3	12	21.4	34	21.3	113	24.3
Total valid responses	173	100.0	76	100.0	56	100.0	160	100.0	465	100.0
Invalid/no response	56	–	7	–	7	–	33	–	103	

2.4 *Impact of the Earthquake on the Business Performance of the Respondent Businesses*

Regarding the impact of the earthquake on the business performance of the respondent businesses (Q2 (9)(1)), as shown in Table 8, the number of responses that said there was an effect was around 90% in each CCI/SCI, and there was not a significant difference between regions.

Table 8 Impact of the earthquake on the respondent businesses (Q2 (9)(1))

	Miyako CCI		Yamada SCI		Otsuchi SCI		Kamaishi CCI		Total	
	No	%	No	%	No	%	No	%	No	%
Had an impact	179	83.6	69	88.5	56	96.6	155	85.2	459	86.3
No impact	31	14.5	7	9.0	1	1.7	22	12.1	61	11.5
Other	4	1.9	2	2.6	1	1.7	5	2.7	12	2.3
Total valid responses	214	100.0	78	100.0	58	100.0	182	100.0	532	100.0
Invalid/no response	15	–	5	–	5	–	11	–	36	–

Regarding the respondent businesses' post-earthquake business performance conditions (Q2 (9)(2)), as shown in Table 9, in each region the responses of "not returned to pre-earthquake level" and "deterioration from pre-earthquake level continuing" combined for more than 50%. However, there was a significant regional difference in the breakdown (*P* value 0.019 in the chi-square test); for example, 30% of the respondent businesses in the Yamada SCI responded with "improved from pre-earthquake level".

Looking further at the post-earthquake performance conditions by industry (cross tabulation of Q2 (1) and Q2 (9)(2)), as shown in Table 10, in all regions the construction industry is the leading industry as the "main industries that have improved from pre-earthquake levels", while the wholesale and retail industry and hospitality industry were at the top as the "main industries that have not returned to pre-earthquake levels" or "main industries where deterioration from pre-earthquake levels has continued".

Next, when looking at the post-earthquake performance conditions by employment size (cross tabulation of Q2 (3) and Q2 (9)(2)), as shown in Table 11, 80% of the small businesses with no employees or 1–4 employees responded as "not returned to pre-earthquake level" or " deterioration from pre-earthquake level continuing", while half of the larger businesses responded as "improved from pre-earthquake level" or "recovered to pre-earthquake level", which was a statistically significant difference (*P*-value 0.019 in the chi-square test).

Looking at the post-earthquake business performance conditions by the pre-earthquake operating format (cross tabulation of Q2 (4) and Q2 (9)(2), as shown in Table 12, the largest number of responses in all asset formats was "not returned to pre-earthquake level". In particular, the respondents who had leased buildings (tenants) are delayed in their business recovery.

Looking at the post-earthquake business performance conditions by the damage suffered (cross tabulation of Q2(5) and Q2(9)(2), the results are as shown in Table 13. Among the businesses whose head office and/or equipment were swept away or completely destroyed, a total of 60% of responses were that the business has "not returned to pre-earthquake level" or "deterioration from pre-earthquake level continuing" and the number of responses were that the business has "improved from pre-earthquake level" or "recovered to pre-earthquake level" was less than 30%, while for those businesses whose head office and/or equipment were partially destroyed, those that have "improved from pre-earthquake level" or "recovered to pre-earthquake level" accounted for a combined 40%, indicating a significant difference depending on the damage suffered (*P*-value 0.000 in the chi-square test).

Looking at the post-earthquake business performance conditions by the form of reconstruction (cross tabulation of Q2(6) and Q2(9)(2), the results are as shown in Table 14. There was not a statistically significant difference (*P*-value 0.274 in the chi-square test), but as mentioned above, while it is thought that the responses of "reconstructing at the original site" were mainly from businesses who suffered damage through being swept away or completely destroyed yet could rebuild on their original site due to being outside of land elevation project areas, however they are the group that is most delayed in their recovery, with the number of responses of

Table 9 Post-earthquake business performance conditions of respondent businesses (Q2 (9)(2))

	Miyako CCI		Yamada SCI		Otsuchi SCI		Kamaishi CCI		Total	
	No	%	No	%	No	%	No	%	No	%
Improved from pre-earthquake level	40	21.7	21	30.0	14	25.5	24	15.2	99	21.2
Recovered to pre-earthquake level	38	20.7	8	11.4	7	12.7	27	17.1	80	17.1
Not returned to pre-earthquake level	57	31.0	28	40.0	24	43.6	56	35.4	163	35.3
Deterioration from pre-earthquake level continuing	37	20.1	9	12.9	7	12.7	29	18.4	82	17.6
Other	12	6.5	4	5.7	3	5.5	22	13.9	41	8.8
Total valid responses	184	100.0	70	100.0	55	100.0	158	100.0	467	100.0
Invalid/no response	45	–	13	–	8	–	35	–	101	–

Table 10 Post-earthquake business performance conditions by industry (Cross tabulation of Q2 (1) and Q2 (9)(2))

	Miyako CCI		Yamada SCI		Otsuchi SCI		Kamaishi CCI	
	Industry	No	Industry	No	Industry	No	Industry	No
Main industries that have improved from pre-earthquake levels	Const Manu W/R	19 7 4	Const Manu Hosp. W/R	6 4 4 2	Const	7	Const Manu Hosp.	10 6 4
Main industries that have recovered to pre-earthquake levels	W/R Const Manu	11 6 6	Const Manu	3 2	W/R Const	3 2	Const Hosp. W/R	7 5 3
Main industries that have not returned to pre-earthquake levels	W/R Manu Hosp.	19 7 7	W/R Fishing Manu Hosp.	11 4 4 4	W/R Hosp. Manu	11 4 2	W/R Manu F/I Hosp.	22 8 4 3
Main industries where deterioration from pre-earthquake levels has continued	W/R Manu Hosp.	14 10 4	W/R Manu	4 2	W/R	4	W/R Hosp. Const Manu	13 4 3 2

Legend Const. = Construction; Manufact. = Manufacturing; W/R = Wholesale/Retail; B/I = Banking/Insurance; Hosp. = Hospitality services

"not returned to pre-earthquake level" or "deterioration from pre-earthquake level continuing" being a combined 70%. This was followed by the "new construction after land readjustment" group, which was forced to wait until the completion of the uplift project to see how their performance would recover. Next, the business recovery of the "new construction on readjusted land" group of respondents, who were forced to wait until the land elevation projects were complete, is poor. Following that, the recovery of the "repair on the original site" group of respondents located near the edge of the areas of tsunami flooding is delayed, and the recovery of the group of respondents that chose to resume their business early by "voluntary relocation" or "leasing" is relatively progressed.

Table 11 Post-earthquake business performance conditions by number of employees (cross tabulation of Q2 (3) and Q2 (9)(2))

		Improved from pre-earthquake level	Recovered to pre-earthquake level	Not returned to pre-earthquake level	Deterioration from pre-earthquake level continuing	Other	Total
Nil	No	7	8	30	17	5	66
	%	9.1	12.1	45.5	25.8	7.6	100.0
1–4	No	29	24	78	42	15	188
	%	15.4	12.8	41.5	22.3	8.0	100.0
5–9	No	17	16	22	7	5	67
	%	25.4	23.9	32.8	10.4	7.5	100.0
10–29	No	33	21	27	11	10	102
	%	32.4	20.6	26.5	10.8	9.8	100.0
30–49	No	4	5	1	2	4	16
	%	25.0	31.3	6.3	12.5	25.0	100.0
50–99	No	7	3	2	0	0	12
	%	58.3	25.0	12.7	0.0	0.0	100.0
100–299	No	2	3	3	0	1	9
	%	22.2	33.3	33.3	0.0	11.1	100.0
Total valid responses	No	98	80	163	79	40	460
	%	21.3	17.4	35.4	17.2	8.7	100.0

2.5 *Factors Behind Deterioration or Recovery of Business Performance*

When the respondents who responded that the earthquake had an impact on their business in Table 8 (Q2 (9)(1)) above were asked about the main causes of the impact (Q2 (9)(3), multiple responses allowed), as shown in Table 15, "loss of customers" was cited as a cause in all regions. The impact of the recession of the Japanese economy as a whole and the loss of facilities due to the earthquake were also cited as a cause by about 20% of the respondents each.

Regarding when business performance recovered after the earthquake (Q2 (9(4)), as shown in Table 16, the most common response was "not recovered yet", by around 30% of respondents in each region. Although not a statistically significant difference, around 20% of respondents from the Miyako CCI and Kamaishi CCI responded that they recovered during "FY 2012", while the responses from the Yamada SCI and Otsuchi SCI were spread across various periods.

Table 12 Post-earthquake business performance conditions by operating format (cross tabulation of Q2 (4) and Q2 (9)(2))

		Improved from pre-earthquake level	Recovered to pre-earthquake level	Not returned to pre-earthquake level	Deterioration from pre-earthquake level continuing	Other	Total
Own land & building	No	45	42	58	31	17	193
	%	23.3	21.8	30.1	16.1	8.8	100.0
Leased land, own building	No	13	11	24	121	3	63
	%	20.6	17.5	38.1	19.0	4.8	100.0
Leased building	No	9	3	16	8	1	37
	%	24.3	8.1	43.2	21.6	2.7	100.0
Combined home and workplace	No	25	19	47	22	11	124
	%	20.2	15.3	37.9	17.7	8.9	100.0
Other	No	6	3	13	8	8	38
	%	15.8	7.9	34.2	21.1	21.1	100.0
Total valid responses	No	98	78	158	81	40	455
	%	21.5	17.1	34.7	17.8	8.8	100.0

The timing of when respondent businesses' performance recovered by industry (cross tabulation of Q2 (1) and Q2 (9)(4)) is as shown in Table 17. Although not statistically significant (*P* value of 0.266 in the chi-square test), differences in recovery status by industry can be read from the fact that in the construction industry, recovery of business performance reached 70% in the first 2–3 years after the earthquake, and only 10% had not yet recovered at the time of the survey, while in the wholesale/retail industry, 50% had not yet recovered at the time of the survey.

When asked about the reasons for the recovery of business performance (Q2(9)(5), multiple responses allowed), as shown in Table 18, 60–70% of the respondents mentioned "reconstruction demand", which stood out in comparison to responses such as "marketing effort" and "recovery by customers", which were only about 20%.

Regarding the reasons for performance recovery by industry (cross tabulation of Q2 (1) and Q2 (9)(5)), the frequency of responses are shown in Table 19. There were statistically significant differences for "reconstruction special procurement", "recovery of the overall Japanese economy" and "marketing effort"; in particular, almost all responses from the construction industry cited "reconstruction special procurement", with 60–70% of wholesale/retail and hospitality service industry respondents also identifying this as a reason, and it was the most common response from manufacturing industry respondents. This was followed by "marketing effort" and "recovery by customers" in the manufacturing and wholesale/retail industries.

Table 13 Post-earthquake business performance conditions by damage suffered (cross tabulation of Q2 (5) and Q2 (9)(2))

		Improved from pre-earthquake level	Recovered to pre-earthquake level	Not returned to pre-earthquake level	Deterioration from pre-earthquake level continuing	Other	Total
Head office & equipment swept away/ completely destroyed	No	19	11	54	26	11	121
	%	15.7	9.1	44.6	21.5	9.1	100.0
Head office swept away/ completely destroyed	No	6	6	13	8	4	37
	%	16.2	16.2	35.1	21.6	10.8	100.0
Equipment swept away/ completely destroyed	No	4	9	16	10	3	42
	%	9.5	21.4	38.1	23.8	7.1	100.0
Head office & equipment partially destroyed	No	9	4	14	5	3	35
	%	25.7	11.4	40.0	14.3	8.6	100.0
Head office partially destroyed	No	7	7	11	5	2	32
	%	21.9	21.9	34.4	15.6	6.3	100.0
Equipment partially destroyed	No	6	12	17	3	3	41
	%	14.6	29.3	41.5	7.3	7.3	100.0
Other	No	39	25	29	20	12	125
	%	31.2	20.0	23.2	16.0	9.6	100.0
Total valid responses	No	90	74	154	77	38	433
	%	20.8	17.1	35.6	17.8	8.8	100.0

Across all industries, there was little mention of “restoration of equipment and machinery”, “support from headquarters and customers” and “support from the government”, and there was no significant difference between industries.

Table 14 Post-earthquake business performance conditions by form of reconstruction (cross tabulation of Q2 (6) and Q2 (9)(2))

		Improved from pre-earthquake level	Recovered to pre-earthquake level	Not returned to pre-earthquake level	Deterioration from pre-earthquake level continuing	Other	Total
Rebuild on original site	No	4	8	25	12	3	52
	%	7.7	15.4	48.1	23.1	5.8	100.0
Repair on original site	No	26	26	55	25	9	141
	%	18.4	18.4	39.0	17.7	6.4	100.0
Construct on readjusted land	No	10	5	17	8	2	42
	%	23.8	11.9	40.5	19.0	4.8	100.0
Construct at voluntary relocation site	No	11	8	16	9	7	51
	%	21.6	15.7	31.4	17.6	13.7	100.0
Leasing	No	7	4	8	8	4	31
	%	22.6	12.9	25.8	25.8	12.9	100.0
Other	No	25	17	25	15	14	96
	%	26.0	17.7	26.0	15.6	14.6	100.0
Total valid responses	No	83	68	146	77	39	413
	%	20.1	16.5	35.4	18.6	9.4	

2.6 Receipt and Effect of Government Administrative Support

Regarding public support received by the respondent businesses (Q2 (7), multiple responses allowed), as shown in Table 20, the "SME Group Subsidy" from the Small and Medium Enterprise Agency was the most common response in all regions. Statistically significant differences were seen between regions in the categories of "SME Group Subsidy", "prefectural subsidies", "temporary shop or factory", and "did not receive public support". Amongst these, the "SME Group Subsidy" was received by more than half of the respondents in Otsuchi, 36.3% in Kamaishi, 32.1% in Yamada, and 21.8% in Miyako. The use of other prefectural and municipal subsidies was also high in the responses from Otsuchi. In Miyako and Yamada, the use of special loans from governmental and private financial institutions was also high, together with the use of subsidies. On the other hand, 40% of respondents in Miyako and over 30% in

Table 15 Reasons for deterioration of respondent businesses' performance (Q2 (9)(3), multiple responses allowed, 394 total valid responses)

	Miyako CCI		Yamada SCI		Otsuchi SCI		Kamaishi CCI		Total	
	No	%	No	%	No	%	No	%	No	%
Damage to buildings & equipment	20	12.8	15	26.3	14	31.1	28	20.6	77	19.5
Loss of customers	90	57.7	38	66.7	30	66.7	87	64.0	245	62.2
Insufficient staff	24	15.4	10	17.5	7	15.6	19	14.0	60	15.2
Insufficient funds	11	7.1	4	7.0	4	8.9	6	4.4	25	6.3
Difficulty obtaining stock	15	9.6	6	10.5	7	15.6	13	9.6	41	10.4
Japan's nationwide recession	35	22.4	9	15.8	11	24.4	38	27.9	93	23.6
Other reasons	22	14.1	12	21.1	6	13.3	23	16.9	63	16.0
Unknown	5	3.2	2	3.5	1	2.2	5	3.7	13	3.3
Performance not deteriorated	19	12.2	5	8.8	4	8.9	11	8.1	39	9.9
Total valid responses	241	154.5	101	177.2	84	186.7	230	169.1	656	166.5

Kamaishi and Yamada did not receive any public support, suggesting that there was a difference in access to subsidies.

Regarding the receipt of public support by damage suffered (cross tabulation of Q2 (5) and Q2 (7)) the frequency is shown Table 21, and there were statistically significant differences in the categories of "municipal subsidy", "prefectural subsidy", "SME Group Subsidy", "temporary shop or factory", "government development finance institution loan", " Corporation for Supporting the Turnaround of Businesses Damaged by the Great East Japan Earthquake", and "did not receive public support". The more severe damage a group of respondents suffered, the more of them received various subsidies; in particular, 60% of the "Head office & equipment swept away/ completely destroyed" group of respondents received the "SME Group Subsidy". There was also a large amount of use of special loans from government-affiliated financial institutions in the group of respondents that suffered severe damage, but this is thought to include the support loans for the 1/4 co-payment for the receipt of the "SME Group Subsidy". Although not shown in this table, there are also regional differences; for example, in Yamada, 80% of the respondents who received the "SME

Table 16 When respondent businesses' performance recovered (Q2 (9)(4))

	Miyako CCI		Yamada SCI		Otsuchi SCI		Kamaishi CCI		Total	
	No	%	No	%	No	%	No	%	No	%
Within one year of earthquake	14	8.4	5	7.7	4	8.0	16	10.8	39	9.1
FY 2012	32	19.3	7	10.8	6	12.0	26	17.6	71	16.6
FY 2013	20	12.0	8	12.3	5	10.0	17	11.5	50	11.7
FY 2014	14	8.4	4	6.2	4	8.0	14	9.5	36	8.4
FY 2015	4	2.4	6	9.2	3	6.0	8	5.4	21	4.9
FY 2016	11	6.6	2	3.1	5	10.0	10	6.8	28	6.5
FY 2017	4	2.4	4	6.2	2	4.0	5	3.4	15	3.5
FY 2018	6	3.6	1	1.5	2	4.0	5	3.4	14	3.3
FY 2019	1	0.6	4	6.2	2	4.0	7	4.7	14	3.3
Not recovered yet	60	36.1	24	36.9	17	34.0	40	27.0	141	32.9
Total valid responses	166	100.0	65	100.0	50	100.0	148	100.0	429	100.0
Invalid/no response	63	–	18	–	13	–	45	–	139	–

Group Subsidy" were from the severely affected group that had buildings swept away or completely destroyed.

Regarding the effect of the public assistance received by the respondent businesses (Q2 (8)), as shown in Table 22, a total of 90% of the respondents in each region responded that it was "very effective" or "somewhat effective".

When the effect of public assistance by the type of assistance (cross tabulation of Q2(7) and Q2(8)) is considered, as shown in Table 23, the "SMG group subsidy" was the type responded as "very effective" in all regions, followed by municipal subsidies.

Looking at the effect of public support by industry (cross tabulation of Q2 (1) and Q2 (8)), although not statistically significant, characteristics are noticeable in each industry as seen in Table 24, such as support being evaluated as especially high in the transportation and real estate/leasing industries, and in the fishing industry 60% of respondents gave a high evaluation but low evaluations were also given by 20% of respondents.

Looking at the effect of public support by level of damage (cross tabulation of Q2 (5) and Q2 (8)), although there is no statistically significant difference, Table 25 shows that the effect of public support tended to be greater for severely damaged businesses.

Table 17 When respondent businesses' performance recovered by industry (cross tabulation of Q2 (1) and Q2 (9)(4))

		Within 1 year	FY 2012	FY 2013	FY 2014	FY 2015	FY 2016	FY 2017	FY 2018	FY 2019	Not Recovered	Total
Agriculture/Forestry	No	0	0	1	0	0	0	0	1	0	1	3
	%	0.0	0.0	33.3	0.0	0.0	0.0	0.0	33.3	0.0	33.3	100.0
Fishing	No	0	1	1	1	0	2	1	1	0	4	11
	%	0.0	9.1	9.1	9.1	0.0	18.2	9.1	9.1	0.0	36.4	100.0
Manufacturing	No	7	10	8	3	4	4	5	1	3	23	68
	%	10.3	14.7	11.8	4.4	5.9	5.9	7.4	1.5	4.4	33.8	100.0
Construction	No	10	21	13	9	5	6	0	2	2	8	76
	%	13.2	27.6	17.1	11.8	6.6	7.9	0.0	2.6	2.6	10.5	100.0
Wholesale/Retail	No	8	17	11	9	5	5	2	3	33	56	119
	%	6.7	14.3	9.2	7.6	4.2	4.2	1.7	2.5	2.5	47.1	100.0
Banking/Insurance	No	1	3	1	2	0	0	1	0	0	3	11
	%	9.1	27.3	9.1	18.2	0.0	0.0	9.1	0.0	0.0	27.3	100.0
Real Estate/Leasing	No	0	1	1	1	0	0	1	1	0	3	8
	%	0.0	12.5	12.5	12.5	0.0	0.0	12.5	12.5	0.0	37.5	100.0
Transport	No	1	0	0	0	0	2	1	0	0	1	5
	%	20.0	0.0	0.0	0.0	0.0	40.0	20.0	0.0	0.0	20.0	100.0
Tele-communication	No	0	0	0	1	0	0	0	0	0	1	2
	%	0.0	0.0	0.0	50.0	0.0	0.0	0.0	0.0	0.0	50.0	100.0
Hospitality services	No	6	9	6	3	2	3	2	4	1	13	49
	%	12.2	18.4	12.2	6.1	4.1	6.1	4.1	8.2	2.0	26.5	100.0
Health, welfare, medical	No	1	1	2	0	1	0	0	0	1	0	6

(continued)

Table 17 (continued)

		Within 1 year	FY 2012	FY 2013	FY 2014	FY 2015	FY 2016	FY 2017	FY 2018	FY 2019	Not Recovered	Total
	%	16.7	16.7	33.3	0.0	16.7	0.0	0.0	0.0	16.7	0.0	100.0
Education	No	0	0	0	0	0	0	0	0	0	4	4
	%	0.0	0.0	0.0	0.0	0.0	0.0	0.0	0.0	0.0	100.0	100.0
Other	No	5	7	6	6	3	5	2	0	4	20	58
	%	8.6	12.1	10.3	10.3	5.2	8.6	3.4	0.0	6.9	34.5	100.0
Total valid responses	No	39	70	50	35	20	27	15	13	14	137	420
	%	9.2	16.7	11.9	8.3	4.8	6.4	3.6	3.1	3.3	32.6	100.0

Table 18 Reasons for recovery of performance of respondent businesses (Q2 (9)(5), multiple responses allowed, 292 total valid responses)

	Miyako CCI		Yamada SCI		Otsuchi SCI		Kamaishi CCI		Total	
	No	%	No	%	No	%	No	%	No	%
Reconstruction special procurement	77	70.6	27	69.2	19	55.9	74	67.3	197	67.5
Economic recovery	8	7.3	6	15.4	2	5.9	11	10.0	27	9.2
Marketing effort	23	21.1	13	33.3	7	20.6	19	17.3	62	15.1
Restoration of equipment and machinery	8	7.3	3	7.7	4	11.8	8	7.3	23	7.9
Support from headquarters and customers	4	3.7	–	–	1	2.9	6	5.5	11	3.8
Recovery by customers	15	13.8	7	17.9	3	8.8	21	19.1	46	15.6
Government support	12	11.0	4	10.3	3	8.8	3	2.7	22	7.5
Other	9	8.3	3	7.7	3	8.8	7	6.4	22	7.5
Total valid responses	156	143.1	63	161.5	42	123.5	149	135.5	410	140.4

3 Respondent Businesses' Perception of the Status of Regional Economic Recovery

3.1 Characteristics of the Regional Economy as Seen by the Respondent Businesses

Prior to the series of questions about the recovery status of the regional economy, we first asked about the core characteristics of the local economy from the perspective of the respondents (Q3 (1)), and a significant difference appeared between towns (*P*-value 0.000 in the chi-square test), as seen in Table 26. Miyako, 50% of the respondents identified the town as a "seafood processing" town, while over 40% of the respondents in Otsuchi also identified the town as such. In Yamada, 40% of respondents identified the town as a "fishing" town, followed by "seafood processing". In Kamaishi, "industrial district" was the most common response at 20%, followed by "shopping street" and "seafood processing".

Table 19 Reasons for recovery of performance by industry (cross tabulation of Q2 (1) and Q2 (9)(5))

		Reconst. special procure	Economic recovery	Marketing effort	Restoration of equipment and machinery	Support from HQ and customers	Recovery by customers	Government support	Other
Agriculture/Forestry	Yes	0	0	1	0	0	1	1	0
	No	2	2	1	2	2	1	1	2
Fishing	Yes	1	1	0	1	0	0	0	4
	No	7	7	8	7	8	8	8	4
Manufacturing	Yes	25	9	15	7	4	7	7	1
	No	19	35	29	37	40	37	37	43
Construction	Yes	71	2	6	1	2	3	4	0
	No	2	71	67	72	71	70	69	73
Wholesale/Retail	Yes	42	7	13	5	3	11	3	8
	No	24	59	53	61	63	55	63	58
Banking/Insurance	Yes	4	2	3	1	1	3	0	0
	No	4	6	5	7	7	5	8	8
Real Estate/Leasing	Yes	3	0	1	0	0	1	0	2
	No	2	5	4	5	5	4	5	3
Transport	Yes	2	1	1	0	0	0	0	0
	No	1	2	2	3	3	3	3	3
Tele-communication	Yes	0	0	0	0	0	1	0	0
	No	1	1	1	1	1	0	1	1
Hospitality services	Yes	24	3	7	2	0	8	2	4
	No	14	35	31	36	38	30	36	34

(continued)

Table 19 (continued)

		Reconst. special procure	Economic recovery	Marketing effort	Restoration of equipment and machinery	Support from HQ and customers	Recovery by customers	Government support	Other
Health, welfare, medical	Yes	1	0	2	0	0	2	0	0
	No	5	6	4	6	6	4	6	6
Other	Yes	21	2	9	6	0	6	3	3
	No	19	38	31	34	40	34	37	38
Total valid responses	Yes	194	27	58	23	10	43	20	22
	No	100	267	236	271	284	251	274	

Table 20 Public support received by respondent businesses (Q2 (7), multiple responses allowed, 542 total valid responses)

	Miyako CCI		Yamada SCI		Otsuchi SCI		Kamaishi CCI		Total	
	No	%	No	%	No	%	No	%	No	%
Municipal subsidy	36	16.6	17	20.7	15	24.9	20	11.0	88	16.2
Prefectural subsidy	21	9.7	14	17.1	17	27.9	20	11.0	72	13.3
SME group subsidy	47	21.7	26	31.7	31	50.8	66	36.3	170	31.4
Temporary shop or factory	4	1.8	13	15.9	9	14.8	10	5.5	36	6.6
Special loan from government development finance institution	42	19.4	15	18.3	9	14.8	20	11.0	86	15.9
Special loan from private financial institution	14	6.5	9	11.0	4	6.6	9	4.9	36	6.6
Industry reconstruction corporation	11	5.1	5	6.1	2	3.3	8	4.4	25	4.8
Corporation for supporting the turnaround of businesses damaged by the great east Japan earthquake	20	9.2	6	7.3	3	4.9	15	8.2	44	8.1
Private restructuring guideline	1	0.5	–	–	–	–	2	1.1	3	0.6
Ministry of agriculture, forestry and fisheries support	5	2.3	2	2.4	–	–	1	0.5	8	1.5
Other	15	6.9	2	2.4	2	3.3	16	8.8	35	6.5
Did not receive public support	85	39.2	26	31.7	12	19.7	63	34.6	186	34.3
Total valid responses	301	138.7	135	164.6	104	170.5	250	137.4	790	145.8

Table 21 Provision of public assistance by damage suffered (cross tabulation of Q2 (5) and Q2 (7))

		Municipal subsidy	Prefecture subsidy	SME group subsidy	Temp. shop, factory	Gov. special loan	Private special loan	* Debt resched. mechanism	MAFF support	Other
Head office & equipment swept away/completely destroyed	Yes	29	26	79	19	30	7	28	1	6
	No	99	102	49	109	98	121	100	127	121
Head office swept away/ completely destroyed	Yes	9	8	19	10	7	5	7	0	3
	No	36	37	26	35	38	40	38	45	42
Equipment swept away/ completely destroyed	Yes	12	8	19	5	12	5	5	3	2
	No	36	40	29	43	36	43	43	45	46
Head office & equipment partially destroyed	Yes	3	3	13	0	8	5	6	0	2
	No	33	33	22	36	27	31	30	36	34
Head office partially destroyed	Yes	7	5	8	0	5	0	5	0	3
	No	26	28	25	33	28	33	28	33	30
Equipment partially destroyed	Yes	5	6	9	0	6	2	7	1	6
	No	40	39	36	45	39	43	38	44	39
Other	Yes	16	10	17	2	14	9	11	2	11
	No	136	142	135	150	138	143	141	150	140
Total valid responses	Yes	81	66	164	36	82	33	69	7	33
	No	406	421	322	451	404	454	418	480	452

(* "Debt resched. mechanism" is the collation of the Industry Reconstruction Corporation, Corporation for Supporting the Turnaround of Businesses Damaged by the Great East Japan Earthquake and Private Restructuring Guideline)

Table 22 Effect of public assistance received by respondent businesses (Q2 (8))

	Miyako CCI		Yamada SCI		Otsuchi SCI		Kamaishi CCI		Total	
	No	%	No	%	No	%	No	%	No	%
Very effective	61	54.0	32	68.1	29	70.7	70	66.0	192	62.5
Somewhat effective	40	35.4	9	19.1	9	22.0	26	24.5	84	27.4
Not very effective	5	4.4	2	4.3	2	4.9	4	3.8	13	4.2
Not at all effective	2	1.8	–	–	–	–	2	0.9	3	1.0
Don't know	5	4.4	4	8.5	1	2.4	5	4.7	15	4.9
Total valid responses	113	100.0	47	100.0	41	100.0	106	100.0	307	100.0
Invalid/no response	116	–	36	–	22	–	87	–	261	–

Legend Develop. fin. inst.: Government development finance institution; Govern. loan: Government loan; Group subsidy: SME Group Subsidy; Industry Reconstruction Corporation: MAFF support: Ministry of Agriculture, Forestry and Fisheries support; Munic. subsidy: Municipal subsidy; Prefect. subsidy: Prefectural subsidy; Restruct. G/L: Private Restructuring Guideline; Temp. shop/fact.: Temporary shop or factory; Turnaround Co.: Corporation for Supporting the Turnaround of Businesses Damaged by the Great East Japan Earthquake

3.2 Level of Recovery of the Regional Economy as Seen by the Respondent Businesses

When we asked about the status of recovery of the regional economy from the perspective of the respondent businesses (Q3 (2)), significant differences were shown by region as shown in Table 27 (*P*-value 0.002 in the chi-square test). Over 40% of Miyako businesses responded that the local economy has recovered to "60–80% of the pre-earthquake level" and over 10% responded that it has "almost completely recovered". In Kamaishi also, just under 40% of respondents said the economy had recovered to "60–80% of the pre-earthquake level". On the other hand, the most common response by businesses in Yamada and Otsuchi was that the economy has recovered to "40–50% of the pre-earthquake level". In particular, 20% of the respondents in Otsuchi said that the recovery is only "20–30% of the pre-earthquake level".

Table 23 Effect of public assistance by type (cross tabulation of Q2 (7) and Q2 (8))

	Miyako CCI		Yamada SCI		Otsuchi SCI		Kamaishi CCI	
	Assistance	No	Assistance	No	Assistance	No	Assistance	No
Main assistance that was very effective	Group subsidy Munic. subsidy Govern. loan Prefect. subsidy Turnaround Co Ind. Recon. Co Private loan MAFF support Temp. shop/fact	25 17 15 10 7 6 6 3 2	Group subsidy Munic. subsidy Prefect. subsidy Govern. loan Temp. shop/fact Turnaround Co Private loan	18 12 10 10 7 5 3	Group subsidy Prefect. subsidy Munic. subsidy Govern. loan Temp. shop/fact Private loan	22 10 6 6 6 4	Group subsidy Munic. subsidy Prefect. subsidy Govern. loan Turnaround Co Temp. shop/fact Private loan Ind. Recon. Co Restruct. G/L	42 13 12 10 8 6 6 5 2
Main assistance that was somewhat effective	Munic. subsidy Group subsidy Govern. loan Turnaround Co Prefect. subsidy Private loan Ind. Recon. Co	12 11 10 9 8 3 2	Group subsidy Prefect. subsidy Govern. loan Munic. subsidy Turnaround Co Ind. Recon. Co Temp. shop/fact Private loan	11 5 5 3 3 2 2 2	Group subsidy Munic. subsidy	6 3	Group subsidy Prefect. subsidy Govern. loan Munic. subsidy Turnaround Co Ind. Recon. Co Temp. shop/fact Private loan	11 5 5 3 3 2 2 2
Main assistance that was not very effective	Munic. subsidy Govern. loan Private loan	3 3 2	Munic. subsidy Govern. loan	1 1	Prefect. subsidy Develop. fin. inst	1 1	Group subsidy Munic. subsidy	3 1
Main assistance that was not at all effective	Govern. Loan MAFF support	1 1					Prefect. subsidy	

Table 24 Effect of public assistance by industry (cross tabulation of Q2 (1) and Q2 (8))

		Very effective	Somewhat effective	Not very effective	Not at all effective	Don't know	Total
Agriculture/Forestry	No	0	2	0	0	0	2
	%	0.0	100.0	0.0	0.0	0.0	100.0
Fishing	No	7	2	1	1	0	11
	%	63.6	18.2	9.1	9.1	0.0	100.0
Manufacturing	No	33	15	2	0	3	53
	%	62.3	28.3	3.8	0.0	5.7	100.0
Construction	No	26	13	2	0	0	41
	%	63.4	31.7	4.9	0.0	0.0	100.0
Wholesale/Retail	No	49	23	5	1	5	83
	%	59.0	27.7	6.0	1.2	6.0	100.0
Banking/Insurance	No	4	2	0	0	1	7
	%	57.1	28.6	0.0	0.0	0.0	100.0
Real Estate/Leasing	No	3	0	0	0	0	3
	%	0.0	0.0	0.0	0.0	0.0	100.0
Transport	No	4	1	0	0	0	5
	%	80.0	20.0	0.0	0.0	0.0	100.0
Tele-communication	No	0	1	0	0	0	1
	%	0.0	100.0	0.0	0.0	0.0	100.0
Hospitality services	No	27	15	1	0	2	45
	%	60.0	33.3	2.2	0.0	4.4	100.0
Health, welfare, medical	No	6	0	0	0	1	7
	%	85.7	0.0	0.0	0.0	14.3	100.0
Education	No	1	2	0	0	0	3
	%	33.3	66.7	0.0	0.0	0.0	100.0
Other	No	27	6	2	1	2	38
	%	71.1	15.8	5.3	2.6	5.3	100.0
Total valid responses	No	187	82	13	3	14	299
	%	62.5	27.4	4.3	1.0	4.7	100.0

Table 25 Effect of public assistance by level of damage (cross tabulation of Q2 (5) and Q2 (8))

		Very effective	Somewhat effective	Not very effective	Not at all effective	Don't know	Total
Head office & equipment swept away/ completely destroyed	No	68	19	3	2	3	95
	%	71.6	20.0	3.2	2.1	3.2	100.0
Head office swept away/ completely destroyed	No	18	12	0	1	2	33
	%	54.5	36.4	0.0	3.0	6.1	100.0
Equipment swept away/ completely destroyed	No	25	8	3	0	1	37
	%	67.6	21.6	8.1	0.0	2.77	100.0
Head office & equipment partially destroyed	No	16	9	0	0	0	25
	%	64.0	36.0	0.0	0.0	0.0	100.0
Head office partially destroyed	No	10	8	0	0	2	20
	%	50.0	40.0	0.0	0.0	10.0	100.0
Equipment partially destroyed	No	13	4	3	0	2	22
	%	59.1	18.2	13.6	0.0	9.1	100.0
Other	No	34	17	2	0	5	58
	%	58.6	29.3	3.4	0.0	8.6	100.0
Total valid responses	No	184	77	11	3	15	290
	%	63.4	26.6	3.8	1.0	5.2	

3.3 *Level of Recovery of Local Shopping Streets as Seen by the Respondent Businesses*

Next, as shown in Table 28, a significant difference appeared when we asked about the status of recovery of the local shopping street from the perspective of the respondent businesses (Q3(3)). In Miyako, Yamada and Kamaishi, the most common response at around 30% of the businesses in each region was that the recovery of the local shopping street was "40–50% of the pre-earthquake level," while in Otsuchi close to 40% of respondents said that the recovery was only "20–30% of the pre-earthquake level".

When looking at the correlation between the recovery of the regional economy and the recovery of the local shopping street (cross-tabulation of Q3 (2) and Q 3(3)), a strong correlation was shown (Spearman's rank correlation coefficient was 0.576 and

Table 26 Characteristics of the regional economy (Q3 (1))

	Miyako CCI		Yamada SCI		Otsuchi SCI		Kamaishi CCI		Total	
	No	%	No	%	No	%	No	%	No	%
Fishing industry	32	17.5	23	38.3	4	8.0	13	8.4	72	16.1
Shopping street	10	5.5	4	6.7	7	14.0	26	16.9	47	10.5
Seafood processing	88	48.1	21	35.0	21	42.0	25	16.2	155	34.7
Industrial district	8	4.4	–	–	4	8.0	31	20.1	43	9.6
Residential area	6	3.3	1	1.7	4	8.0	9	5.8	20	4.5
Other	8	4.4	–	–	2	4.0	12	7.8	22	4.9
Don't know	31	16.9	11	18.3	8	16.0	38	24.7	88	19.7
Total valid responses	183	100.0	60	100.0	50	100.0	154	100.0	447	100.0
Invalid/no response	46	–	23	–	13	–	39	–	121	–

the Kendall rank correlation coefficient was 0.522). This suggests that the scope of the "regional economy" subjectively considered by the respondents tends to overlap with the trading area of the local shopping street.

3.4 *Private Organizations that Led Regional Economic Recovery*

Regarding the organizations that led the recovery of the regional economy, as shown in Table 29, around half of the respondents in each regions said "chamber/society of commerce and industry", which was the most common response, but it is thought that this is also influenced by the fact that the survey questionnaire was distributed through the chambers and societies of commerce and industry. On the other hand, about 40% of respondents replied that they "don't know". There was a significant difference in between the regions in the responses of "shopping street association", "fishery cooperative" and "community-building association"; the most common response was "fishery cooperative" (18.3%) in Miyako, "shopping street association" (26.3%) in Yamada and "community-building association" (23.2%) in Kamaishi, which reflects an aspect of the differences in the nature of recovery in each region.

In addition, when asked about the factors that have contributed to the recovery of the regional economy (Q3 (7), multiple responses), as seen in Table 30, 40–50% of respondents in each region mentioned the role of the "government" which showed

Table 27 Level of recovery of the regional economy (Q3 (2))

	Miyako CCI		Yamada SCI		Otsuchi SCI		Kamaishi CCI		Total	
	No	%	No	%	No	%	No	%	No	%
10% of pre-earthquake level	4	1.8	1	1.3	2	3.3	4	2.2	11	2.0
20–30% of pre-earthquake level	15	6.7	10	12.8	13	21.7	15	8.2	53	9.7
40–50% of pre-earthquake level	55	24.4	28	35.9	20	33.3	43	23.5	146	26.7
60–80% of pre-earthquake level	97	43.1	20	25.6	16	26.7	72	39.3	205	37.5
Almost completely recovered	25	11.1	4	5.1	1	1.7	13	7.1	43	7.9
Exceeded pre-earthquake level	1	0.4	3	3.8	2	3.3	3	1.6	9	1.6
Don't know	28	12.4	12	15.4	6	10.0	33	18.0	79	14.5
Total valid responses	225	100.0	78	100.0	60	100.0	183	100.0	546	100.0
Invalid/no response	4	–	5	–	3	–	10	–	22	–

interest towards public assistance such as subsidies, followed by the chamber/society of commerce and industry and new employment. A significant difference between regions appeared for the responses of "shopping street association" and "don't know" responses, with over 20% of respondents in the Yamada region responding with "leadership of the shopping street association", which was also prominent in the responses from Miyako.

3.5 Status of Regional Population Recovery

When asked about the status of the recovery of the regional population from the viewpoint of the respondent businesses (Q 3(8)), as shown in Table 31, the most common response in each region was that the regional population had recovered to "70% of the pre-earthquake level". However, there were also 10% of the total respondents who viewed it as "30% of the pre-earthquake level" or less. By region,

Table 28 Level of recovery of local shopping streets (Q3 (3))

	Miyako CCI		Yamada SCI		Otsuchi SCI		Kamaishi CCI		Total	
	No	%	No	%	No	%	No	%	No	%
10% of pre-earthquake level	5	2.2	–	–	5	8.3	10	5.5	20	3.7
20–30% of pre-earthquake level	34	15.2	14	17.9	23	38.3	38	20.8	109	20.0
40–50% of pre-earthquake level	66	29.6	26	33.3	16	26.7	56	30.6	164	30.1
60–80% of pre-earthquake level	64	28.7	20	25.6	7	11.7	40	21.9	131	24.1
Almost completely recovered	22	9.9	7	9.0	1	1.7	10	5.5	40	7.4
Exceeded pre-earthquake level	–	–	–	–	1	1.7	1	0.5	2	0.4
Don't know	32	14.3	11	14.1	7	11.7	28	15.3	78	14.3
Total valid responses	223	100.0	78	100.0	60	100.0	183	100.0	544	100.0
Invalid/no response	6	–	5	–	3	–	10	–		–

although there was no statistically significant difference (*P*-value 0.198 in the chi-square test), in Otsuchi responses such as "50% of the pre-earthquake level" and "30% of the pre-earthquake level" accounted for 40% of the total.

Regarding the reasons for this negative view of population recovery (Q3 (9), multiple responses), as seen in Table 32, the most common response was "lack of places for work opportunities" at 80% of the responses. In Miyako, this was followed by "inconvenience of transport" and "lack of lifestyle-related facilities", which are seen as problems continuing from since before the earthquake, while in Otsuchi 70% of responses raised "waiting for reconstruction projects", which was also identified as a factor in close to half of the responses in Yamada and Kamaishi.

Table 29 Private organizations that led regional economic recovery (Q3 (6), multiple responses allowed, 535 total valid responses)

	Miyako CCI		Yamada SCI		Otsuchi SCI		Kamaishi CCI		Total	
	No	%	No	%	No	%	No	%	No	%
Chamber/society of commerce and industry	123	55.9	40	51.9	33	54.1	86	48.6	282	52.7
Shopping street association	32	14.5	20	26.0	5	8.2	10	5.6	67	12.5
Agricultural cooperative	8	3.6	2	2.6	2	3.3	2	1.1	14	2.6
Fishery cooperative	40	18.2	5	6.5	3	4.9	8	4.5	56	10.5
Community-building association	24	10.9	11	14.3	6	9.8	41	23.2	82	15.3
NPO	3	1.4	1	1.3	2	3.3	6	3.4	12	2.2
Other	8	3.6	5	6.5	6	9.8	9	5.1	28	5.2
Don't know	83	37.7	29	37.7	23	37.7	78	44.1	213	39.8
Total valid responses	321	145.9	113	146.8	80	131.1	240	135.6	754	140.9

4 Results of Responses About the Recovery Calendar

4.1 Recovery Calendar, Overall Total and Related Factors

The "recovery calendar" is a research tool devised during the recovery process after the Great Hanshin-Awaji Earthquake that focuses on changes over time in the subjective perception of recovery of disaster victims. It has currently settled as a survey of twelve items ((1) grasped overall damage, (2) thought it is now safe, (3) resolved to live an inconvenient life, (4) restarted work, (5) have finally resolved housing problems, (6) household budget has recovered, (7) daily life has settled down, (8) local activities have returned to normal, (9) self-perception as a disaster victim has disappeared, (10) Regional economy has escaped the effects of the disaster, (11) local roads have been repaired, and (12) local schools have recovered). The "recovery calendar" was also used as a means of assessing the degree of recovery of the entire region in the five-year survey conducted in cooperation with the Reconstruction Agency and the affected prefectures after the Great East Japan Earthquake Recovery Survey Team (2016). In this survey, the "recovery calendar" was incorporated into the questionnaire for the purpose of identifying the characteristics of the evaluation of recovery by businesses, in contrast to the previous survey which mainly focused on regular households.

The overall "recovery calendar" of this survey is shown in Fig. 1. A cross-verification of this was conducted in relation to the attributes of the respondent businesses, the recovery status of the regional economy, and the attributes of the

Table 30 Decisive factors of regional economic recovery (Q3 (7), multiple responses allowed, 529 total valid responses)

	Miyako CCI		Yamada SCI		Otsuchi SCI		Kamaishi CCI		Total	
	No	%	No	%	No	%	No	%	No	%
Government role	116	53.2	43	55.1	30	50.8	74	42.5	263	49.7
Chamber/society of commerce and industry leadership	84	38.5	30	38.5	22	37.3	52	29.9	188	35.5
Shopping street association leadership	27	12.4	19	24.4	4	6.8	10	5.7	60	11.3
New employment	57	26.1	22	28.2	15	25.4	43	24.7	137	25.9
Other	9	4.1	6	7.7	3	5.1	13	7.5	31	5.9
Don't know	43	19.7	15	19.2	11	18.6	59	33.0	128	24.2
Total valid responses	336	154.1	135	173.1	85	144.1	251	144.3	807	152.6
Invalid/no response	116	53.2	43	55.1	30	50.8	74	42.5	263	49.7

Table 31 Level of regional population recovery (Q3 (8))

	Miyako CCI		Yamada SCI		Otsuchi SCI		Kamaishi CCI		Total	
	No	%	No	%	No	%	No	%	No	%
10% of pre-earthquake level	6	2.8	–	–	1	1.7	3	1.7	10	1.9
30% of pre-earthquake level	16	7.6	4	5.6	9	15.3	21	11.9	49	9.7
50% of pre-earthquake level	21	10.0	11	15.3	14	23.7	31	17.6	77	14.9
70% of pre-earthquake level	115	54.5	44	61.1	25	42.4	86	48.9	270	52.1
Almost completely recovered	8	3.8	–	–	1	1.7	5	2.8	14	2.7
Exceeded pre-earthquake level	1	0.5	–	–	–	–	1	0.6	2	0.4
Don't know	44	20.9	13	18.1	9	15.3	29	16.5	95	18.3
Total valid responses	211	100.0	72	100.0	59	100.0	176	100.0	518	100.0
Invalid/no response	18	–	11	–	4	–	17	–	50	–

respondents themselves, and the significant items are shown in Table 33 (◎: 1% significant, ○: 5% significant).

Looking at the attributes on the horizontal axis, differences in the region of the business' location had a large effect on the responses to lifestyle aspects such as "(5) housing", "(6) household budget" and "(7) daily life has settled down", as well as regional aspects such as "(8) Local activities," "(11) local roads" and "(12) local schools". The responses to the business' damage status (Q2 (5)) and status reconstruction status (Q2 (6)) had a large effect on their responses to questions such as "(5) housing", "(6) household budget" and "(8) local activities". In addition, the responses regarding the recovery of the regional economy and local shopping streets (Q3 (2) and Q3 (3)) had a large effect on many of the categories such as "(2) safety", "(4) resumption of work", "(6) household budget", "(7) daily life has settled down", "(8) local activities", "(9) sense of being a disaster victim", and "(10) regional economy". The responses to the question about the status of population recovery (Q3 (8)) had a large effect on the items of "(3) resolved to live an inconvenient life", "(5) housing", "(7) daily life has settled down", and "(12) reopening of schools". Looking at the personal attributes of the respondents, age (Q1 (1)) had a large effect on "(1) overall image of damage", "(3) resolved to live an inconvenient life", and "(9) sense

Table 32 Causes of population reduction (Q3 (9), multiple responses allowed, 456 total valid responses)

	Miyako CCI		Yamada SCI		Otsuchi SCI		Kamaishi CCI		Total	
	No	%	No	%	No	%	No	%	No	%
Waiting for public recovery projects	46	26.1	33	47.8	37	69.8	72	45.6	188	41.2
Lack of safety measures	16	9.1	4	5.8	11	20.8	6	3.8	37	8.1
Lack of places for employment opportunities	144	81.8	53	76.8	38	71.7	124	78.5	359	78.7
Lack of lifestyle-related facilities	55	31.3	18	26.1	20	37.7	46	29.1	139	30.5
Inconvenience of transport	58	33.0	21	30.4	12	22.6	32	20.3	123	27.0
Other	12	6.8	4	5.8	2	3.8	14	8.9	32	7.0
Don't know	5	2.8	5	7.2	–	–	10	6.3	20	4.4
Total valid responses	336	190.9	138	200.0	120	226.4	304	192.4	898	196.9

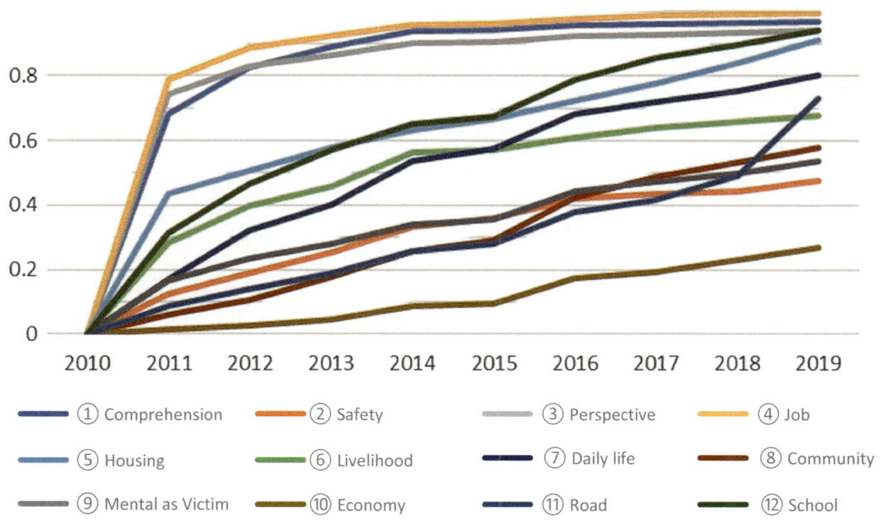

Fig. 1 Overall Recovery Calendar

Table 33 Relationship between recovery calendar and various attributes

	Attributes of business						Regional economy			Attributes of respondent				
Question No	Region	2(1) Industry	2(3) Number of employees	2(5) Damage status	2(6) Rebuild status	2(9) Business recovery	3(2) Econ. recovery	3(3) Shop. street recovery	3(8) Pop. recovery	1(1)(1) Age	2(1)(1) Gender	1(4) Housing damage	1(5) Housing rebuild	1(7) Role
(1) Grasped overall damage									○	◎		○		
(2) Thought it is now safe			○				◎	◎	○		◎			
(3) Resolved to live an inconvenient life							○	○	◎	◎		◎		
(4) Restarted work							◎							
(5) Have resolved housing problems	◎			◎	◎		○	○	◎	○		◎	◎	◎
(6) Household budget has recovered	◎			○		◎	◎	◎	○	○		◎	○	◎
(7) Daily life has settled down	◎			◎	◎		◎	○	◎		◎	◎	◎	

(continued)

Table 33 (continued)

	Attributes of business						Regional economy			Attributes of respondent				
Question No	Region	2(1) Industry	2(3) Number of employees	2(5) Damage status	2(6) Rebuild status	2(9) Business recovery	3(2) Econ. recovery	3(3) Shop. street recovery	3(8) Pop. recovery	1(1)(1) Age	2(1)(1) Gender	1(4) Housing damage	1(5) Housing rebuild	1(7) Role
(8) Local activities have returned to normal	◎			◎	◎		◎	◎	○		○			
(9) Self-perception as a disaster victim has disappeared			○				○	◎		◎		◎		
(10) Regional economy has escaped the effects of the disaster		◎	○				◎	◎	○					
(11) Local roads have been repaired	◎						○	◎						
(12) Local schools have recovered	◎		○				◎	○	◎			◎		

Legend ◎ = 1% significance; ○ = 5% significance

of being a disaster victim"; gender (Q2 (1)) had a significant effect on "(2) safety", and "(7) daily life has settled down"; status of damage to housing (Q1 (4)) had a large effect on "(3) resolved to live an inconvenient life", "(5) housing", "(6) household budget", and "(7) daily life has settled down" and sense of being a disaster victim"; status of housing reconstruction (Q1 (5)) had a large effect on "(5) housing" and "(7) daily life has settled down"; and the employment role (Q1 (7)) had a large effect on "(5) housing" and "(6) household budget". All of these points require more detailed analysis in the future.

4.2 *Attributes of the Respondents*

Before displaying the "recovery calendar" for each region, the results of the questionnaire regarding the demographics of the respondents are shown below.

The age of the respondents (Q1-1 (1)) is as shown in Table 34, and there was no significant difference between the regions. (*P*-value 0.400 in the chi-square test).

Regarding the gender of the respondents (Q1-1 (2)), as shown in Table 35, the majority of respondents were male and there was no significant difference between the regions (*P*-value 0.262 in the chi-square test).

Regarding the respondents' pre-earthquake residential status (Q1-1 (3)), as seen in Table 36, the proportion of respondents who lived in their own house on their own land was the highest in all of the regions, but in Miyako and Yamada, the proportion of respondents who lived in their own house on rented land was also high, and there was a significant difference between the regions (*P*-value 0.002 in the chi-square test).

As shown in Table 37, there was a significant difference between regions (*P*-value 0.000 in the chi-square test) in the housing damage status of the respondents (Q1-1 (4)), with 70% of the respondents in Otsuchi, 60% in Yamada, less than 40% in

Table 34 Age of respondents (Q1-1 (1))

	Miyako CCI		Yamada SCI		Otsuchi SCI		Kamaishi CCI		Total	
	No	%	No	%	No	%	No	%	No	%
Under 40	6	2.7	2	2.4	1	1.6	5	2.7	14	2.5
40–49	33	14.7	10	12.0	8	13.1	21	11.2	72	12.9
50–59	46	20.5	13	15.7	15	24.6	49	26.1	123	22.1
60–69	70	31.3	25	30.1	20	32.8	57	30.3	172	30.9
70–79	54	24.1	31	37.3	17	27.9	49	26.1	151	27.2
80 or older	15	6.7	2	2.4	–	–	7	3.7	24	4.3
Total valid responses	224	100.0	83	100.0	61	100.0	188	100.0	556	100.0
Invalid/no response	5	–	–	–	2	–	5	–	12	–

Table 35 Gender of respondents (Q1-1 (2))

	Miyako CCI		Yamada SCI		Otsuchi SCI		Kamaishi CCI		Total	
	No	%	No	%	No	%	No	%	No	%
Male	175	76.8	57	68.7	42	66.7	134	70.9	408	72.5
Female	53	23.2	26	31.3	21	33.3	55	29.1	155	27.5
Total valid responses	228	100.0	83	100.0	63	100.0	189	100.0	563	100.0
Invalid/no response	1	–	–	–	–	–	4	–	5	–

Table 36 Pre-earthquake residential status of respondents (Q1-1 (3))

	Miyako CCI		Yamada SCI		Otsuchi SCI		Kamaishi CCI		Total	
	No	%	No	%	No	%	No	%	No	%
Own land/ house	159	70.0	72	87.8	54	85.7	145	77.1	430	76.8
Leased land/ own house (registered)	33	14.5	2	2.4	2	3.2	14	7.4	51	9.1
Leased land/ own house (unregistered)	6	2.6	1	1.2	–	–	1	0.5	8	1.4
Leased house/ apartment	18	7.9	7	8.5	4	6.3	21	11.2	50	8.9
Public housing	4	1.8	–	–	3	4.8	1	0.5	8	1.4
Other	7	3.1	–	–	–	–	6	3.2	13	2.3
Total valid responses	227	100.0	82	100.0	63	100.0	188	100.0	560	100.0
Invalid/no response	2	–	1	–	–	–	5	–	8	–

Kamaishi and less than 20% in Mayako suffering severe damage such as being swept away or completely destroyed.

The form of reconstruction of the respondents' houses (Q1-1 (5)), as seen in Table 38, was similar to the form of reconstruction of businesses (Q2 (6)) shown in Table 7 above; for the respondents in Miyako and Kamaishi "repair on the original site" was common, while in Yamada and Otsuchi there was a variation such "new construction on a voluntarily relocated site", "new construction on the original site" and "new construction on adjusted land". The results of the cross-verification by region were significant (*P*-value 0.000 in the chi-square test).

Regarding the status of the respondents' household budget (Q1-1 (6), (1)–(4)), as shown in Tables 39–42, the prominent responses were that household income

Table 37 Status of damage to respondents' residences (Q1-1 (4))

	Miyako CCI		Yamada SCI		Otsuchi SCI		Kamaishi CCI		Total	
	No	%	No	%	No	%	No	%	No	%
Swept away	8	3.8	3	3.8	7	12.3	6	3.5	24	4.6
Completely destroyed	40	19.0	43	54.4	32	56.1	58	34.1	173	33.5
Mostly damaged	20	9.5	4	5.1	6	10.5	13	7.6	43	8.3
Half-damaged	10	4.8	2	2.5	–	–	3	1.8	15	2.9
Partially damaged	17	8.1	–	–	3	5.3	17	10.0	37	7.2
Not assessed (damaged)	12	5.7	2	2.5	1	1.8	27	15.9	42	8.1
Not assessed (undamaged)	101	47.9	25	31.6	7	12.3	44	25.9	177	34.2
Not assessed (no response)	3	1.4	–	–	1	1.8	2	1.2	6	1.2
Total valid responses	211	100.0	79	100.0	57	100.0	170	100.0	517	100.0
Invalid/no response	18	–	4	–	6	–	23	–	51	–

and savings have decreased, and that expenses and debts have increased. Cross-verification by region shows significant differences in that regarding income, the number of respondents in Otuschi that had a decrease was large (P-value 0.011 in the chi-square test), and regarding debts, the number of respondents in Yamada that had an increase was large (P-value 0.014 in the chi-square test).

The respondents' pre-earthquake employment status is as shown in Table 43, with significant differences such as the high proportion of respondents in Yamada who were "self-employed with employees" and the high proportion in Kamaishi who were a "company director" (P-value 0.001 in the chi-square test).

Regarding changes to employment after the earthquake (Q1-1 (8)), as shown in Table 44, the number of respondents who answered that they continued to work in the same job before and after the earthquake was largest at 80%, and there was no significant difference by region (P-value 0.208 in the chi-square test).

4.3 "Recovery Calendar" of the Businesses in Each Region

Regarding the "recovery calendar" of this survey, Figs. 2–5 show the average results of the responses by region. In all of the regions, the number of responses that the three categories of "(1) have grasped the overall image of the damage", "(3) resolved

Table 38 Status of rebuilding of respondents' residences (Q1-1 (5))

	Miyako CCI		Yamada SCI		Otsuchi SCI		Kamaishi CCI		Total	
	No	%	No	%	No	%	No	%	No	%
New construction on original site	10	6.7	12	17.9	11	20.0	23	15.9	56	13.5
Repair on original site	62	41.6	11	16.4	9	16.4	51	35.2	133	32.0
New construction on adjusted land	5	3.4	9	13.4	11	20.0	14	9.7	39	9.4
New construction at group relocation	11	7.4	7	10.4	4	7.3	1	0.7	23	5.5
Self-relocation	15	10.1	12	17.9	13	23.6	13	9.0	53	12.7
Disaster public housing	2	1.3	–	–	2	3.6	7	4.8	11	2.6
Private lease	2	1.3	5	7.5	–	–	10	6.9	17	4.1
Temporary housing	–	–	–	–	–	–	2	1.4	2	0.5
Other	42	28.2	11	16.4	5	9.1	24	16.6	82	19.7
Total valid responses	149	100.0	67	100.0	55	100.0	145	100.0	416	100.0
Invalid/no response	80	–	16	–	8	–	48	–	152	–

Table 39 Status of respondents' household budget: Income (Q1-1 (6)(1))

	Miyako CCI		Yamada SCI		Otsuchi SCI		Kamaishi CCI		Total	
	No	%	No	%	No	%	No	%	No	%
Increased	42	18.8	27	32.5	10	16.1	29	15.7	108	19.5
Unchanged	81	36.3	16	19.3	18	29.0	68	36.8	183	33.1
Decreased	100	44.8	40	48.2	34	54.8	88	47.6	262	47.4
Total valid responses	223	100.0	83	100.0	62	100.0	185	100.0	553	100.0
Invalid/no response	6	–	–	–	1	–	8	–	15	–

that an inconvenient life would continue for a while" and "(4) my job has returned to normal" were achieved at a relatively early stage after the earthquake were over 80%, while the responses regarding achievement of the other categories were low.

It is noteworthy that the categories which have not reached 50% achievement even after nine years of reconstruction include "(10) the local economy has recovered

Table 40 Status of respondents' household budget: Expenses (Q1-1 (6)(2))

	Miyako CCI		Yamada SCI		Otsuchi SCI		Kamaishi CCI		Total	
	No	%	No	%	No	%	No	%	No	%
Increased	113	52.6	54	66.7	37	62.7	97	52.7	301	55.8
Unchanged	82	38.1	22	27.2	17	28.8	68	37.0	189	35.1
Decreased	20	9.3	5	6.2	5	8.5	19	10.3	49	9.1
Total valid responses	215	100.0	81	100.0	59	100.0	184	100.0	539	100.0
Invalid/no response	14	–	2	–	4	–	9	–	29	–

Table 41 Status of respondents' household budget: Savings (Q1-1 (6)(3))

	Miyako CCI		Yamada SCI		Otsuchi SCI		Kamaishi CCI		Total	
	No	%	No	%	No	%	No	%	No	%
Increased	26	12.2	17	21.3	8	13.6	24	13.0	75	14.0
Unchanged	80	37.6	16	20.0	16	27.1	60	32.6	172	32.1
Decreased	107	50.2	47	58.8	35	59.3	100	54.3	289	53.9
Total valid responses	213	100.0	80	100.0	59	100.0	184	100.0	536	100.0
Invalid/no response	16	–	3	–	4	–	9	–	32	–

Table 42 Status of respondents' household budget: Debts (Q1-1 (6)(4))

	Miyako CCI		Yamada SCI		Otsuchi SCI		Kamaishi CCI		Total	
	No	%	No	%	No	%	No	%	No	%
Increased	83	42.6	42	60.0	25	48.1	75	42.9	225	45.7
Unchanged	87	44.6	25	35.7	22	42.3	65	37.1	199	40.4
Decreased	25	12.8	3	4.3	5	9.6	35	20.0	68	13.8
Total valid responses	195	100.0	70	100.0	52	100.0	175	100.0	492	100.0
Invalid/no response	34	–	13	–	11	–	18	–	76	–

from the effects of the disaster", "(2) I thought it is safe now", "(8) local activities have returned to normal," and "(9) I no longer have a self-perception as a disaster victim". Among these, "(10) local economy" had the lowest rate of achievement among the twelve categories. As of when the survey was conducted in 2019, the rate of achievement in each region was remarkably low at 30.4% in Miyako, 20.6% in Yamada, 14.8% in Otsuchi, and 29.1% in Kamaishi.

Table 43 Pre-earthquake employment status of respondents (Q1-1 (7))

	Miyako CCI		Yamada SCI		Otsuchi SCI		Kamaishi CCI		Total	
	No	%	No	%	No	%	No	%	No	%
Permanent employee	54	24.1	6	7.3	14	22.2	51	27.4	125	22.5
Part-time/ casual employee	7	3.1	1	1.2	3	4.8	4	2.2	15	2.7
Company director	61	27.2	14	17.1	14	22.2	53	28.5	142	25.6
Self-employed with employees	67	29.9	40	48.8	17	27.0	40	21.5	164	29.5
Self-employed with no employees	32	14.3	17	20.7	14	22.2	30	16.1	93	16.8
Other	3	1.3	4	4.9	1	1.6	8	4.3	16	2.9
Total valid responses	224	100.0	82	100.0	63	100.0	186	100.0	555	100.0
Invalid/no response	5	–	1	–	–	–	7	–	13	–

It is also worth noting that the responses regarding achievement of "(2) safety" remains stagnant at a low level in each region. The percentages were remarkably low at the time of the survey in 2019, with 45.4% in Miyako, 49.3% in Yamada, 35.7% in Otsuchi, and 54.7% in Kamaishi.

Apart from this, another category that shared a low level of achievement responses is "(9) I no longer have a self-perception as a disaster victim", with 59.9% in Miyako, 49.3% in Yamada, 37.3% in Otsuchi, and 54.6% in Kamaishi at the time of the survey in 2019.

When looking at the categories that had not reached 50% achievement as of 2019 in each region, in ascending order, in Miyako (Fig. 2) it was the two categories of "(10) the local economy has recovered from the effects of the disaster" and "(2) I thought it is safe now". In Yamada (Fig. 3) it was the three categories of "(10) the local economy has recovered from the effects of the disaster", "(8) local activities have returned to normal," and "(9) I no longer have a self-perception as a disaster victim". In Otsuchi (Fig. 4), it was "(10) the local economy has recovered from the effects of the disaster", "(8) local activities have returned to normal," "(2) I thought it is safe now" and "(9) I no longer have a self-perception as a disaster victim". In Kamaishi (Fig. 5), the only category was "(10) the local economy has recovered from the effects of the disaster".

Table 44 Post-earthquake changes to employment of respondents (Q1-1 (8))

	Miyako CCI		Yamada SCI		Otsuchi SCI		Kamaishi CCI		Total	
	No	%	No	%	No	%	No	%	No	%
Continued previous employment	190	84.1	60	72.3	47	74.6	149	78.8	446	79.5
Employment interrupted but resumed	17	7.5	15	18.1	6	9.5	17	9.0	55	9.8
Changed employer/business due to earthquake	4	1.8	5	6.0	5	7.9	4	2.1	18	3.2
Resigned/ceased business due to earthquake	1	0.4	1	1.2	–	–	3	1.6	5	0.9
Commenced business due to earthquake's effect	6	2.7	1	1.2	1	1.6	4	2.1	12	2.1
Changed employer/business due to personal circumstances	3	1.3	–	–	2	3.2	3	1.6	8	1.4
Resigned/ceased business due to personal circumstances	–	–	–	–	–	–	1	0.5	1	0.2
Other	2	0.9	–	–	1	1.6	2	1.1	5	0.9
Total valid responses	3	1.3	1	1.2	1	1.6	6	3.2	11	2.0
Invalid/no response	226	100.0	83	100.0	63	100.0	189	100.0	561	100

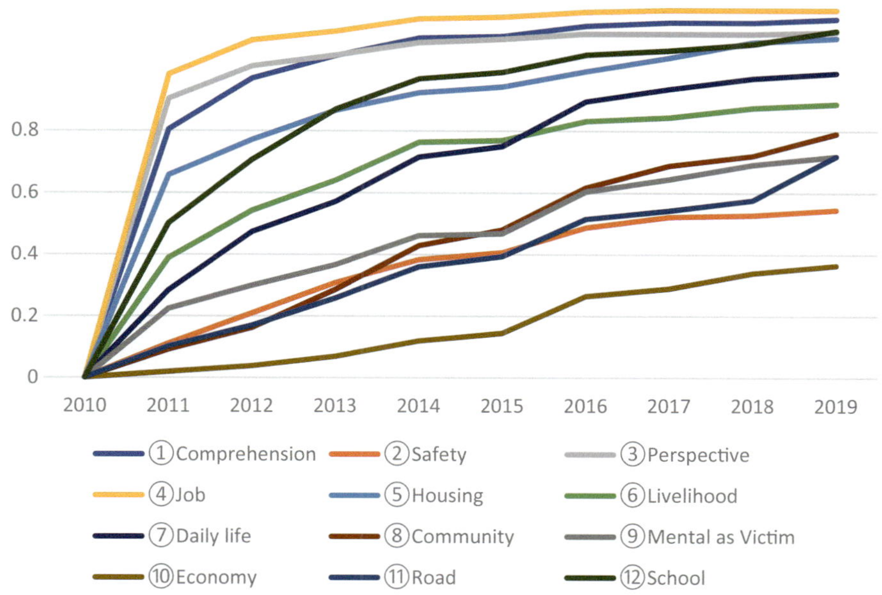

Fig. 2 Recovery Calendar (Miyako respondents). *Remarks* The number of valid responses and the rate of achievement as of 2019 for each item: (1) 212 (96.7%); (2) 207 (45.4%); (3) 206 (93.2%); (4) 208 (99.0%); (5) 190 (91.6%); (6) 195 (73.5%); (7) 212 (82.2%); (8) 185 (65.9%); (9) 177 (59.9%); (10) 191 (30.4%); (11) 177 (59.9%); (12) 170 (93.5%)

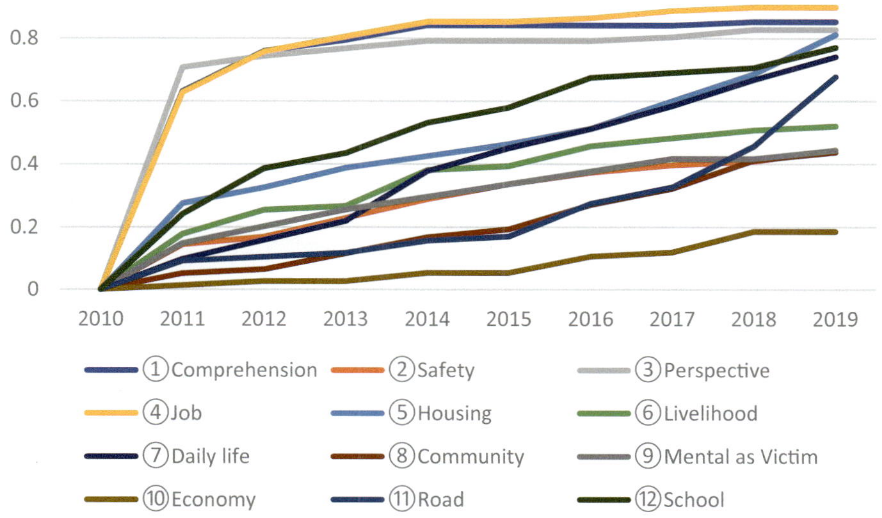

Fig. 3 Recovery Calendar (Yamada respondents). *Remarks* The number of valid responses and the rate of achievement as of 2019 for each item: (1) 77 (94.8%); (2) 75 (49.3%); (3) 75 (92.0%); (4) 76 (100.0%); (5) 72 (90.3%); (6) 71 (57.7%); (7) 74 (82.4%); (8) 70 (48.6%); (9) 67 (49.3%); (10) 68 (20.6%); (11) 69 (75.3%); (12) 56 (85.7%)

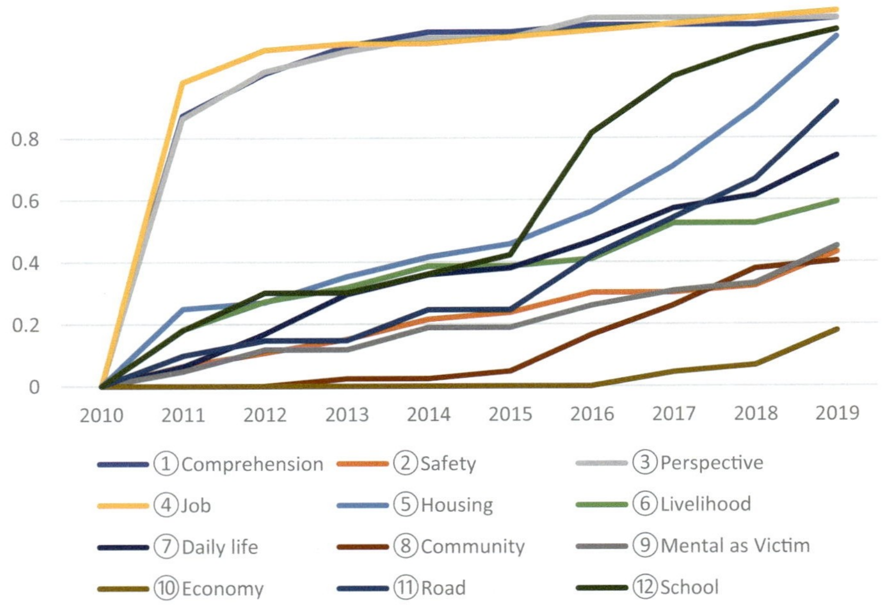

Fig. 4 Recovery Calendar (Otsuchi respondents). *Remarks* The number of valid responses and the rate of achievement as of 2019 for each item: (1) 54 (98.1%); (2) 56 (35.7%); (3) 56 (98.2%); (4) 58 (100.0%); (5) 58 (93.1%); (6) 53 (49.1%); (7) 57 (61.4%); (8) 51 (33.3%); (9) 51 (37.3%); (10) 54 (14.8%); (11) 49 (75.5%), (12) 40 (95.0%)

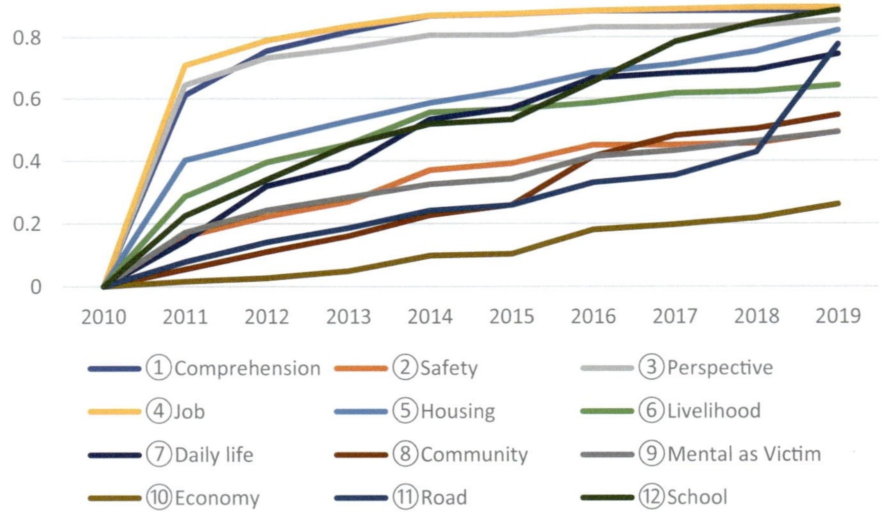

Fig. 5 Recovery Calendar (Kamaishi respondents). *Remarks* The number of valid responses and the rate of achievement as of 2019 for each item: (1) 175 (98.3%); (2) 170 (54.7%); (3) 173 (94.8%); (4) 179 (99.4%); (5) 172 (91.3%); (6) 175 (71.4%); (7) 174 (82.8%); (8) 163 (60.1%); (8) 163 (60.1%); (9) 152 (54.6%); (10) 165 (29.1%); (11) 160 (86.3%); (12) 132 (98.5%)

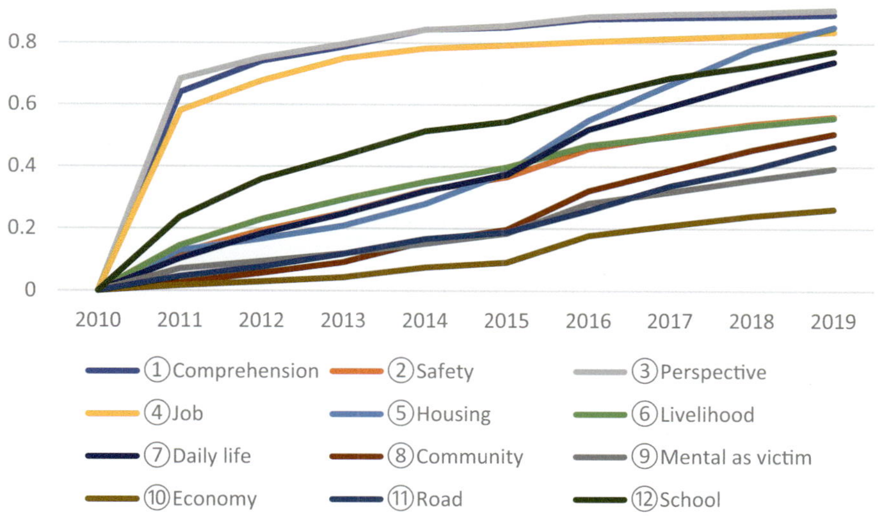

Fig. 6 Recovery calendar from five-year recovery survey. *Source* Great East Japan Earthquake Lifestyle Recovery Research Team (2016)

5 Some Consideration

5.1 Regional Economy and Perception of Disaster Victims

In this survey, a common point in the "recovery calendar" of each region was that "(10) local economy" had the lowest result of the 12 categories and, as shown above, the percentage of respondents who said it had been achieved as of 2019 was extremely low: 30.4% in Miyako, 20.6% in Yamada, 14.8% in Otsuchi, and 29.1% in Kamaishi.

In the above-mentioned 5-year recovery survey by the Reconstruction Agency (Fig. 6),[4] the only one of the 12 categories that had not achieved 50% in the five years after the earthquake was "(10) the local economy has recovered from the effects of the disaster", but the figure was 43.3%. Compared to the 5-year recovery survey that was a survey of general households conducted in the entire prefectures of Iwate, Miyagi and Fukushima, including their inland areas, it is thought that this survey more clearly showed the actual feelings of businesses in the directly affected areas.

[4] See East Japan Earthquake Lifestyle Recovery Survey Team (2016). Professor Reo Kimura of the University of Hyogo, who supervised the survey, kindly assisted with the provision of the original data, etc.

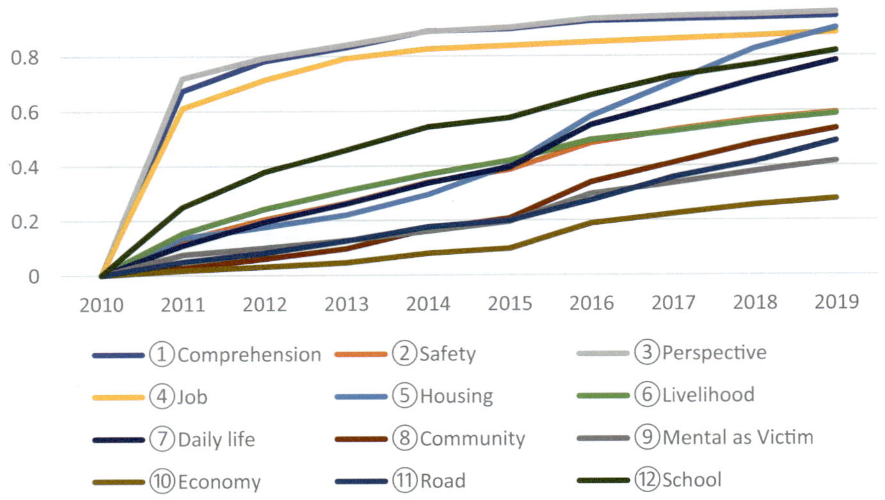

Fig. 7 Recovery calendar (Results of Household Survey in 16 Districts of 13 Cities and Towns). *Source* Hokugo, Kaneko, Honjo, Toyoda, Siomi, Pineiro and Iegane (2021b)

On the other hand, another noteworthy result of this survey is the low achievement of "(9) I no longer have a self-perception as a disaster victim", and this category is moving in almost parallel with the curve of "(10) local economy". This trend is shared with the results of the author's group's survey of people's perception of lifestyle recovery after the disaster, which was conducted in 16 districts from 13 cities and towns along the coast of Iwate and Miyagi prefectures at the same time as this survey (Fig. 7).[5] Further, the NHK survey, which was conducted around the same time as this survey, also shows the slow recovery of the local economy as well as a low perception of recovery from being disaster victims.[6]

In the prior research following the Great Hanshin-Awaji Earthquake, which brought about the emergence of the "recovery calendar," the delay in responses about achieving "(10) local economy" was identified, but the trend concerning "(9) self-perception as a victim" conversely was reported as being achieved earlier in the post-disaster period, along with "(1) have grasped the overall image of the damage", "(3) resolved that an inconvenient life would continue for a while" (Kimura et al. 2004). Therefore, "(9) self-perception as a victim" is thought to require further analysis as an aspect that reflects the difference in the nature of recovery between the Great Hanshin-Awaji Earthquake and the Great East Japan Earthquake.

What this survey focuses on is the shape of the curve of each category with the passage of time and their interrelationships. In all of the regions where this survey was

[5] Corresponds to Fig. 7–1 in Hokugo, Kaneko, Honjo, Toyoda, Siomi, Pinheiro and Ghezelloo (2021b).

[6] According to the report on NHK's website, under the supervision of Professor Reo Kimura (University of Hyogo), the survey was distributed to about 4,000 people in Iwate, Miyagi and Fukushima prefectures during 2019, and 1,965 responses were received.

conducted, the categories of "(9) self-perception as a victim" and "(10) local economy" showed a low level of achievement for a while after the earthquake, in parallel with other categories such as "(11) local roads have been restored" and "(8) local activities have returned to normal". However, it is noteworthy that even though the categories "(11) local roads" and "(8) local activities" showed a rapid improvement around 2018, "(9) self-perception as a victim" did not follow these and remained stagnant. This suggests that the source of the long-lasting "(9) self-perception as a victim" of the businesses in the disaster area are factors in the background, other than the improvement of infrastructure or actions to rebuild local activities such as the revival of festivals.

The other categories that show a flat recovery curve along with "(9) self-perception as a victim" are "(10) local economy", "(6) Impact of the disaster on household budget" and "(2) thought that it was safe now".

5.2 *Impact of the Reconstruction Development Policy on "Livelihood"*

It is worthy of note that in the "recovery calendar" of this survey targeting businesses, along with "(10) local economy" and "(9) self-perception as a victim", the responses of achievement for "(6) household budget" was low. For the businesses affected by the disaster, the investigation of the cause of the delay in the recovery of both the local economy and household budgets remains as an issue.

Table 27 (level of recovery of the regional economy) and Table 28 (level of recovery of local shopping streets) of this paper display the severe perception of the respondents regarding the recovery of the local economy, which is a result that is consistent with the low feeling of recovery of "(10) local economy" in the "recovery calendar". On the other hand, "population outflow" was strongly indicated in Table 29, which showed correlation with Table 27 and Table 28, and in Table 32, "lack of places for employment opportunities" followed by "waiting for public recovery projects" were identified as the causes of this. These tendencies in the responses suggest the possibility that population outflow, sluggish employment, and the state of the reconstruction development policy are connected in the background of the low feeling of recovery of "(10) regional economy".

On the other hand, in relation to "(6) household budget" in the "recovery calendar," as seen in Table 4 (number of employees of respondent businesses) and Table 5 (operating format of respondent businesses), 60% of the businesses that responded to the survey were small businesses with four employees or less, and many of them had a "combined home and workplace" form of business, and in Table 6 (damage suffered by respondent businesses) it was identified that many of them suffered damage to their joint home and business assets. For these small-scale, combined home-and-business operators that were affected by the disaster, the ten years of recovery following the earthquake means they have had to bear the two problems of rebuilding both their business performance and their family budget from the human and physical damage they suffered; accordingly, the "(6) household budget" curve in the "recovery calendar" is thought to reflect the changes in the foundation of their livelihood, namely the combination of their household budget and business. On the other hand, considering that the curve of "(4) work has returned to normal" does not necessarily mean the period of full-scale reconstruction but also includes temporary business, the curves of "(6) household budget" and "(7) daily life has settled down" are thought to represent the "livelihood" that encompasses both business and household budget. From the results of this survey's questions about business conditions, as seen in Table 11 (Business Performance Conditions by Number of Employees), the delay in recovery was distinct for small businesses, and in Table 12 (Business Performance Conditions by Operating Format), the recovery was delayed for tenant businesses and businesses with a combined home and workplace; in Table 10 (Business Performance Conditions by Industry) and Table 17 (When Respondent Businesses' Performance Recovered by Industry), recovery was particularly delayed for wholesale and retail businesses and hospitality service industries, but it can be thought to be meaningful to analyse these results in relation to "(6) household budget" and "(7) daily life has settled down " in the "recovery calendar".

On the other hand, in particular for the small-scale, combined home-and-workplace businesses, the curve of "(5) housing problems have been resolved" is thought to mean not only the period of rebuilding their home, but also the time when full-scale reconstruction of their business together with their home became possible due to the progress of reconstruction work. In that sense, the curve of "(5) housing" can be read as an indicator representing the impact of the reconstruction development policy on businesses and households.

Looking at the "recovery calendar" for each area with these categories as the main focus, the trend for Miyako (Fig. 2) and Kamaishi (Fig. 5) is that the category of "(4) work returned to normal" appeared to lead and the categories of "(1) grasped overall image of damage" and "(3) resolved to live an inconvenient life" were achieved at an early stage and categories such as "(6) household budget" and "(7) daily life has settled down" followed suit in showing improvement in the form of being led by "(5) resolved housing problems"; on the other hand, the group of categories such as "(8) local activities", "(9) self-perception as a disaster victim", and "(11) local roads" were still sluggish at the time of the survey, with "(10) regional economy" at the bottom. In this way, the recovery curve for Miyako and Kamaishi can be read as splitting into three overall groups, since the "(4) work" curve resumes early and is soon followed by the achievement of the recovery development projects represented by "(5) home", this connects to the recovery of "(6) household" and "(7) settling down of life" that suggests the full-scale rebuilding of "livelihood", which parts from the sluggish feeling of recovery of "(10) regional economy".

In contrast to this, the recovery curve based on the responses from the businesses from the Yamada SCI (Fig. 3) and Otsuchi SCI (Fig. 4) is largely split in two, with the three categories of "(1) overall image of the damage", "(3) resolved to live an inconvenient life" and "(4) work" leading and the stagnated group of categories such as "(10) regional economy", "(9) self-perception as a disaster victim" and "(8) local activities". In the middle of these two groups, the curve for the item (5) "housing" shows a large delay in rising up, but the categories such as "(6) household budget" and "(7) settling down of life" do not follow suit, and continue to stagnate in parallel with the curve for "(10) local economy". This bifurcation is even more pronounced in the responses from Otsuchi than in those from Yamada. The recovery curves for Yamada and Otsuchi can be read as "(4) work" resuming for the time being in temporary facilities, while the recovery development projects delayed full-scale reconstruction for several years, as represented by "(5) housing", which meant the categories of "(6) household budget" and "(7) life has settled down" that display the actual feeling of business conditions were stagnant and are connected to the sluggish sense of recovery in the region as a whole.

The possibility that the longer-term reconstruction projects affected the recovery of businesses and households is an issue to be examined in the future, but one piece of evidence is that the differences in the direction of the reconstruction project policies shown in Table 7 (reconstruction form of respondent businesses by region) of this survey can be read as having affected the differences in business performance recovery shown in Table 14 (business performance conditions by form of reconstruction). In the responses from Miyako and Kamaishi, reconstruction by "repairing at the original site" was most common at 40%, which may be read as reflecting the conditions of the businesses that were able to achieve full-scale reconstruction early without getting caught up in reconstruction projects because, as will be discussed below, Miyako chose to build floodgates and Kamaishi chose to rebuild the breakwaters at the entrance to the bay as the safety measures to protect the central area of each city. In contrast, in Yamada and Otsuchi, the responses to the question in Table 7 (reconstruction form of respondent businesses by region) were scattered, which seems to reflect the situation that in these regions the recovery development policy was centred on wide-ranging height-raising land readjustment projects in the central commercial and industrial districts, which meant businesses in the relevant areas had no choice but to wait for the projects to be completed, and that there were also businesses which chose to voluntarily relocate to inland areas and conduct full-scale reconstruction of their business. In the "recovery calendar" of Yamada and Otsuchi, the resumption of "(4) work" rose at a comparatively early stage, but is thought that most were temporary resumption in temporary shops and factories. The curve of "(5) housing" which represents the progress of recovery development projects was significantly delayed, and the trend that the curves for "(6) household budget" and "(7) settling of lifestyle", which reflect the feeling of substantial business conditions, continue to be stagnant even when "(5) housing" finally entered underlying recovery, also matches the tone in the results in Table 11 (business performance conditions by number of employees) and Table 12 (business performance conditions by operating format) of this paper.

5.3 *Recovery Community Building Entities*

As seen above, it was identified that in the recovery curves of Yamada (Fig. 3) and Otsuchi (Fig. 4), even when the reconstruction development projects, which are thought to be represented by the curve of "(5) housing", enter the final stage, the categories such as "(6) household budget" and "(7) settling down of life", which are related to the "livelihood" of businesses, still tend to remain low. However, this tendency is more pronounced in the recovery curve for Otsuchi than for Yamada. The difference in the level of recovery between Yamada and Otsuchi is also reflected in Table 27 (level of recovery of the regional economy), Table 28 (level of recovery of local shopping streets), and Table 31 (level of regional population recovery) of this survey, and is one of the issues that require closer examination in the future.

As one factor, it is noteworthy that in Table 29 of this survey (private organizations that led regional economic recovery), the responses from Yamada were notable for the role of the "society of commerce and industry" and the "shopping street association," and in Table 30 (decisive factors of regional economic recovery), the role of the "shopping street association" was cited alongside government support, particularly in Yamada. According to the author group's separate interviews in the field,[7] in the reconstruction of the central area of Yamada Town, commercial interests such as the society of commerce and industry and the shopping street association proactively submitted proposals to the town administration, raised the "living town" concept that is a shopping street recovery concept that would connect the shopping street with transportation access to the Sanriku Railway and public disaster housing complexes and residential areas, which is a rare example of business-led reconstruction community building that achieved realization. In the process, the government took into consideration the wishes of the businesses, and in order to incorporate into the "living town" concept the reconstruction of businesses in the integrated house-and-store form, which was not accepted by the national tsunami reconstruction base project, the land readjustment project involved repeated detailed changes, such as placing the land readjustment project around the base project and consolidating the plots using the scattered replotting method.

Also, it was identified in Table 21 (provision of public assistance by damage suffered) above that the more severely damaged businesses tended to receive more public assistance, and especially when examining the responses from Yamada, 80% of the businesses that received the "SME Group Subsidy" were severely damaged businesses that were swept away or completely destroyed. This can be seen as an example of how differences in support could be avoided through the joint receipt of the "SME Group Subsidy" and other public support for industry in the process of realizing the "living town" concept mentioned above.

The activity of businesses stood out in Otsuchi Town's recovery process, such as the attention which was given to the "Kirari Shopping Street" that gathered together temporary shops, however, a trend that businesses were deeply involved in recovery community building did not appear, at least not in the results of this survey. Recovery

---

[7] Based on interviews with the Yamada SCI in March 2018 and March 2020.

community building is the foundation that affects the reconstruction of businesses, and the decision-making process should not be left to the government or consultants[8]; local businesses being involved themselves suggests a contribution to recovery.

5.4 *Non-Achievement of "Safety"*

One of the noticeable trends common to all the regions in this survey's "recovery calendar" is the low percentage of responses of having achieved "(2) I feel safe now". As of the time of the survey in 2019, Otsuchi had the lowest percentage at 35.7%, followed by Miyako at 45.4%, Yamada at 49.3%, and Kamaishi at 54.7%, which were remarkably low numbers. Among these, "(2) safety" was the second lowest category after "(10) regional economy" in the responses from businesses in both Miyako and Kamaishi.

In the above mentioned NHK survey too, the response for achieving "(2) safety" was below 50% at the time of the survey. However, in the author group's survey of households regarding the recovery of livelihoods (Fig. 7), the percentage of respondents who answered that they had achieved "(2) safety" reached the 50% line between 2015 and 2016, and while remaining flat, reached 60% at the time of the survey. In addition, in the 5-year assessment of recovery by the Reconstruction Agency (Fig. 5), the percentage of respondents who had achieved "(2) safety" already exceeded 80% at the 5-year point of recovery. The feeling of recovery from the aspect of "safety" in this survey of businesses has found a severe trend when compared to answers from regular households.

The causes for why businesses' view regarding "(2) safety" was more severe than those of households requires further investigation. One hypothesis is that the "multi-level disaster prevention" approach adopted by the government in its basic reconstruction policy after the Great East Japan Earthquake has had an impact on safety measures. "Multi-level disaster prevention" refers to the idea of using hard measures such as the construction of seawalls and land readjustment projects taken according to the safety standards based on the Meiji-Sanriku tsunami class (level 1), and using soft measures such as warnings and evacuation when a future Great East Japan Earthquake class disaster (level 2) occurs.[9] Areas near seawalls are designated as a disaster risk area (subject to residential restrictions under Article 39 of the Building Standards Act), but since the disaster prevention group relocation promotion

[8] There is a risk that recovery community-building led by consultants from urban areas may become detached from the needs of local businesses. For example, according to an interview conducted in August 2018 with Kyassen Ofunato, the company responsible for area management of the site development of the disaster risk area in Ofunato-cho, Ofunato City, the company was weary of the combined shop-and-home form of business as a cause of the shuttering of streets, and consciously adopted a tenancy model. As a result, the town development became devoid of continuity with the residential area, and the opening of local businesses has been sparse.

[9] See Kaneko (2018) and Kaneko (2019) regarding safety measures in the recovery after the East Japan Earthquake.

projects target only residences, for the small-scale businesses with integrated home-and-business facilities, they were forced to separate their home from their business as shown in Table 4 and 5 of this paper. As a result, the shops and factories that were forced to remain and rebuild in the disaster risk area have to face the heavy safety issue of evacuating their employees and customers to higher ground in the event of a future level 2 tsunami. On the other hand, the businesses that have been included in height-raising land readjustment projects have been forced to wait several years for the construction to be completed, but the raised land is only in response to a level 1 tsunami (2-m depth of inundation), which means that they will still have to secure the safety of their employees and customers in the event of a future level 2 tsunami.

The fact that a significant difference in Table 14 (business performance conditions by form of reconstruction) occurred in the results of this survey suggests that the intervention of the reconstruction projects affected the rebuilding of businesses and caused a "recovery gap" both economically and in terms of safety. Strictly speaking, further detailed consideration is required because reconstruction policies differ from district to district within the same city or town. To give an example, in Miyako City, construction of floodgates on the Heigawa River was chosen as a safety measure to protect the center of the city, and businesses inside the floodgates were not eligible for reconstruction projects, which led to the main response being "repair on the original site". However, also in the same Miyako City, seawall levees were raised as a giant experimental device at the same time as a disaster-prevention group relocation project and a height-raising land readjustment project in the Taro district, and the schedule of the height-raising land readjustment project in the Kuwagasaki district became delayed, which meant that businesses were included in the reconstruction work, creating a recovery gap with the centre of the city. In Kamaishi too, the center of the city was protected by the rebuilding of the seawall at the entrance of Kamaishi Bay, so the businesses in the center were able to "repair on the original site", while those outside the bay, such as those in the Unosumai district, had to wait several years for the completion of the height-raising land readjustment project. On the other hand, cases also stood out where businesses in districts where the entire central area has been subject to a height-raising land readjustment project, such as the Yamada district of Yamada Town and the Machikata district of Otsuchi Town, have given up on rebuilding on the original site and have chosen to relocate inland to safer areas, as shown in Table 7 (reconstruction form).

The fact that "(2) safety" had the lowest result in this survey, along with "(10) regional economy" and "(9) self-perception as a disaster victim", can be read as an expression of doubts by businesses about the adequacy of the government's safety measures. One of the lessons learned from this survey is that recovery policy planning, which defines the course of recovery community building including safety aspects, should not be set by the government or consultants, but should be carried out through the disclosure of information and participation in a way that is acceptable to businesses and civilians.

References

Great East Japan Earthquake Livelihood Recovery Survey Team (2016) *Survey on the Recovery of Livelihoods after Five Years from the Great East Japan Earthquake and Tsunami*, Reconstruction Agency.

Haruo, Hayashi (Ed.). 2000. *Kobe City Disaster Recovery Overview and Validation – Livelihood Reconstruction Topic Report*, Research Center for Disaster Reduction Systems Technical Report, Disaster Prevention Research Institute, Kyoto University

Hokugo, Akihiko, Yuka Kaneko, Yuichi Honjo, Toshihisa Toyoda, Yumi Shiomi, Abel Táiti Konno. Pinheiro, and Yegane Ghezelloo. 2021a. Resident questionnaire survey on the lives and livelihoods recovery in the Devastated area after ten years from the great east Japan earthquake and Tsunami; overall results review. *Journal of International Cooperation Studies* 28 (2): 23–62.

Hokugo, Akihiko, Yuka Kaneko, Yuichi Honjo, Toshihisa Toyoda, Yumi Shiomi, Abel Táiti Konno. Pinheiro, and Yegane Ghezelloo. 2021b. Resident questionnaire survey on the lives and livelihoods recovery in the Devastated area after ten years from the great east Japan earthquake and Tsunami; integrated results review. *Journal of International Cooperation Studies* 29 (1): 1.

Kawawaki, Yasuo. 2014. Does social capital in the community promote residents' mutual aids after disasters?: The empirical analysis based on local residents' survey in the areas affected by the great east Japan earthquake. *The Nonprofit Review* 14 (1 & 2): 1–13.

Kimura, Reo, Haruo Hayashi, Shigeo Tatsuki, Keiko Tamura, et al. 2004. "Psychologically defined life reconstruction processes of disaster victims in the 1995 Hanshin-Awaji earthquake." *Journal of Social Safety Science* 6: 241–250.

NHK. 2020. *Questionnaire of Victims Nine Years After the Great East Japan Earthquake*, NHK website, https://www3.nhk.or.jp/news/special/shinsai9portal/questionnaire/

Tamura, Keiko, Haruo Hayashi, Shigeo Tatsuki, and Reo Kimura. 2001. "A quantitative verification of the seven elements model of socio-economic recovery from the Kobe earthquake." *Journal of Social Safety Science* 3: 1–8.

Tatsuki, Shigeo. 2013. "What is important for reconstructing livelihoods? A comparison of the results of livelihood recovery surveys after the Hanshin-Awaji earthquake and the great east Japan earthquake." *Toshi Seisaku* 161: 86–103.

Toshihisa ,Toyoda, Yuichi, Honjo, Akihiko, Hokugo, Yuka, Kaneko, and Yumi, Shiomi. 2021. "The reality of economic recovery in areas Devasated by disaster—A survey of commerce and industry", *Kokumin Keizai Zasshi* (not yet published).

Yuichi, Honjo, Akihiko, Hokugo, Yuka, Kaneko, Yuichi, Honjo, Toshihisa, Toyoda, Yumi, Shiomi, Abel Táiti Konno, Pinheiro, and Yegane, Ghezelloo. 2021. *Resident Questionnaire Survey on the Lives and Livelihoods Recovery in the Devastated Area after Ten years from the Great East Japan Earthquake and Tsunami; Results and Review*, Hyogo Earthquake Memorial 21st Century Research Institute (not yet published).

Yuka, Kaneko. 2018. "State's Obligation to Ensure Safety and Issues of Mutual Assistance", *Report of Research Center for Urban Safety and Security, Kobe University*, No. 22, pp. 95–103.

Yuka, Kaneko. 2020. "Safety Standards Reviewed in Proportion to the Restriction of Civil Properties", *Report of Research Center for Urban Safety and Security, Kobe University*, No. 24, pp. 266–278.

Aceh Post 2004 Tsunami Recovery: Strategies and Implications

Teuku Alvisyahrin, Taqwaddin Husin, Rizki Wan Oktabina, and Risma Sunarty

1 Introduction

Post mega-disaster recovery remains a very challenging effort for many disaster-prone countries and requires proper strategies for its sustainability. The destructive impacts of a disaster can create a serious set-back of the development of a country, which subsequently lowers the prosperity level of its society. The incidence of the 2004 Indian Ocean 9.1 M earthquake followed by the tsunami in Aceh, Indonesia, caused impact and devastation on an unprecedented scale. The Agency for the Reconstruction and Rehabilitation of Aceh-Nias (BRR) reported that the massive tsunami disaster impact in Aceh included, among others, over 200,000 fatalities and the destruction of 139,195 houses, 13,828 fishing boats, 73,869 ha of farmland, 104,500 small-medium enterprises, 2,618 km of roads, 3,415 school buildings, 517 health facilities, and 119 bridges (BRR 2009). The estimated total damage and loss from this disaster was US$4.5 billion, which was equivalent to roughly 80% of Aceh's gross domestic product and primarily associated with private assets and revenues (Masyrafah and McKeon 2008).

T. Alvisyahrin (✉)
Graduate Program in Disaster Science, Syiah Kuala University, Banda Aceh, Indonesia
e-mail: talvisyahrin@gmail.com; teuku.alvisyahrin@usk.ac.id

Tsunami and Disaster Mitigation Research Center, Syiah Kuala University, Banda Aceh, Indonesia

T. Husin
Faculty of Law, Syiah Kuala University, Banda Aceh, Indonesia

High Court of Aceh, Banda Aceh, Indonesia

R. W. Oktabina
Health Polytechnic, Ministry of Health, Banda Aceh, Indonesia

R. Sunarty
Aceh Disaster Risk Reduction Forum, Banda Aceh, Indonesia

Y. Kaneko et al. (eds.), *Recovery of Disaster Victims*, Kobe University Monograph Series in Social Science Research, https://doi.org/10.1007/978-981-99-2957-3_4

With this scale of destruction, rebuilding Aceh posed substantial multi-sectoral challenges. Despite the difficult circumstances, the post-tsunami reconstruction effort in Aceh proceeded with a determination to adopt the Build-Back-Better philosophy (BRR 2005) backed by strong support from both strategic national and international stakeholders. Along with elaborating the concept of Build-Back-Better in post-disaster reconstruction, Clinton (2006) emphasized the importance of creating livelihood opportunities and reviving private businesses and employment for the impacted communities in order to achieve a sustainable recovery.

Approaching the 19th anniversary of the mega-disaster event, Aceh has seen a multitude of achievements as far as the recovery results are concerned. That said, questions still arise as to if and how these results can be sustained over time, particularly with respect to opting for a reconstruction strategy in favor of safety (relocation) in contrast to rebuilding on the original land. This paper examines the long-term post-tsunami recovery status of three villages of Aceh.

2 Survey Approach

To assess the long-term impacts of Aceh's post-2004 tsunami recovery efforts, a field survey was conducted in three selected villages. Lambada Lhok village and Neuheun village-Jackie Chan complex (Neuheun-JC) are located in Aceh Besar District, while Lambung village is located in Banda Aceh Municipality. Each of these three villages had a unique main strategy for post-tsunami recovery. Lambada Lhok Village is a fishing village with most of the heads of households working as fishermen, making their livelihoods the most important recovery lesson. In addition, the Reconstruction of Aceh Land Administration System (RALAS) project for land certification, which includes a community-driven adjudication process, was successfully implemented in this village (Husin and Alvisyahrin 2016).

Neuheun-JC village had housing relocation as its recovery strategy, where a site on higher ground was prepared for a new housing development for tsunami victims that relocated from tsunami-impacted villages in Banda Aceh municipality such as Uleelheu and Deah Glumpang, and from Aceh Besar District such as Kajhu and Mon Singet. Relocation to a safer residential area away from hazard zones is often a preferred strategy in post-disaster housing reconstruction, in anticipation of potential future disaster events.

The highlight of the recovery strategy in Lambung village was assisting livelihoods backed by a land consolidation policy. Before the tsunami, the landscape of the village was such that it did not provide sufficient infrastructure for emergency vehicle access, nor did it have a good drainage system. During the village reconstruction planning phase, the community was directly involved in redesigning the spatial unit allocation that includes both private and public spaces, making Lambung the model village for Aceh's post-tsunami recovery (BRR 2009). Prior to the 2004 tsunami, Lambung village was noted for its highly valued products such as traditional Aceh wedding costumes and equipment as well as cookies and snacks.

Thirty three tsunami-survivor respondents from each of the three villages were purposely interviewed using a questionnaire prepared by the Kobe University Center for Social Systems Innovation. The survey questionnaire focused on selected elements of socio-economic recovery according to different recovery strategy implementation.

3 Profile of the Respondents

The survey respondents from Lambada Lhok, Neuheun-JC, and Lambung villages represented their respective community members well in terms of age group and gender equality. Most of the respondents from Lambada Lhok and Lambung villages were originally from the same village prior to the tsunami. In contrast, 79% of the respondents from Neuheun-JC village came from Banda Aceh, and 31% from other villages in Aceh Besar District. Respondents from all three villages had their original homes destroyed by the tsunami. While all respondents from Lambada Lhok and Lambung villages had owned a house before the tsunami, 48% of Neuheun-JC village were renters in their original villages. Respondents from Lambada Lhok and Lambung villages have lived in their current house for 10–75 years, while 91% of respondents from Neuheun-JC village relocated to their current residence within 1–2 years after it was constructed. In addition, 84% of the respondents from Lambada Lhok village had their aid house built on the same land parcel, while all respondents from Lambung village had theirs built on consolidated lands.

The main employment for Lambada Lhok community is in the fishery sector, whereas for Neuheun-JC and Lambung villages it is multi-sectoral. After the tsunami, 50% of Lambada Lhok, 52% of Neuheun-JC, and 61% of Lambung village respondents changed their jobs. The tsunami disaster impacted the household economy of 81% of Lambada Lhok, 79% of Neuheun-JC, and 67% of Lambung village respondents. After the tsunami, 44% of the respondents of Lambada Lhok and 79% of those in Neuheun-JC villages experienced a decrease in income. On the contrary, 64% of the respondents in Lambung village saw an increase in their income after the tsunami. All three villages had 90–94% of the respondents report an increase in household expenses after the tsunami.

4 Population Recovery

The 2004 tsunami took the lives of most of the residents in all three villages surveyed. The majority (75%) of the respondents in Lambada Lhok thought that the current village population is still 40–50% of that before the tsunami. However, only 48% of Lambung respondents believed the population recovery rate was the same in their village. These population recovery estimates appear to be related to the high number of 2004 tsunami fatalities in these two villages. While the population of

Lambada Lhok and Lambung villages appear to have recovered to only about half of that before tsunami, the majority (67%) of the respondents in Neuheun-JC believed that the current population of their wider area village is more than that before the tsunami. The Chief of Neuheun-JC village, Mr. Faizan, confirmed (via authors' personal communication) that the increase in the village population is very significant which, for the most part, could be attributed to an increase in the number of new residents in other relocated housing sites existing in the village, such as the Buddha Tzu Chi, UMCOR, and Saudi Charity housing complexes.

5 Economic Recovery

The status of economic recovery in the three surveyed villages is presented in Figs. 1 and 2. It is noteworthy that, for Neuheun-JC village, the respondents' perception on the village economic and business area recovery includes the wider area of the Neuheun village beyond the Jackie Chan Complex. Overall, 50% of Lambada Lhok, 51% of Neuheun-JC, and 69% of Lambung village respondents believed that their village economic recovery was between *'almost completely recovered'* and recovery *'better than before tsunami'* (Fig. 1). Looking at the economic recovery achievement *'better than before tsunami'* alone, Lambung village stands out with the number of respondents nearly doubling or tripling those in Lambada Lhok and Neuheun JC villages. This can be explained by the fact that both pre- and post-tsunami reconstruction, Lambung village residents had much better access to education and training, market infrastructure, and business opportunities around the city of Banda Aceh compared to the other two villages.

Fig. 1 Perceived village economy recovery (%)

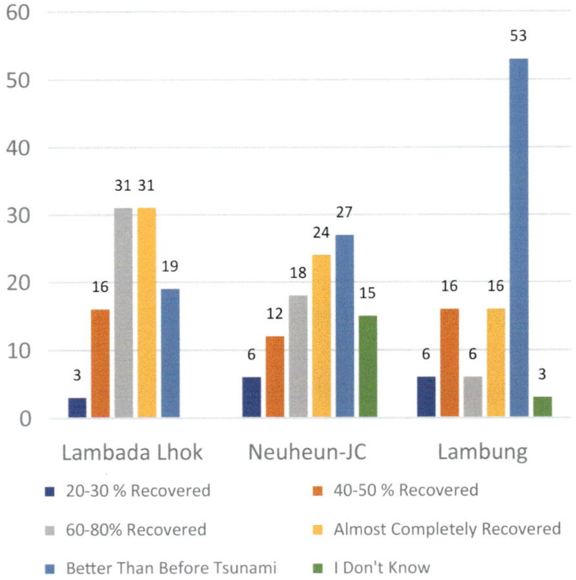

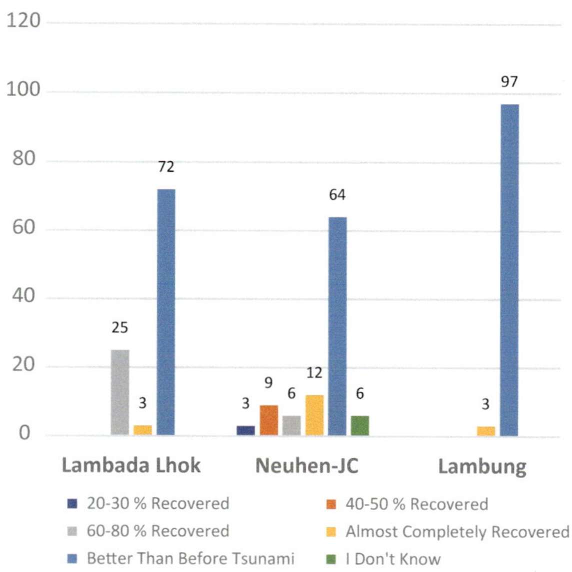

Fig. 2 Perceived business area recovery (%)

The majority of respondents from all three villages agreed that business area reconstruction efforts in their village have produced a better result than that before the tsunami (Fig. 2). As with its economic recovery, Lambung village respondents, again, surpassed those in the two other villages in their perception of a better business area recovery in their village. The significant improvement of business area facilities and other infrastructure in Lambung village could be closely linked to the land consolidation policy that was successfully implemented during the village reconstruction. Among the three villages surveyed, Neuheun-JC showed the lowest perceived economic and business area recovery.

The provision of aid by donors played a very important role in the socio-economic and physical reconstruction of the 2004 tsunami-impacted areas of Aceh. While the majority (69%) of the respondents in Lambada Lhok and Lambung villages received support for their business, more than half of the respondents in Neuheun-JC village did not (Fig. 3). This could help explain in part why the perceived economic recovery in Neuheun-JC village was lower compared to that in both Lambada Lhok and Lambung villages.

The majority of respondents in all three villages who received business support stated that the support from donors was effective (Fig. 4). Lambada Lhok and Neuheun-JC villages had a higher level of effectiveness than that of Lambung village. The effectiveness of support in Lambada Lhok village could be related to its established fishing community, while for Neuheun-JC village it might be due to new business initiatives that were temporary in nature. As for Lambung village, the lower effectiveness of support could be associated with the difficulties in reestablishing its collapsed home industry after the tsunami, besides lacking in skilled workers and a mentoring program. Results of a study by Daly et al. (2020) show that aid programs

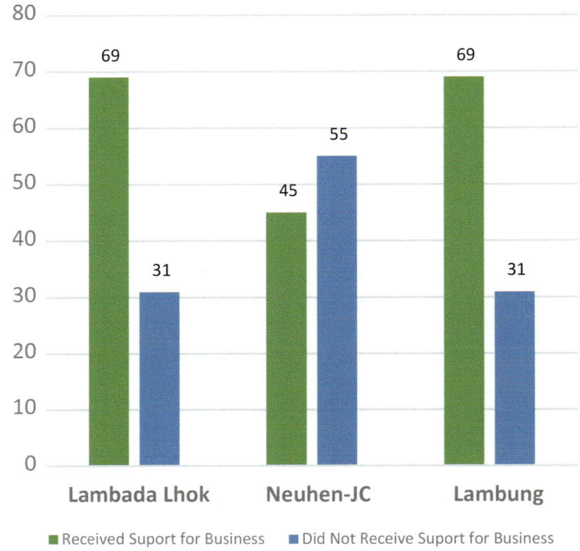

Fig. 3 Recipients of support for business (%)

were temporarily able to support some recipients without pre-disaster livelihood experience, but were not effective for developing these recipients' full-time new livelihoods.

A larger decrease in income, limited employment opportunities, lower perceived economic recovery, and less support for business reported by Neuheun-JC respondents may suggest that the needs of the relocated tsunami survivors in terms of essential services had not been adequately addressed, if at all. Vale et al. (2014)

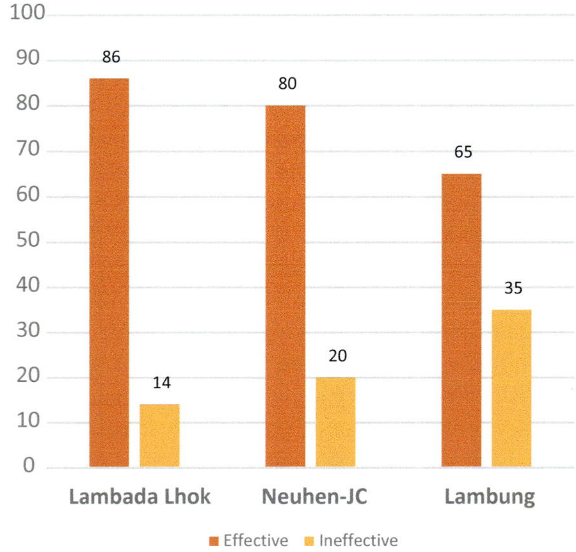

Fig. 4 Effectiveness of support for business (%)

Table 1 Time factor in attitude changes toward post-tsunami recovery

Recovery element	Lambada Lhok (Years)	Neuheun-JC (Years)	Lambung (Years)
Grasping the total image of tsunami devastation	< 1	< 1	< 1
Started feeling safe	3	3	< 1
No longer as a victim	3	3	3
Job resumed	2	4	1
Village economy recovered	6	4	4
Housing issues resolved	4	3	3
School restored	3	3	3

stated that Neuheun-JC's location 17 km away from Banda Aceh and a lack of public services and transportation creates more burdens on the lives of the various workers and entrepreneurs who resettled there.

6 Time Factor in Post-tsunami Recovery

The communities in all three villages were able to come to terms with the reality of the 2004 tsunami's massive destruction practically within less than one year (Table 1). Furthermore, it took respondents of all three villages three years to cope with the impacts of the disaster and move on with their lives. It is interesting to note, however, it took the respondents of Lambada Lhok and Neuheun-JC villages thrice as much time to start feeling safe from the implications of the tsunami's impact compared to that of Lambung village. In addition, more challenging circumstances appeared to have been faced by the respondents of Lambada Lhok and Neuheun-JC in resuming their job after the tsunami compared to those from Lambung village. The matter was even more serious for Neuheun-JC respondents due to their very limited access to employment and public services at the new residential location. In general, the community members in Lambung village have better education and training on top of more employment opportunities during the post-tsunami reconstruction of Aceh. This could also help explain in part why it took Lambung village respondents a lot less time to feel safe and secure after dealing with the impacts of the tsunami. While all three villages had their schools rebuilt within three years, it took longer for Lambada Lhok village to recover from their economic and housing issues compared to that of Lambung village. As the data in Table 1 indicates, it generally took longer for economic and physical reconstruction to complete compared to that of the psycho-social recovery.

7 Pre- and Post-tsunami Community Activities

Typical community activities during the pre- and post-tsunami periods more or less stayed the same and are quite similar for all three villages, and are dominated by those of a cultural, environmental, developmental, and religious nature. In Lambung village, disaster mitigation became an added practice after a tsunami evacuation building was erected during the village reconstruction. The community activities in all three villages usually take place once a week, using mosque yards or a village community building as the venue. For Lambung village, the tsunami evacuation building provides another convenient venue for its activities. Community activities for Lambada Lhok and Neuheun-JC villages are basically conducted within the village's range, while for Lambung village, they extend toward Banda Aceh city and Aceh Besar District areas. All three villages use the same communication media for community activity notification, i.e., a public address system available at the mosque and more recently after the tsunami, social media broadcast via cellular phones. The fact that Lambung village is located within the City of Banda Aceh, with better access to various resources and facilities, gives the village some added advantages in conducting their community programs.

8 Conclusion and Implications

Economic recovery in Lambada Lhok (Livelihood + RALAS strategy) and Lambung (Livelihood + Land consolidation strategy) villages was better that in Neuheun-JC (Relocation) village. This suggests that the choice for relocating the tsunami survivors to Neuheun-JC village was not accompanied by a comprehensive strategy. Limited access to employment and public services at the relocation site may have contributed to this shortfall. In the meantime, physical recovery in all three villages with regard to housing and village schools have generally been satisfactorily accomplished. This was somewhat lacking for the economic sector. Better identification of financial aid recipients and the suitability of their proposed business plan, among others, would be needed for a sustainable economic recovery.

The adopted land consolidation policy coupled with access to more resources and employment opportunities available to tsunami survivors may well be the driving factors for the better recovery results in Lambung village compared to the other two villages. Comments received from most respondents in all villages surveyed suggest that training and mentoring in business management as well as further access to financing would continue to help rebuild and strengthen the sustainability of their household economy. In this regard, the Indonesian government will need to continue to provide technical and, to some extent, financial assistance to ensure the sustainability of recovery of the tsunami-impacted communities.

Acknowledgements We would like to express our sincere thanks and appreciation to Kobe University Center for Social Systems Innovation (KUSSI), Kobe University Research Center for Urban

Safety and Security (RCUSS), Iwate University Research Center for Regional Disaster Management (RCRDM), and The Asian Disaster Reduction Center (ADRC), for their support and leadership in this research. Our sincere gratitude also goes to the late Mr. Faizan (the former Chief of Neuheun village), Mr. A. Kadir (the Chief of Lambada Lhok village), Mr. Yasir (the Chief of Lambung village), and Mr. A. Wahid (the Chief of Mukim Lamnga) for their kind assistance and facilitation during the field survey conducted in their respective villages.

References

BRR. 2009. STORY: Feat of the Daunting Launch. BRR book 1. The Agency for the Reconstruction and Rehabilitation of Aceh-Nias.

BRR. 2005. Rebuilding a Better Aceh and Nias—Stocktaking of the Reconstruction Effort. The Agency for the Reconstruction and Rehabilitation of Aceh-Nias

Clinton, W. J. 2006. Key Propositions for Building Back Better. A Report by the UN Secretary-General's Special Envoy for Tsunami Recovery. Office of the UN Secretary-General's Special Envoy for Tsunami Recovery.

Daly, P., Mahdi, S., McCaughey, J., Munzir, I., Halim, A., Ardiansyah, Nizamuddin, and Srimulyani. 2020. Rethinking relief, reconstruction and development: Evaluating the effectiveness and sustainability of post-disaster livelihood aid. *The International Journal of Disaster Risk Reduction* 49 (2020): 101650.

Husin, T., and Alvisyahrin, T. 2016. The legal framework of community-based land administration in tsunami-impacted areas of Aceh: A case study in Baitussalam Sub_district, Aceh Besar District, Indonesia. p. 97–113. In Y. Kaneko et al. (eds.) *Asian Law in Disasters: Toward a human-centered recovery*. Routledge Taylor & Francis Group. London and New York.

Masyrafah, H., and McKeon, J. MJA. 2008. Post-tsunami aid effectiveness in Aceh: Proliferation and coordination in reconstruction. Working Paper 6. Wolfensohn Center for Development.

Vale, L., Shamsuddin, S., and Goh, K. 2014. Tsunami + 10: Housing Banda Aceh After Disaster. Places Journal. https://doi.org/10.22269/141215

Survey Report on Resilience of Wenchuan Earthquake-Affected Areas

Jianping Wang and Jingyi Liao

1 Background of the Survey on "Resilience Project in Wenchuan Earthquake-Affected Areas"

The Wenchuan Earthquake that occurred on May 12, 2008, with a magnitude of Ms 8.0, was the most destructive since the founding of the People's Republic in 1949, with the widest geographical range of effect and causing the most serious amount of disaster-induced losses, including more than 69,000 deaths, 375,000 injuries, 18,000 missing, and direct economic losses of 845.2 billion yuan.[1] After the earthquake, the CPC Central Committee and the State Council urgently deployed earthquake relief work, and the government, military, professional rescue teams, enterprises, social organizations and others fought hard to carry out the rescue work.

On June 8, marked by the State Council's announcement of the "Regulations on Post-Wenchuan Earthquake Restoration and Reconstruction" ("Restoration Regulations"), the Wenchuan earthquake response entered the post-disaster reconstruction phase that follows the disaster relief phase. On September 19, the State Council released "The Overall Planning for Post-Wenchuan Earthquake Restoration and Reconstruction" ("Restoration Overall Planning"), which explicitly proposed to "achieve the major task of restoration and reconstruction in approximately three years".

On May 10, 2011, the State Council Information Office held a press conference to announce that by the end of September 2010, the objectives of the "three-year task to

[1] As of August 25, 2008.

J. Wang · J. Liao (✉)
Sichuan University—The Hong Kong Polytechnic University Institute for Disaster Management and Reconstruction, Section 2, Chuanda Road, Shuangliu District, Chengdu, Sichuan, China
e-mail: 365236504@qq.com

J. Wang
e-mail: wangjianping@scu.edu.cn

Y. Kaneko et al. (eds.), *Recovery of Disaster Victims*, Kobe University Monograph Series in Social Science Research, https://doi.org/10.1007/978-981-99-2957-3_5

be completed basically in two years" had been achieved, and completed projects now account for 95% of the planned projects. Since then, the post-disaster reconstruction of Wenchuan earthquake has entered a new reconstruction era.

It has been more than ten years since the restoration and reconstruction from the Wenchuan earthquake, and this decade also coincides with a decade of rapid social, economic, and cultural development in China. Under the idea of high-quality development in the new era, new development concepts and new economic models have penetrated the vast land of the disaster-affected areas and promoted the development and revitalization of the disaster-affected areas. At the same time, driven by policies such as "One Belt, One Road", poverty alleviation and rural revitalization, the disaster-affected areas have used their own strengths to achieve strong economic growth, constructing a post-disaster restoration and reconstruction model with unique Chinese characteristics. This new model brings new academic enlightenment implications for reassessing the scale and intensity of resilience and legal mechanisms in the Wenchuan earthquake-affected area.

At the end of 2020, on the eve of the 10th anniversary of the March 11, 2011 earthquake in Japan, Professor Yuka Kaneko of Kobe University, Japan, and Professor Wang Jianping of Sichuan University, China, reached a collaborative agreement to conduct a systematic study of the state of post-disaster reconstruction in Asia. After thorough discussion and communication, Professor Wang formed a special research team and undertook a collaborative research task on social resilience in post-Wenchuan Earthquake affected areas, i.e., the "Resilience Project in Wenchuan Earthquake-Affected Areas", to conduct systematic research, analysis, and summary of the post-disaster reconstruction in Beichuan County and Anzhou District (formerly named An County),[2] in Mianyang City, Sichuan Province.

The design of the "Resilience Project in Wenchuan Earthquake-Affected Areas" is based on three academic theories: (1) the relationship between resilience and the support of the central and local governments, i.e., the role of administrative power on resilience; (2) the collaborative relationship among resilience, government, and the affected population; (3) the intrinsic correlation between resilience and resource integration.

2 Organization and Implementation of the Survey

Beichuan County and Anzhou District, both under the jurisdiction of Mianyang City, Sichuan Province, were extremely hard-hit disaster areas in the Wenchuan earthquake. Beichuan County is located in the northwestern part of the Sichuan basin and is the only Qiang autonomous county in China. In the Wenchuan earthquake, more than 15,000 people in the Beichuan old county were killed, more than 141,000 people were left homeless, and more than 40,000 houses collapsed, which

[2] In March 2016, the State Council officially approved the abolition of the "An County" in Mianyang City, Sichuan Province and renamed it as "Anzhou District".

was the most concentrated area of disaster-bearing bodies damaged in the Wenchuan earthquake.

Due to the devastating destruction of the old county of Beichuan County (Old Beichuan), the State Council approved the overall relocation and off-site reconstruction following the disaster, and the Old Beichuan was preserved as a site museum of the Wenchuan earthquake. So far, this earthquake site museum is a unique in-situ preservation of the world's largest, most comprehensive type of damage, and is also a very typical secondary disaster earthquake disaster site area, which allows the observation of the full picture of the hazard-inducing environment of Old Beichuan before and after the Wenchuan earthquake.

Anzhou District, located in the northwestern part of the Sichuan Basin, in the southwestern part of Mianyang City and adjacent to Beichuan County, is one of the main urban areas of Mianyang City. In the Wenchuan earthquake, more than 1,500 people died and more than 13,000 were injured in An County, making it another extremely hard-hit area.

The theoretical and practical basis for selecting Beichuan County and Anzhou District (hereinafter referred to collectively as the "County and District") for the "Resilience Project in Wenchuan Earthquake-Affected Areas" are: (1) both are extremely hard-hit areas and their disaster-bearing bodies and hazard-inducing environments are typical and irreplaceable; (2) both places received counterpart assistance in the process of post-disaster reconstruction; (3) their different methods of post-disaster reconstruction. The Old Beichuan was preserved as a site museum and the new county was reconstructed off-site, while the Anzhou District was reconstructed in situ, with contiguity and comparability.

After systematic preparation, the "Resilience Project in Wenchuan Earthquake-Affected Areas" research team, under the guidance of Professor Wang Jianping, visited Beichuan County and Anzhou District from February to September 2021, distributing questionnaires, conducting talks and occasional interviews, and so on.

The research team distributed a total of 200 questionnaires (100 each in Beichuan and Anzhou), all of which were returned. After validity verification, 183 valid questionnaires were determined (92 in Beichuan and 91 in Anzhou), meaning that 183 respondents were eligible. Among the 183 respondents, 50.27% were male and 49.73% were female; 3.82% were 25 years old or younger, 79.23% were 26 to 55 years old, and 16.94% were 56 years old or older. The respondents were randomly selected and evenly distributed in terms of gender, age, occupation, and address, and can be used objectively to evaluate the resilience of local post-disaster reconstruction.

3 Results and Analysis of the Survey

Based on the results of relevant academic research on disaster resilience,[3] combined with research ideas, methods, data, and assumptions based on government administrative power as a core factor, the research team analyzed the resilience of the Wenchuan earthquake area in four dimensions: physical resilience, organizational resilience, economic resilience, and social resilience.

Before the specific analysis of this project, three points need to be highlighted in particular: (1) the background of rapid economic development and high-quality growth in China. This is an important background factor that has led the economy, society, and culture of the disaster-affected areas to maintain high growth, and should be considered comprehensively in the research. (2) The "national system" and the objective of "high-speed reconstruction". Driven by the objective of the "three-year task to be completed basically in two years", most of the reconstruction projects were completed in around 2011. Therefore, 2011 is an important time point for resilience observation. (3) The agricultural attributes of the "County and District". The agricultural attributes of Beichuan County and Anzhou District determine the ease of implementation of post-disaster reconstruction projects and the predominance of physical resilience.

According to official statistics, before the Wenchuan earthquake in 2008, Beichuan and Anzhou both had a relatively large agricultural population and a large proportion of agricultural workers, and most of them lived in rural self-built houses with weak earthquake resistance. Over the past ten years of post-disaster reconstruction, although the "County and District" have been vigorously developing secondary and tertiary industries, based on the above objective of resource allocation, they still retain strong customs and cultural traditions of agricultural production. At the same time, common issues in rural areas in China existed in Beichuan and Anzhou as well, such as the outflow of young laborers, the decrease of the resident population, the high proportion of left-behind children, and the aging problem of the countryside, which are also variables that need special attention when conducting analysis and data summarization.

3.1 Physical Resilience

The physical resilience of the disaster-affected areas mainly refers to the resilience of roads, communications, houses, land, and its attached crops in the disaster-affected areas. The massive destruction of these disaster-bearing bodies seriously affected the basic production and livelihoods of the victims. Therefore, for post-disaster infrastructure construction, the central and local governments issued several documents requiring disaster areas to prioritize the restoration and reconstruction of housing for the affected people and public service facilities, such as schools and hospitals,

[3] Bruneau et al. (2003); Liu et al. (2006b).

to ensure the basic production and livelihoods of urban and rural residents, which was a requirement for the physical resilience of damaged livelihood projects as disaster-bearing bodies.

On November 7, 2008, the National Development and Reform Commission (NDRC) released the "Special Plan for Post-Wenchuan Earthquake Rehabilitation and Reconstruction Infrastructure" ("Reconstruction Infrastructure Plan"), which provided a three-year plan for the restoration and reconstruction of disaster-bearing bodies in the aspects of transportation, communication, energy and water conservation, which are a part of the life and production of residents, and sought to restore the level and capacity of infrastructure services in the disaster-affected areas to or in excess of the pre-disaster level within the three-year recovery period. According to the survey data, 72.13% of the respondents believed that the roads were reopened in 2011, while 91.80% of the respondents believed that the schools were reopened in 2011, which indicates that the physical resilience of public facilities is extremely strong.

In terms of housing of the disaster-affected population, 53.55% of houses were severely damaged (completely destroyed; immediate demolition; not reparable) after the earthquake, 26.78% were moderately damaged (out of service before retrofitting), 12.02% were negligible to slight damage (operational), and 7.65% thought that they had not received a house damage assessment (Fig. 1).

Indeed, the People's Government of Sichuan Province has issued documents on post-Wenchuan earthquake urban and rural housing damage assessment. In view of the fact that a small number of houses have not been assessed for disaster damage, this reflects the inadequate implementation of grassroots measures.

Under the government's objective of "three-year task to be completed basically in two years", the post-disaster restoration and reconstruction work in the Wenchuan earthquake area has proceeded at a high speed. According to the survey data, 79.78% of the respondents moved into new homes three years after the earthquake.

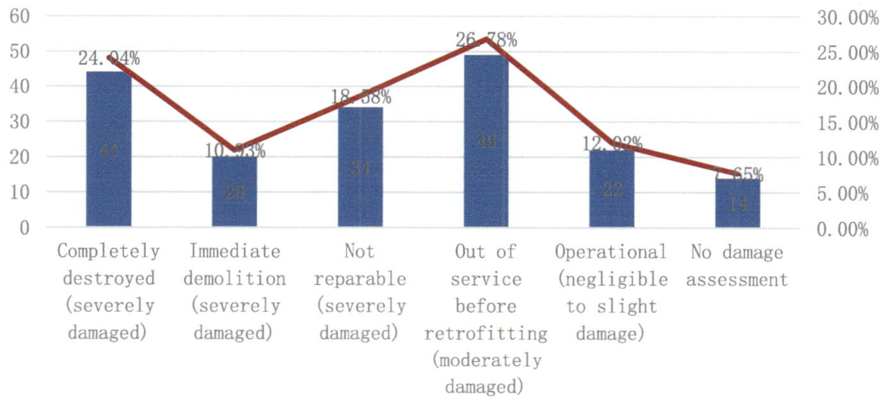

Fig. 1 Post-disaster housing damage assessment

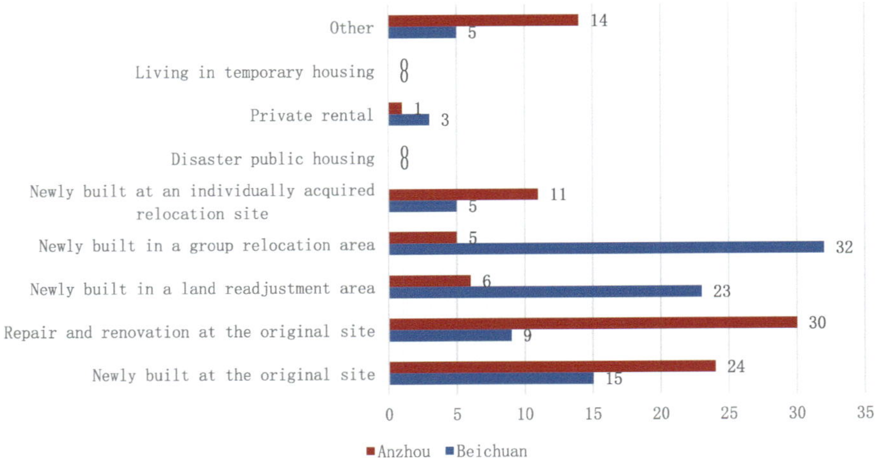

Fig. 2 Reconstruction status of houses

However, Beichuan and Anzhou issued different housing reconstruction policies for the disaster-affected populations, because the Old Beichuan as a whole was rebuilt off-site. Among the 92 respondents in Beichuan County, 40.21% of homes were the subject of off-site reconstruction, including collective relocation (34.78%) and individual relocation (5.43%). In Anzhou District, only 17.58% were the subject of off-site reconstruction, which is much lower than Beichuan County (Fig. 2).

From the beginning of the reconstruction in 2008, the task of reconstruction or reinforcement and repair of permanent housing has been completed by 2021, and the temporary housing and disaster public housing provided as post-earthquake transitional housing have been vacated and demolished,[4] so it is no longer possible for people to be living in disaster temporary housing.

3.2 *Organizational Resilience*

The organizational resilience of a disaster-affected area mainly refers to the ability of the government and social organizations in the affected area to participate in disaster management, organization, and decision-making. In China, understanding this organizational resilience requires an awareness of the structure of administrative functions and administrative power from the perspective of collaboration between the central government and local governments, and in particular, an understanding

[4] The reconstruction of housing after earthquakes and other types of disasters in China can be roughly divided into three stages: emergency housing (tents, stadiums, inside cars, etc.), transitional housing (mainly centrally housed mobile homes or farmer-built houses) and permanent housing.

of the unity and efficiency of the CPC leadership that can enable organizational resilience to effectively overcome the forces of disintegration and create a strong synthetic force.

3.2.1 Government-Led: The Core of Administrative Power

The formation and the transmission of effective decisions in the event of a disaster is an important aspect of the resilience of government organizations. When an earthquake causes local communication interruptions and traffic disruptions, thereby forming "information-isolated islands", it is difficult to fully demonstrate the government's disaster relief capabilities if there is no effective information transfer, even if the earthquake relief headquarters makes effective disaster relief decisions. With the restoration of communication and traffic, the information can be passed and circulated up and down properly, so that the decisions and measures for disaster prevention, mitigation and relief can be effectively implemented.

In the Wenchuan earthquake, the State Council immediately set up the national headquarters for earthquake relief, followed by the Sichuan Province and other cities' earthquake relief headquarters, taking full responsibility for the organization and command of the earthquake relief work. The establishment of such temporary command institutions is an organizational response made in accordance with China's "Emergency Response Law", "Law of Protecting Against and Mitigating Earthquake Disasters" and earthquake disaster contingency plans, and is a concrete manifestation of the recovery of organizational capacity after a disaster. After the emergency relief work of the earthquake is completed, the earthquake relief duties of the government and social organizations are transferred to post-disaster reconstruction.

Generally speaking, the central and local governments, especially the governments of the disaster-affected areas, are the core subjects of post-disaster restoration and reconstruction, while other subjects include juridical persons, other organizations and the affected populations.[5] However, the research team found that the provincial government, which is in an intermediate position in the administrative structure of the central and local governments, still had absolute dominance in the post-Wenchuan earthquake restoration and reconstruction. It is an inevitable manifestation of both the CPC's unified leadership and the Chinese hierarchy at the level of administrative power allocation, which manifested in the central government as the core and local governments at all levels as the executive power.

The research team found that 134 out of 183 respondents, 73.22% of the total, believed that government leadership was decisive for the recovery of the local economy (Fig. 3).

This assessment was a high recognition of the integration ability of the central and local governments, as well as the implementation of the counterpart assistance system at all levels of government.

[5] Wang (2008).

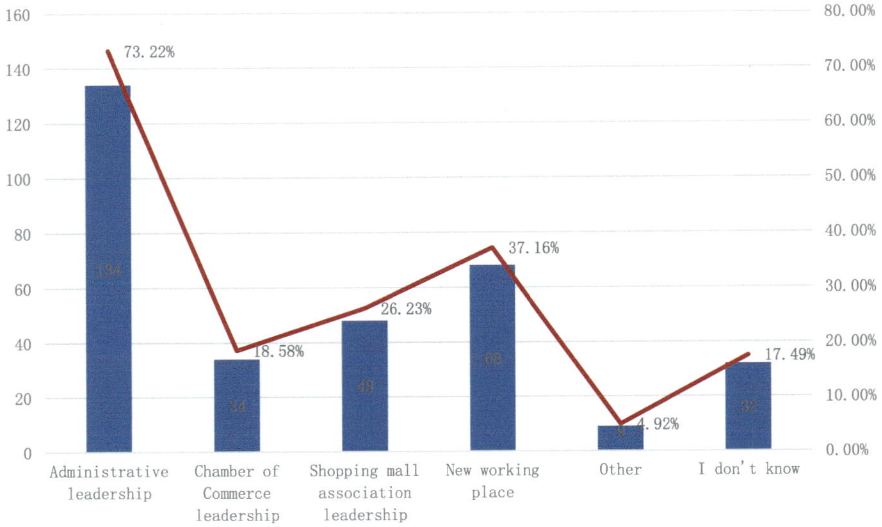

Fig. 3 Decisive factors in regional economic recovery

3.2.2 Participation of Social Organizations: One of the Synthetic Forces

Social organizations are an indispensable component of disaster prevention, mitigation, and relief in China. The Earthquake Disaster Prevention and Mitigation Law, which was revised on December 27, 2008, made the "combination of government-led, social participation and market operation" as the basic principle of post-earthquake restoration and reconstruction.[6]

Meanwhile, the central government has issued various regulations and rules on disaster prevention, mitigation, and relief in recent years, constantly emphasizing the important role of social organizations, and at the same time, more committed to vigorously fostering and encouraging social organizations to participate in disaster prevention, mitigation, and relief. For example, the "Guidelines on Promoting the Reform of the Institutional Mechanism for Disaster Prevention, Mitigation and Relief" ("Guidelines on Disaster Prevention Mechanism"), published on December 19, 2016, specifically stipulate the obligations of social organizations to participate in disaster prevention and mitigation.

The research team found that many respondents acknowledged that some business associations and enterprises were participating in post-disaster reconstruction, but little was known about other social organizations. For example, among the 183 people surveyed, only 14 of them consulted with NPOs or NGOs in post-disaster reconstruction, which is a very small percentage. It shows that social organizations' participation in post-disaster reconstruction was still relatively small in terms of depth and breadth.

[6] See "Earthquake Disaster Prevention and Mitigation Law", Article 72.

3.2.3 Legal Power: Enforceability to Guarantee the Implementation of Policies and Measures

In post-disaster restoration and reconstruction, legal power is mainly used to illustrate the protective capacity of reconstruction policy and measures. In other words, it refers to the compulsion to make all subjects involved in the reconstruction, such as governments, assistance providers, social organizations, and disaster victims, to comply with laws, regulations, and policies, fulfill their obligations and responsibilities, and promote the completion of the restoration and reconstruction, which can be observed in three dimensions, i.e., starting point, process, and result evaluation.

In the process of resilience research, legal power is easily neglected. From the perspective of sociology of law, it may be because scholars studying post-disaster reconstruction lack knowledge of institutional economics, which leads to neglect or ignorance of the role of institutions. According to the experience of the sociology of law, this contempt for the legal system also happens to lead to the indulgence of the deficiencies in the configuration of the executive power of the government, i.e., the indulgence of the incompetence of the administrative synthetic power. In China, it is the enforcement provided by institutions such as the "Emergency Response Law", "Law of Protecting Against and Mitigating Earthquake Disasters", "Restoration Regulations", "Restoration Overall Planning", and their specific enforcement through the counterpart assistance system, that made the post-earthquake reconstruction a strong institutional achievement and an inevitable manifestation of the superiority of socialism.

3.3 Economic Resilience

Economic resilience refers to the ability to promote the recovery of national economic production levels by allocating resources to the economic system, industries, employment, and population in the affected areas, thus becoming a combined resource force, which is an important component of the overall resilience of the affected society. This can be specifically divided into the following areas.

3.3.1 Economic Recovery of Disaster-Affected Areas

According to the "5.12 Wenchuan Earthquake-Affected area 10-year Economic Development Report", in the past ten years of post-Wenchuan earthquake restoration and reconstruction, the comprehensive power of the disaster-affected areas had increased significantly. 39 extremely hard-hit areas had a higher economic growth rate than the average level of Sichuan Province, urban and rural residents' income had increased significantly, urban and rural construction had increased speed and efficiency, investment consumption demand had further expanded, and the development of the disaster-affected areas was more adequate. Meanwhile, according to

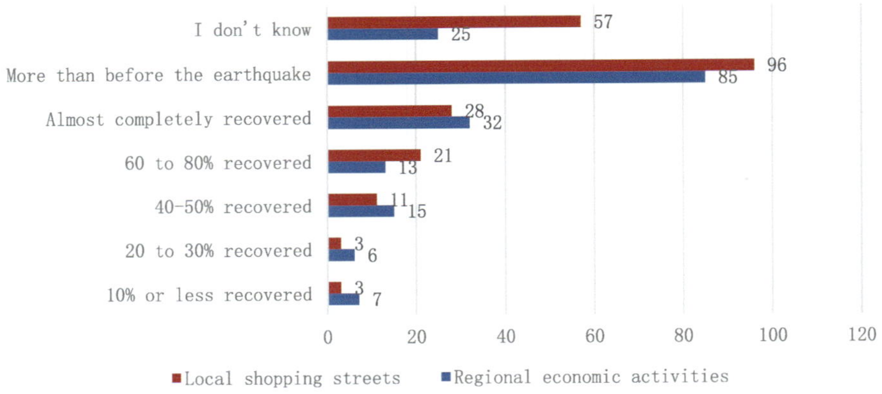

Fig. 4 Recovery situation of regional economic activities and local shopping streets

Mianyang City Yearbook data, Beichuan County and Anzhou District achieved a GDP of 5.594 billion yuan and 14.635 billion yuan respectively in 2018, an increase of 3.25 times and 1.88 times over the pre-Wenchuan earthquake period.[7]

The project data also shown that 46.45% of respondents believed that the local economy had surpassed the pre-earthquake level, and 52.46% of respondents thought the reconstruction status of local shopping streets had exceeded the pre-earthquake level (Fig. 4).

As for the impact of economic recovery in the disaster-affected areas on personal business performance, of the 106 respondents who believed that their business performance was affected, 43.4% believed that their performance improved because of the improved economic situation, which was the most common response (Fig. 5).

3.3.2 Personal Employment and Income

During the post-Wenchuan earthquake restoration and reconstruction, governments and human resource departments at all levels in Sichuan Province adopted a series of employment assistance measures. For example, through measures such as strengthening employment training, encouraging entrepreneurship, and supporting the restoration and reconstruction of enterprises, the stability of the employment situation in the disaster-affected areas has been maintained.

It is known that, in the initial period after the Wenchuan earthquake, few jobs were available in the disaster-affected areas. But with the promotion of post-disaster reconstruction work and the resumption of production and operation of enterprises, local jobs gradually increased. According to the project survey data, 51.98% of the respondents believed that their company's performance started to improve during 2011. Further, 59.02% of the respondents found jobs again one year after the earthquake; among them, 51.91% of the respondents remained in their original jobs (including

[7] Statistics source: 2008 and 2019 Mianyang City Yearbook.

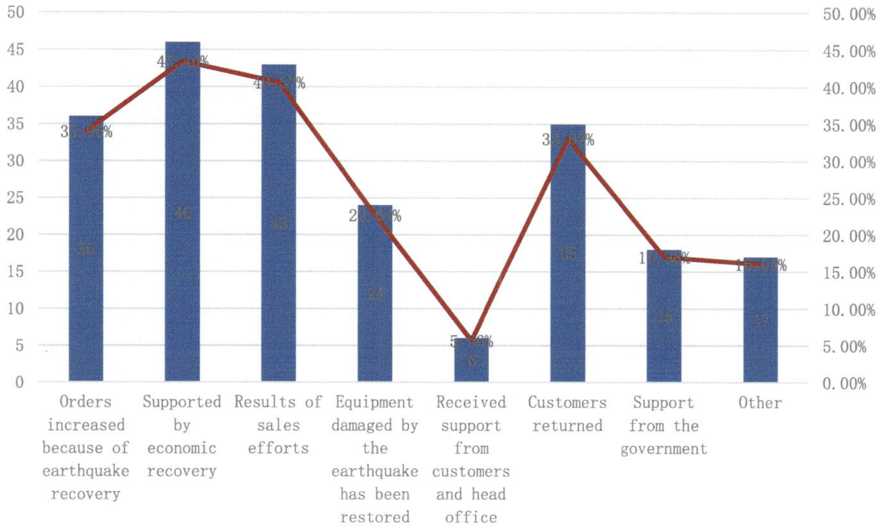

Fig. 5 Reasons for sales and performance recovery

resuming after a suspension), and only 6.01% changed jobs or stopped working and lost their jobs due to the earthquake. The remaining respondents either resigned, stopped working, changed careers for other reasons, have not been working, or had other changes.

Meanwhile, the project research team found that 106 respondents believed that their performance had been affected by the Wenchuan earthquake. 42.45% of the respondents believed that their performance had returned to the pre-earthquake level, 29.25% believed that it had not returned, and 2.83% believed that their operating income performance had gradually declined since before the Wenchuan earthquake. In addition, 25.48% of the respondents chose "other changes" (Fig. 6).

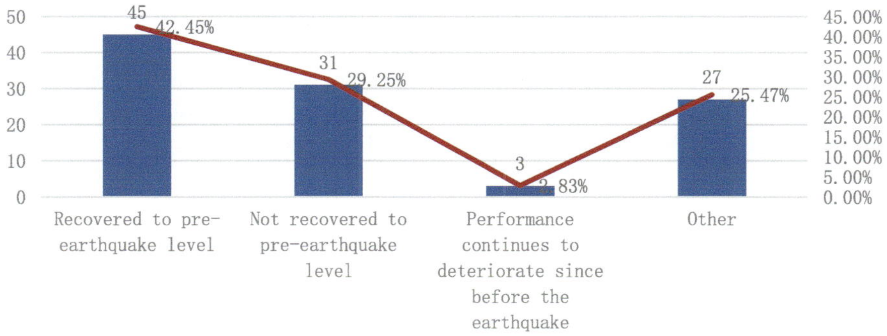

Fig. 6 Changes in sales and performance recovery before and after the disaster

The research team also found that, unlike the significant economic growth presented by the official statistics, not more than half of the respondents believed that their performance had returned to the level they were at before the Wenchuan earthquake. The reasons for this may be a combination of differences between industries and personal management.

3.3.3 Population Recovery and Migration

After the Wenchuan earthquake, the government took many measures to promote the recovery of the population in the disaster-affected areas. For example, the Standing Committee of the Sichuan Provincial People's Congress issued "Decision on the Reproduction of Families with Members Casualties in the Wenchuan Earthquake" (July 25, 2008), which relaxed the fertility policy and provided policy support for families with earthquake casualties, in order to reduce the continuation of damage to the disaster-bearing bodies, which originated from the changes in family structure caused by the earthquake.

Specifically, in terms of population recovery, the research team found some differences between Beichuan and Anzhou. In Beichuan County, 68.48% of respondents believed that the population had not returned to its pre-earthquake number, while only 31.87% of respondents in Anzhou District believed so. Although the above data on the population of the disaster-affected areas were subjective perceptions of the respondents, combined with the data from the sixth (2010) and seventh (2020) national censuses,[8] the population growth of Beichuan County in the last ten years after the Wenchuan earthquake was −1.17%, while that of Anzhou District was 1.68%, which proves that the subjective perceptions of the respondents were basically in line with the objective situation.

As for the reasons of population outflow from the "County and District", the research team found that the destruction of the social structure as a disaster-bearing body after the Wenchuan earthquake, resulting in the "lack of job and places", was considered one of the most important reasons for population outflow, accounting for 55.24% of the 105 respondents who thought the population had not recovered (Fig. 7).

According to official statistics, the proportion of the urban population in Mianyang had risen by 11.81% in the last decade, indicating that more people were leaving the countryside to live and work in towns, which was detrimental to the growth of economic resilience in the affected areas.

---

[8] Statistics source: Bureau of Statistics, Mianyang City, Sichuan Province.

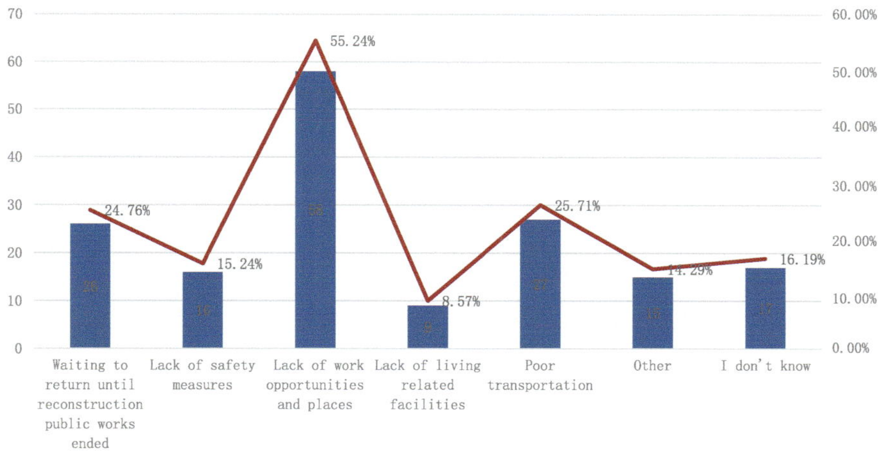

Fig. 7 Causes of population outflow

3.4 *Social Resilience*

Social resilience mainly refers to the restoration and enhancement of social trust, social interaction, sense of security, and disaster awareness after a disaster. The realization of social resilience relies on the government's administrative power and post-disaster reconstruction measures to help disaster victims' sense of security recover, learn from the disaster, and subsequently enhance disaster prevention, mitigation, and relief awareness, as well as improve social trust. Specifically, this includes the following.

3.4.1 Restoration of the People's Feeling of Safety

Undoubtedly, catastrophes not only cause huge casualties and economic losses, but also have serious effects on the physical and mental health of the survivors. Therefore, the psychological recovery of the victims, especially the recovery of their feeling of safety, is also an important factor in the evaluation of resilience.

There are three items related to the psychology of victims in the questionnaire, when they were no longer afraid (returned to a normal life), when they thought they were safe, and when they thought they were no longer victims. The survey results have shown that the 5th year after the earthquake, i.e. 2013, is an important time demarcation point and observation point for safety recovery, with 79.78%, 76.50% and 81.42% of the respondents respectively believing that they were no longer afraid, thought they were safe and thought they were no longer disaster victims five years after the earthquake. This indicates that five years after the Wenchuan earthquake, most of the victims were no longer psychologically affected by the catastrophe (Fig. 8).

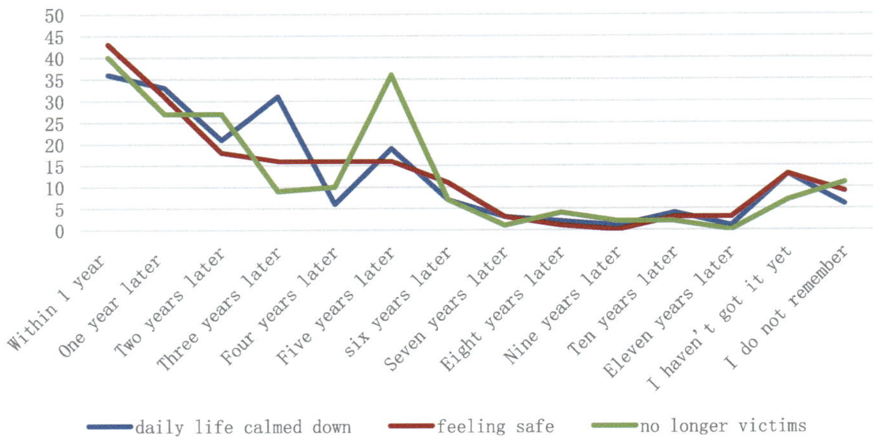

Fig. 8 Timeline of returning to daily life

It is necessary to point out that, according to some studies, due to cultural differences between Asia and the West, for Asian post-disaster survivors to reveal their personal feelings to strangers would make them feel uncomfortable and admitting to mental health problems would bring them a sense of humiliation.[9] Based on the above results, if respondents may be embarrassed to express their feelings, then the real psychological feelings of the victims after the completion of the post-Wenchuan earthquake reconstruction may be more worrying than the situation shown by the survey data.

3.4.2 Generation of Victims' Awareness of Disaster Prevention, Mitigation and Relief

The increased awareness of disaster prevention, mitigation and relief is due, on the one hand, to the introspection of the victims after their experiences. On the other hand, it also depends on the strong promotion of the government and related departments. After the Wenchuan earthquake, the State Council decided to designate May 12 every year as "National Disaster Prevention and Mitigation Day" to further enhance national awareness of disaster prevention, mitigation, and relief, and to promote the whole society to improve disaster prevention, mitigation, and relief capacity. Recently, around May 12 every year, governments, enterprises, and other social organizations carry out activities such as disaster prevention and mitigation publicity, disaster education and escape drills around the theme of disasters to arouse and strengthen public awareness of disaster prevention, mitigation, and relief, and continuously strengthen it.

[9] Zhao et al. (2009).

During the research, the research team observed that governments at all levels, from the central to local governments, had significantly strengthened publicity and education on disaster prevention, mitigation and relief, and the proportion of activities that involved disaster prevention, mitigation and relief education, drills, and skills training in communities, such as village committees and neighborhood committees, had increased significantly, from 36.61 to 52.46%. Specifically, the willingness of the respondents to participate in activities such as the "5.12" disaster prevention and mitigation campaign, the "11.9" fire prevention campaign, and various disaster memorial days, mourning days and post-disaster reconstruction days (Fig. 9).

The participation of respondents before and after the disaster had increased from 25.14 to 42.08%, showing that the public's awareness of disaster prevention, mitigation and relief had been effectively raised and a positive atmosphere of participation had been formed in the whole society (Fig. 10).

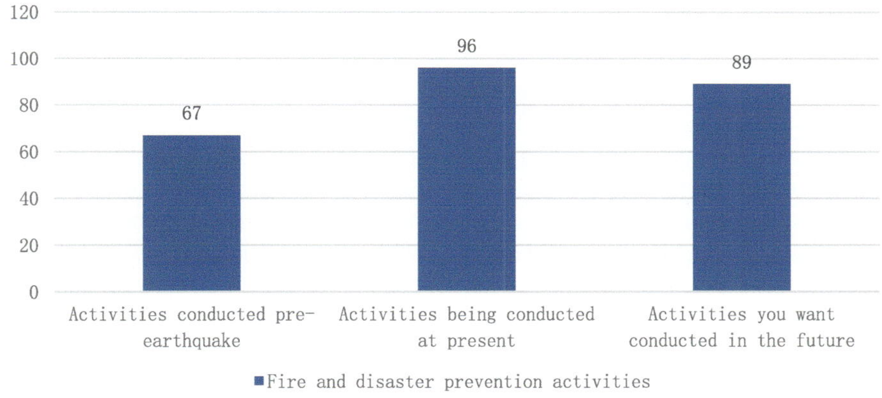

Fig. 9 Implementation of fire and disaster prevention activities in the community

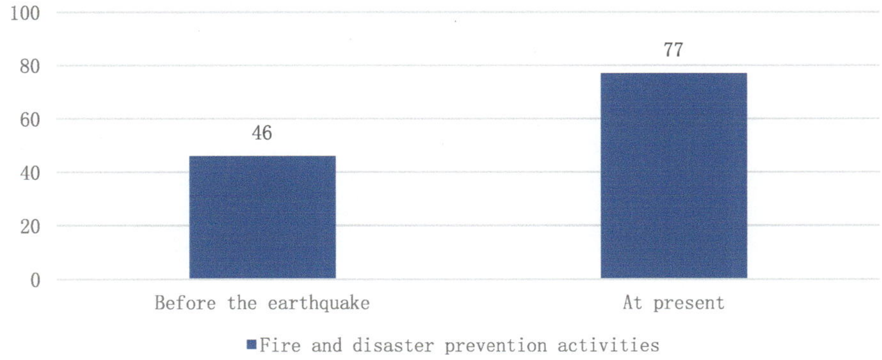

Fig. 10 Participation before and after the earthquake

3.4.3 Social Activities and Social Trust

Social attributes are the fundamental attributes of human beings. Under non-emergency conditions, people are socially connected to each other through participation in a variety of social activities, such as going to school, working, playing, and visiting friends and family. When emergency situations occur due to disasters, these social connections may be temporarily interrupted and some non-essential social activities may be delayed, suspended, or cancelled. For example, many social events involving a high concentration of people were postponed or cancelled during the outbreak of Covid-19, a typical example being the postponement of the Tokyo Olympics from 2020 to 2021.

Social activities are an important part of showing the vitality of society. Beichuan County and Anzhou District are not only geographically close to each other, but also have similar traditional customs and life attitudes, therefore there are many similarities in the types of social events, frequency of events, and the participation methods. With the continuous process of post-disaster restoration and reconstruction, various social events that were briefly stopped have started to be held again.

The project's questionnaire covers social activities that can be divided into two types: "government-run" and "private-run". The "private-run" activities were mostly organized by the people themselves and were not affected much by the earthquake, including weddings, funerals, chess activities, village fairs and other traditional events. As an important part of the social connections between people, they remained highly organized and were actively participated in before and after the earthquake. Influenced by local culture and custom,[10] people in Beichuan County and Anzhou District were likely to participate in recreational activities such as mahjong and poker, which were usually held in village or community activities rooms and tea houses, as well as at home. The rally and temple fair are typical rural social activities, which are an important part of traditional Chinese folk culture. With the restoration of production and life in the disaster-affected areas, such rural social activities have long since returned to a completely normal state.

Activities such as children's activities, caring for the elderly, environmental protection, security, and fire- and disaster-prevention activities have a relatively obvious "government-run" character and are usually organized and promoted by the local government. As left-behind children and the aging problem have gradually become important issues in China's social and livelihood governance in recent years, a large number of activities related to them have been carried out. The project research data show that the proportion of these two types of on-going local activities has increased from 25.14% and 35.52% before the earthquake to 30.60% and 46.45%, respectively (Fig. 11).

During the project survey, the research team also discovered that many elders in the affected areas had a very urgent need for activities of caring for left-behind children and the elderly.

---

[10] This mainly refers to the leisure-related cultural tradition of Sichuan people who like to play mahjong for folk entertainment in this case.

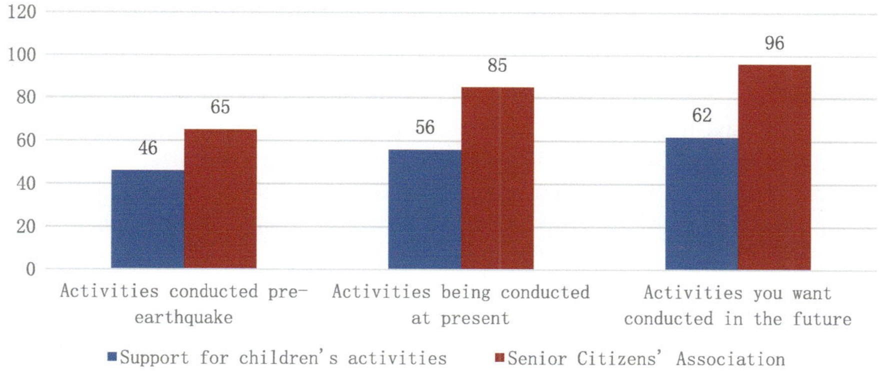

Fig. 11 Implementation of social activities in the community

It is important to emphasize that 62.84% of the respondents chose WeChat and QQ as the publicity methods for social activities, compared to 12.57% before the Wenchuan earthquake, indicating that WeChat and QQ have been widely used for communication between people as a new product of the Internet era. As can be seen, the restoration and reconstruction of the post-Wenchuan earthquake has distinctive Chinese characteristics that carry the mark of the times (Fig. 12).

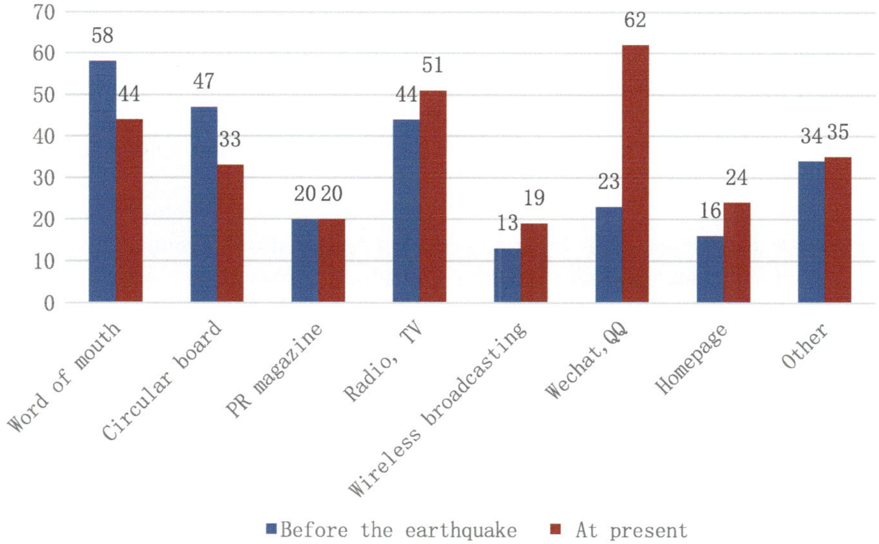

Fig. 12 Media for community notifications

4 Conclusion

From the perspective of resilience theory of the disaster-affected areas, the existence, scale, and intensity of resilience are inevitably affected by factors such as the economic level, regional policies, population structure and size, and cultural differences of the disaster-affected areas.[11] In China, the resilience of the disaster-affected area is more affected by vertical and horizontal administrative powers, which are regarded as core powers. After quantitative analysis, the resilience of the two extremely hard-hit areas, Beichuan County and Anzhou District, were considered strong by the project research team. The factors that determine the strong resilience of these two disaster areas are multiple; among them, there are two more prominent factors, i.e., government-led reconstruction and the counterpart assistance system, which are specific manifestations of "administrative power" and "legal power" respectively.

The research team believes that during the earthquake relief and post-disaster reconstruction process of the Wenchuan earthquake, the nation immediately took strong response measures, used its political power and social organization system, extensively mobilized various social forces, quickly assembled a large amount of material resources, and formulated a series of regulations, policies, and specific measures. The "national system", in which the central government and high-level governments effectively guide the emergency relief actions of the low-level governments and mobilize resources in a short period of time, has a distinctive political character and is recognized as an important political reason for the rapid post-disaster restoration and reconstruction of the "County and District". It is still being used as an advantage of the socialist system in the response to major national emergencies, such as the emergency response to the outbreak of the Covid-19 epidemic, making China, with a population of 1.4 billion, the most successful example of epidemic control.

In other words, the "strong government" model, which effectively combines "administrative power" and "legal power", can form a strong administrative force to deal with various major emergencies and achieve outstanding results. But once the state of emergency ends and it enters the normalized post-disaster reconstruction phase, the issue of the boundary of public power arises and needs to be studied specifically.

In China, the post-disaster counterpart assistance system is another outstanding advantageous system. It was developed under the "strong government" mode and is a unique economic, social, and cultural system with Chinese socialist characteristics, which is essentially a legal system. In the post-Wenchuan earthquake restoration and reconstruction, the basic operation of the counterpart assistance system is that a province assists a hard-hit county (city or district), in which it first helps solve the reconstruction and repair of housing and public facilities, and then helps the

[11] Liu et al. (2006a).

disaster-affected areas with production, management and construction.[12] Therefore, the resilience of the disaster-affected areas can be expressed as a kind of ability to integrate the internal and external resources of the disaster-affected areas, which can be achieved by the counterpart assistance system with the help of "administrative power" and "legal power".

According to the theory of disaster resilience, the counterpart assistance system should be regarded as an act of assistance from outside the disaster-affected areas for the elimination and reduction of damage to the disaster-stricken body. In other words, with the help from outside the disaster-affected areas and the legal power, the economic, social, and cultural recovery of the disaster affected area is rapidly recovered in a comprehensive way by importing and integrating resources. Based on this, the restoration and reconstruction of Beichuan County and Anzhou District can become a typical model with exceptional economic, social, and cultural resilience.

References

Bruneau, M., S. Chang, R. Eguchi, et al. 2003. A Framework to Quantitatively Assess and Enhance the Seismic Resilience of Communities. *Earthquake Spectra* 19 (4): 733–752.

Liu, Jing, Peijun Shi, and Yi Ge. 2006a. A Review of Advances in Disaster Resilience Research. *Advances in Earth Sciences* (2)

Liu, Jing, Weihua Fang, and Yi Ge. 2006b. Regional Flood Resilience and Flood Risk Management: A Case Study on Dongting Lake Region. *Journal of Natural Hazards* (6)

Wang, Jianping. 2008. *Research on the Legal Issues of Natural Disaster Mitigation*, 479. Beijing: Law Press

Zhao, Gaofeng, Yanchun Yang, and Qiang Zhang, et al. 2009. Incidence of Post-Traumatic Stress Disorder and Influencing Factors of Community Residents in the Extremely Hard-Hit Areas of Wenchuan Earthquake. *Stress and Mental Health* (7)

[12] On June 11, 2008, the State Council issued the "Counterpart Assistance Scheme for Post-Wenchuan Earthquake Restoration and Reconstruction", which is based on the principle of "one province helping one hardest-hit county" and stipulates the implementation methods and specific contents of counterpart assistance.

Recovery Status from the 2013 Typhoon Yolanda: Results of a Survey in Two Typical Barangays in Tacloban City

Ebinezer R. Florano

1 Introduction

This chapter describes the results of a survey conducted in two *barangays* ("village") in Tacloban City in Leyte Province in the Philippines in February 2021. In order to understand the context of this paper, brief descriptions of the disaster brought by the super typhoon that occurred in November 2013, and the affected areas, including the two barangays, are provided. The methods of conducting the survey are explained, followed immediately by the presentation and analysis of the results of the survey. The conclusions summarize the state of recovery in the two barangays, and how was this was achieved by the residents.

2 Super Typhoon Yolanda/Haiyan Disaster

On 8 November 2013, Super Typhoon Yolanda, also known as as Typhoon Haiyan under the international naming system, struck the central Visayas region of the Philippines. It brought heavy rains, strong winds and floods, as well as the previously largely-unknown phenomenon of a storm surge, which caught the people surprised and unprepared. Eighty percent of the land hit by the typhoon's destructive power was damaged, which displaced thousands of families and left thousands dead, injured, or missing. In the whole region, around 1.14 million houses were either partially or totally damaged (NDRRMC, 2013).

E. R. Florano (✉)
National College of Public Administration and Governance, University of the Philippines, Quezon, Philippines
e-mail: erflorano@up.edu.ph

Y. Kaneko et al. (eds.), *Recovery of Disaster Victims*, Kobe University Monograph Series in Social Science Research, https://doi.org/10.1007/978-981-99-2957-3_6

Picture 1 The Damaged Barangay Hall of Barangay 90. *Photo Credit* Takayuki Ii, March 2014

In Tacloban City, considered as the regional economic hub, it was estimated that there were more than 3,000 deaths and around US$130 million (Philippine Peso 6.95 billion) worth of damage and loss. In addition, it was also estimated that 58,823 houses were damaged (12,270 totally damaged and 46,553 partially damaged), which affected at least 58,000 families or around 553,000 persons (NDRRMC, 2013).

3 Profiles of the Barangays

Among the 138 barangays of Tacloban City, Barangay 60-A and Barangay 90 were among the hardest hit by the storm surge because both are located in coastal areas (see Picture 1 for a scene of the devastation in Barangay 90).[1] The former is along the Cancabato Bay while the latter is along the San Pedro Bay (see Fig. 1 for the exact locations of the barangays in Tacloban City). Unfortunately, due to the chaos in the aftermath of the typhoon, no records were kept about the number of casualties, injuries, and loss and damage to properties in either barangay. When a team from Kobe University interviewed residents and officials of the two barangays in March 2014, they said that "many died and got injured" but "no records were kept."

[1] No related pictures taken in March 2014 are available for Barangay 60-A.

Picture 2 The Residential and Commercial Areas in Barangay 60-A. *Photo Credit* Orlando Vinculado et al., February 2021

Picture 3 The Seawall in San Pedro Bay and Residential Area in Barangay 90. *Photo Credit* Orlando Vinculado et al., February 2021

Picture 4 Survey Interviews in February 2021. *Photo Credit* Orlando Vinculado et al., February 2021

Barangay 60-A is at Old Road in Sagkahan District in the northwestern part of the city, while Barangay 90 is at Baybay, San Jose on the east coast (see Fig. 1 for the exact locations). Being near the San Pedro and Cancabato Bays, many of the residents are involved in fishing. However, Barangay 60-A also has many commercial establishments and a few factories. Before Typhoon Yolanda, the 2010 population census revealed that Barangay 60-A had 1,640 residents. This was reduced to 923 residents (a 44% decrease) in 148 households according to the 2015 census. Meanwhile, Barangay 90's population suffered the most in the same period. In 2010 it had 382 residents, but the 2015 census estimated that this had decreased to 61 residents (an 84% decrease) in 11 households (see Table 1). According to interviews conducted by the survey team among the respondents, many of the former residents moved out due to economic hardships brought by the disaster. Lastly, in both barangays, many do not have own their houses and/or lands. Unfortunately, there are also no records that could break down the status of land/house ownership of the residents. However, one of the questions in the survey questionnaire is able to reveal this important information (read in "Housing/Dwelling Situation and the Immediate Effects of the Typhoon").

Table 1 Profiles of Barangay 60-A and Barangay 90

	Barangay 60-A	Barangay 90
Major economic activities	Fishing, commerce	Fishing, resort
Location	Old Road, Sagkahan District	Baybay, San Jose
Land area	0.056 km^2	0.0548 km^2
Surrounding water body	Cancabato Bay	San Pedro Bay
Elevation	1.2 m above sea level	4.3 m above sea level
Natural hazards	Storm surge, liquefaction	Storm surge, liquefaction
Population census in 2010	1,640	382
Population census in 2015	923	61
No. of households in 2015	148	11

Sources of data City Population, n.d.; PhilAtlas, n.d.; Philippine Statistics Authority (PSA), n.d.; Tacloban City, n.d

Figure 1. **Locations of Barangay 60-A and Barangay 90 on the UN-OCHA's Map (2013) of Typhoon Yolanda's Damage in Tacloban City.**

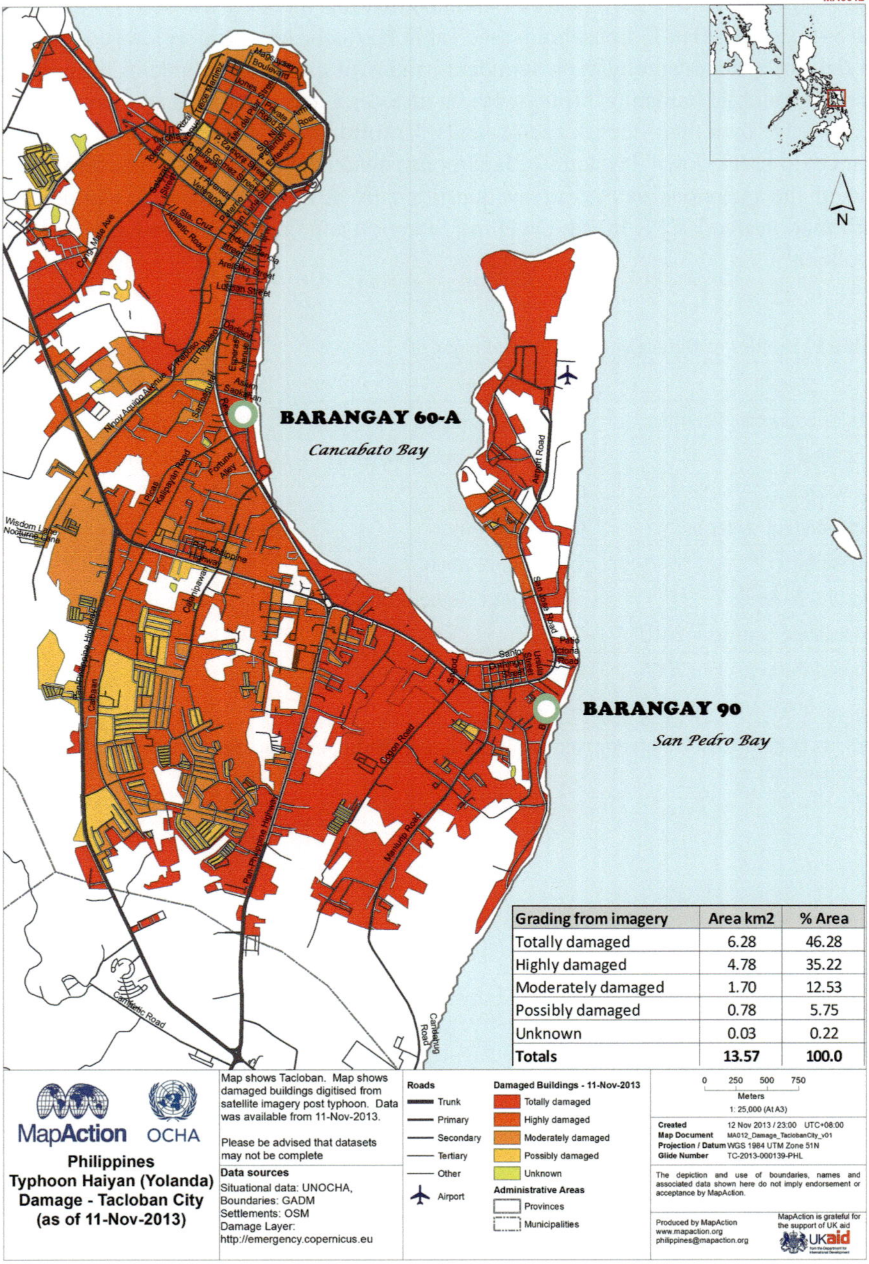

Grading from imagery	Area km2	% Area
Totally damaged	6.28	46.28
Highly damaged	4.78	35.22
Moderately damaged	1.70	12.53
Possibly damaged	0.78	5.75
Unknown	0.03	0.22
Totals	**13.57**	**100.0**

Picture 5 Interview with Barangay 60-A Officials and residents by Kobe university professors in 2014. *Photo Credit* Takayuki Ii, March 2014

Note The map shows that the two barangays are located where many of the houses were in the red zone, i.e., totally damaged.

Given the similarities and differences between the two barangays, it is interesting to examine their recovery status and the residents' perceptions, attitudes, and behaviors towards recovery and reconstruction years after the deadly disaster brought by Typhoon Yolanda. Do they share the same sentiments? Why or why not? Does their housing status affect their sentiments? How?

4 Methodology

The survey was undertaken in the first two weeks of February 2021 by a survey team headed by a local college instructor,[2] who obtained a permit from the Tacloban City Hall to conduct the survey in the two barangays. In compliance with the directives of the city government, the field enumerators wore face masks and face shields, and practiced social distancing at all times when conducting face-to-face interviews (see Picture 4).

---

[2] Mr. Orlando Vinculado of Leyte Normal University.

Picture 6 Interview with the Barangay 90 chairman by Kobe university professors in 2014. *Photo Credit* Takayuki Ii, March 2014

For ease of understanding, the survey questionnaire was translated from English to the local dialect *Waray-Waray* by a local language expert. The survey team purposively selected household heads from among the barangay residents, with the criterion that they should have been residents before and after the occurrence of Typhoon Yolanda in 2013.

The head of the survey team encoded and cleaned the data in Excel before emailing it to the author for processing using IBM-SPSS. The author performed descriptive analyses, i.e., percentage analysis and tabular analysis to analyze the results. The analyses in this report were supplemented from the interviews with barangay officials and residents conducted by the Kobe University team in March 2014 (see Pictures 5 and 6).

5 Findings and Analysis

5.1 Profile of the Respondents

The survey yielded a total of 100 responses. 62% came from Barangay 60-A and the other 38% came from Barangay 90. Even though the survey team aimed to get 50 respondents from each barangay, it was not possible to get that number from Barangay 90 because many of its pre-Yolanda residents moved out to other places.

Picture 7 Market scene in Barangay 60-A. *Photo Credit* Orlando Vinculado et al., February 2021

The majority of the respondents were female and the average age was 44 years old. The average residency period in the barangays was 39 years (see Table 2).[3]

5.2 *Housing/Dwelling Situation and the Immediate Effects of the Typhoon*

All were living in their respective barangays when the typhoon struck, but a few had moved out after that and are now working somewhere else (i.e., they were interviewed for the survey because they are still working in the barangay but live in nearby areas). A majority of those who stayed in the barangays are still working in Tacloban City. However, the housing situation for most of the population in the two barangays differ. In Barangay 60-A, almost half of them were (and still are)

[3] From here onwards, unless totally necessary, the frequency distributions and percentage numbers are no longer cited in the text because they are already written in the tables. Only the patterns and modal answers (e.g., majority, many, few, half, a third, etc.) are discussed. This is to make reading of the analyses unfettered by the figures.

Throughout the manuscript, unless stated otherwise, the patterns and modal answers refer to both barangays. Separate analyses are made when there are substantial differences in the results for both barangays.

Picture 8 A family picnic at the coast in Barangay 90. *Photo Credit* Orlando Vinculado et al., February 2021

Table 2 Profile of the respondents

	Barangay 60-A (%)	Barangay 90 (%)
No. of respondents	62	38
Sex	Female–60 Male–40	Female–66 Male–34
Average age	36 years old	47 years old
No. of years living in the current area	33 years	42 years

unregistered land/house owners, which are called "informal settlers" or pejoratively called "squatters," i.e., people who build houses on vacant lots using light materials like plywood, galvanized iron sheets, tarpaulin, etc. In Barangay 90, where there were (and still are) fewer residents, a majority of the respondents own their lands/houses (see Table 3).

As for the immediate effects of the typhoon on housing, a majority of the residents of both barangays suffered the same fate, i.e., their houses were washed away either by floods or the storm surge. Luckily, at the time of the survey, almost all of them had rebuilt their houses (see Table 3). It was relayed to the 2021 survey team and to the 2014 Kobe University visitors that informal settlers were able to rebuild their shanties using light materials immediately after the typhoon in the same areas, compared to

Table 3 Housing/Dwelling situation

	Barangay 60-A (%)	Barangay 90
Living in the same city during the typhoon?	Yes–100	Yes–100
Living and working in the same city during the typhoon?	Yes–88	Yes–76
Living in the same city at present?	Yes–90	Yes–97
Living and working in the same city at present?	Yes–87	Yes–79
Housing situation before the typhoon	Leasehold land/owned house (no registration)–47	Owned land/owned house–79
Damage assessment	House washed away–81	House washed away–76
House rebuilding status	Newly-built on the original site –71	Newly-built on the original site –71

those whose houses were made of solid wood and concrete. It was implied that this shows the "resilience" of the informal settlers because they were able to rebuild their shanties faster than those who had sturdier cemented houses.

5.3 *Immediate Effects of the Disaster on Household Finances and Expenditures*

Almost a third of the respondents were housewives, followed by part-time employees (see Table 4). In the Philippines, most of those who stay in houses at daytime are housewives. Hence, it is not surprising that many or a majority of the respondents of the survey were housewives who continued their duties after the disaster.

In households where income depends on business, a majority them were affected by the typhoon, especially in Barangay 60-A (many of them were engaged, and still are engaged, in retail selling in *sari-sari* ("variety") stores and/or selling fish in the markets. Intuitively, the decrease in sales or incomes were caused mostly by: (1) decrease in the number of customers, (2) cannot obtain funding, and (3) building/ stalls and equipment were destroyed.

Table 4 Employment before and after the typhoon

	Barangay 60-A (%)	Barangay 90
Employment status & employment position before the disaster	Part-time job–23 Housewife–23	Housewife–40
Job changed after the typhoon?	Same job–40	Same job–50
When job resumed after the disaster?	Not applicable–95	Not applicable–95

Table 5 Business performance before and after the typhoon

	Barangay 60-A (%)	Barangay 90 (%)
Sales & performance of the workplace affected by the typhoon?	Were affected–85%	Were affe–52
Top 3 reasons why performance decreased (multiple responses)	1. Number of customers has decreased–47 2. Could not get funds–34 3. Building & equipment destroyed–27	1. Building & equipment destroyed–29 2. Number of customers has decreased–26 3. Could not get funds–27
Pattern of recovery before and after the typhoon	Recovered to pre-typhoon level –65	Recovered to pre-typhoon level –67
When did sales and performance begin to recover?	1 year after the typhoon–34	1 year after the typhoon–83%
Top 3 reasons why sales & performance of the workplace have recovered	Supported by the city economic recovery–57 Orders increased because of the typhoon recovery–50 Customers returned–36	1.5. Supported by the city economic recovery–29 1.5. There was support from the government–29 3. Orders increased because of the typhoon recovery–18

Table 6 Household finance and expenditure after the typhoon

	Barangay 60-A (%)	Barangay 90 (%)
Change in income	Increased–37 Reduced–34	Reduced–66
Change in spending	Increased–83	Increased–74
Change in deposits & savings	Reduced–61	Reduced–50
Change in debts/loans	Increased–63	Increased–53

The good news is that many of them had already recovered to their pre-typhoon level one year after the disaster. However, a majority of those in Barangay 90 recovered in a year's time while only more than a third recovered in Barangay 60-A. Among others, the main factors that helped them recover were the city's economic recovery, increased orders, returning customers, and government support (see Table 5).

Immediately after the typhoon, their household financial conditions worsened. Generally, incomes decreased but spendings increased. However, in the case of Barangay 60-A, more than a third of the respondents also experienced an increase in income. This could be explained by the fact that many of them engaged in retail selling of essential goods (e.g., rice, fish, grocery items, candles, etc.) in their *sari-sari* stores or in the market, which profited a lot immediately after the typhoon. Lastly, savings/deposits also decreased while loans/debts increased among the residents in the two barangays (see Table 6).

5.4 Perceptions About Recovery and Reconstruction

Barangay 60-A residents recovered faster in many aspects compared to those in Barangay 90. Within the first year, those in Barangay 60-A had psychologically recovered by recognizing the disaster and the hardships it brought, and at the same time, they had already felt safe and their lives had calmed down. They also saw some economic and infrastructural restorations (i.e., roads and schools). In the succeeding years, their financial situations improved with the resumption of their jobs, and the return to normalcy of local activities.

Recovery in Barangay 90 came slower compared to that in the other barangay. A majority of them had learned to accept the reality of the disaster in the first year. Socio-economic and infrastructural recovery took from one year up to four years.

The only commonality about the feelings of the residents of the two barangays is that many of them took more than four years to stop feeling sorry for themselves as victims (see Table 7).

The relatively faster recovery of Barangay 60-A residents in many aspects proves that "there is resilience in numbers." Life may have been hard for them even before Yolanda, and made harder after it, but they were able to rebuild their lives after the typhoon's devastation with the help of their neighbors and relatives through what is called the spirit of *bayanihan,* i.e., Filipinos' sense of communal unity and cooperation.[4]

5.5 Economic Recovery Situation and Population Out-Migration

More than a third of the residents of both barangays felt that Tacloban City had recovered between 40–50% and 60–80%. Almost half of them believe that shopping streets had been reconstructed better than before the typhoon. They cited that NGOs or civil organizations participated in the recovery efforts. They attributed the economic recovery of their city to the leadership of the city government (see Table 8).

As for the recovery of their businesses, a majority said that they did not receive support. Those who received support stated that NGOs assisted them in their recovery efforts. A majority believed that the support that they received was "moderately effective" (see Table 9).

Many residents believed that the city population has recovered between 40–50% and 60–80%. But, before that, there was massive out-migration immediately after the disaster. This was due to, among others, the following factors: (1) lack of basic life-sustaining facilities, (2) lack of work opportunities, and (3) long wait until reconstruction works had ended (see Table 10).

---

[4] A concise description of *bayanihan* can be read at http://groups.csail.mit.edu/cag/bayanihan/bayanword.html.

Table 7 Perceptions about Recovery and Reconstruction

Time period	Barangay 60-A (%)	Barangay 90
Within 1 year	Roads have been restored–66% Grasped the total image of the disaster–57% Gave up on one's inconvenient life lasting long –37% Thought oneself as safe–32% Local school education has been restored–32% Local economy has survived the disaster–29% Daily life has calmed down–26%	1. Grasped the total image of the disaster–71%
1 to 4 years after	Housing problem was finally solved–34% Impact of the disaster on households has ceased–27% Job resumed–26% Local activities returned as before–26%	1. Roads have been restored–63% 2. Local activities have returned as before–57% 3. Local school education has been restored–50% 4. Job resume–37% 5. Housing problem was finally solved–37% 6. Local economy has survived the disaster–53% 7. Thought oneself as safe –32% 8. Impact of the disaster on households had ceased–32% 9. Daily life has calmed down–37%
Have not yet thought about it	1. No longer recognizes oneself as a victim–29%	1. Gave up on one's inconvenient life lasting long–37% 2. No longer recognizes oneself as a victim–37%

5.6 Participation in Community Activities

Filipinos are generally warm people and socialize a lot in their communities. The survey validates this when residents in both barangays stated that they hold yearly events and festivals like *fiesta* ("festival"), environmental cleaning, and community development in the neighborhood block. They had been doing these activities before the disaster and have continued doing so after the disaster (see Table 11).

A majority of the residents said that they joined their community residents' associations in their barangays, and were involved in their activities once every six months

Table 8 Economic recovery of the city

	Barangay 60-A (%)	Barangay 90 (%)
Perception about the recovery situation of regional economic activities	40–50% recovered–33	60–80% recovered–44%
Perception about the reconstruction status of local shopping streets	More than before the typhoon–52%	• More than before the typhoon–36% • 60–80% recovered–36%
Participation of private or civil organizations	NGOs–52 Several private or civil organizations–31	NGOs–87 Several private or civil organizations–5
Top 3 decisive factors in regional economic recovery (multiple responses)	1. Leadership of the administration – 66 2. I don't know–24 3. Others–21 (Help from NGOs)	1. Leadership of the administration–82 2. Others–50 (Local and international NGOs, e.g., Tzu Chi, Oxfam, ESA, Green Mindanao) 3. I don't know–13

Table 9 Support for the business recovery of the residents

	Barangay 60-A (%)	Barangay 90 (%)
No, did not receive support	86	92%
If received support, from whom?	Group grants–52 NGOs–78 Corporations–11 Government–7 Did not identify–4	Others–53 NGOs–75 Government–19 Barangay–6
Effectiveness	Moderately effective–78	Moderately effective–62

Table 10 Population recovery

	Barangay 60-A (%)	Barangay 90 (%)
Perception about the regional population recovery situation	• 40–50% recovered–24 • 60–80% recovered–23	• 60–80% recovered–37
Top 3 causes of population outflow (multiple responses)	Lack of work opportunities and places–52 Lack of living-related facilities–34 Waiting to live there until the reconstruction public works ended–32	1. Lack of living-related facilities–66 2. Lack of work opportunities and places–32 3.5. Others–18 3.5. I don't know–18

Table 11 Community activities before and after the typhoon

	Barangay 60-A (%)	Barangay 90
Top 3 local activities before the typhoon (multiple responses)	Community development–66 2.5. Traditional events & festivals–53 2.5. Senior citizens' association–53	Traditional events & festivals–73 Athletic events–66 Environmental maintenance & cleaning–40
Top 3 local activities at present (multiple responses)	Environmental maintenance & cleaning–77 Community development–50 3.5. Traditional events & festivals–40 3.5. Athletic events–40	Traditional events & festivals–73 Athletic events–70 Community development–50
Top 3 local activities would like to do in the future (multiple responses)	Community development–67% Traditional events & festival–53% Environmental maintenance & cleaning–46%	Traditional events & festivals–78% Environmental maintenance & cleaning–50% Athletic events–34%

before the typhoon, as well as at present, even though a majority of them were not officers before the typhoon, nor at present. These activities are done at the neighborhood block, specifically in (1) nearby private homes, (2) buildings of their organizations, and (3) either barangay halls or barangay basketball courts, which are a 5–15 min or less walk away. Because many of them rebuilt their houses in the same areas where the typhoon destroyed them, the activities and venues remained the same (see Table 12).

Before the typhoon and even up to now, residents get information from: (1) word of mouth, (2) radio/TV, and (3) community/circle boards (see Table 13). These information sources are popular in remote areas due to the non-availability of modern communication facilities and/or lack of electricity. Social media and the internet became popular sources of information only recently.

According to a majority of the respondents, their community activities received no public support before the typhoon, nor even at present. In the reconstruction of their communities, the residents consulted their (1) neighbors, (2) community leaders, (3) NGOs/NPOs, (4) and government (see Table 14).

6 Conclusions

The characteristics of the two barangays, their residents, and their recovery situation and perceptions (except for psychological recovery) are almost the same.

The respondents felt that to a great extent, they have partially recovered economically, financially, and psychologically, that their city is on the way to full recovery, and life has gradually normalized. However, the memories of having been a victim of the disaster brought by the super typhoon still linger.

Table 12 Affiliation with local associations before and after the typhoon

	Barangay 60-A (%)	Barangay 90
Pre-typhoon affiliation with local associations	Community residents' association–61	Community residents' association–66
Present affiliation with local associations	Community residents' association–61	Community residents' association–63
Pre-typhoon officer of the community organization?	Was a board member–21	Was a board member–5
Present officer of the community organization?	Board member–22	Board member–11
Pre-typhoon participation in local activities	Every quarter–26	Once every six months–42
Pesent participation in local activities	Others–24 (Only when needed/called, busy, sickness, etc.)	Once every six months–42
Pre-typhoon extent of area where local activities are held	Neighborhood block–69	Neighborhood block–53
Present extent of area where local activities are held	Neighborhood block–52	Neighborhood block–71
Top 3 places before the typhoon (multiple responses)	Nearby private homes–42% Schools–24% Buildings owned by activity organization – 18%	Others–42% (barangay basketball courts) Buildings owned by activity organization–29% Gymnasium–24%
Top 3 places at present (multiple responses)	Nearby private homes–40% Schools–24% Others–23% (barangay basketball courts, barangay halls)	Buildings owned by activity organization–40% Gymnasium–16% Schools–11%
Before the typhoon, distance walked to local associations	Within 5 min or less walk from home–52%	Within 5–15 min on foot–66%
At present, distance walked to local associations	Within 5 min or less walk from home–53%	Within 5–15 min on foot–68%

Table 13 Types of media notification in the community

	Barangay 60-A (%)	Barangay 90
Top 3 media used before the typhoon (multiple responses)	Word of mouth–90 Radio/TV–53 Circular boards–11	Word of mouth–97 Circular boards –40 Radio/TV–13
Top 3 media used at present (multiple responses)	Word of mouth–58 Radio/TV–50 Wireless broadcasting–29	1. Word of mouth–71 2. Circular boards –40 3. Others–6 (Facebook)

Table 14 Presence of public support for communities

	Barangay 60-A (%)	Barangay 90
Pre-typhoon presence of public support for community activities	Yes–36	Yes–95
Present presence of public support for community activities	Yes–39	Yes–97
Conducted consultation/discussion with regard to the reconstruction in the community	Neighbors–68 NPOs and NGOs–32 Community leaders–24 Government–23	1.5. Neighbors–61 1.5. Community leaders–61 3. NPOs and NGOs–16 4. Government–11

Aside from self-help, residents received assistance from people closest to them (neighbors, community leaders), NGOs, corporations, and the government.

The survey reveals two important aspects about the recovery in the two barangays, which may affect the way "resilience" is perceived. These are:

- The informal settlers were able to rebuild their houses faster in the same areas where the storm surge hit them, compared to higher-income families. The reason behind this is that their shanties were made of light materials like plywood, galvanized sheets, and tarpaulin, which were easily recycled. Not to romanticize "poverty," does this manifest "resilience"—the ability to put a roof over one's head immediately after a disaster to continue to survive?
- Respondents in Barangay 60-A, many of whom were informal settlers, recovered faster in many aspects compared to those in Barangay 90, who are mostly owners of their houses and lands but are fewer in numbers. It is claimed that "there is resilience in numbers" because the Filipino's spirit of *bayanihan* might have helped neighbors assist each other in the midst of the disaster, even though most of them were also hard up financially.

Appendix

Survey of the current state of the local economy and community building after the mega-disaster

We are a collaborative research team of _(your organization name)_ and the Japanese university consortium between Kobe University Center for Social Science Innovation, the Research Center for Urban Safety and Security of Kobe University, Iwate University Research Center for Regional Disaster management, and the Asian Disaster Reduction Center.

This time, we are conducting a survey on the state of the livelihood reconstruction and the local economy and community rebuilding after (disaster name of your region) for the comparison of the status of the 10th year of the Great East Japan Earthquake and Tsunami in Japan. We would appreciate your cooperation for future community development.

November 2020

(Your name, title, and affiliation)

I. Questions About the Respondents Themselves

(1) For your age and gender, please fill in the boxes that apply.

① Age: years ② Gender: 1. Male 2. Female.

(2) Please fill in your home address. For ② and ③, please mark the applicable one

① At the time of the earthquake: Prefecture city/town /village.

② The location of your home is the same as the location of your office, workplace or school at the time of earthquake?:

1. Same municipality 2. Other municipalities(name) 3. Not working/studying at that time.

③ At present: Prefecture city/town /village.

④ Location relationship between your current home and your workplace/office/school location.

1. Same municipality 2. Other municipalities(name) 3. Not working/studying now.

⑤ How many years have you lived in the current place: about years.

(3) Check the applicable housing situation before the earthquake. (Single Answer).

① Age: years ② Gender: 1. Male 2. Female.

1. owned land/ owned house 2. Leasehold land/owned house (registered)

3. Leasehold land/owned house (no registration)

4. Private Rental house/Apartment 5. Public housing 6. Other (Please Specify)

(4) Please put a check mark on one of the damage assessments on the "disaster damage certificate" of your house indicated by the government office after the disaster. (Single Answer)

1. House washed away 2. Completely destroyed 3. Largely destroyed 4. Half destroyed 5. Partially damaged 6. I have not received a damage assessment of my house from the government office (There a."was" b."was not" house damage).

(5) Regarding the rebuilding status of your house, please mark one that applies. (Single Answer)

1. newly built in the original site 2. Repair and renovation at the original site 3. New construction at land readjustment area 4. New construction at group relocation area 5. Newly built at the individually acquired relocation site 6. Disaster public housing 7. Private rental 8. Living in temporary housing 9. Other (Please specify)

(6) What was your workplace / business type before the disaster? Please mark one with ○. (Single Answer)

1. Agriculture and forestry 2. Fishery 3. Manufacturing 4. Construction industry 5. Wholesale and retail business 6. Finance / Insurance 7. Real estate and rental 8. Transportation industry9. Information and communication industry 10. Lodging and Food Service 11. Health / Welfare / Medical 12. Education Related 13. Government Office 14. Unemployed 15. Other (Please Specify)

(7) Please mark one of the following that best describes your employment status and employment position before the earthquake. (Single Answer)

1. Regular staff and employee 2. Leased employee 3. Part-time job.

4. Hand manufacturing work at home 5. Company executive 6. Self-employed with employees 7. Self-employed without employees 8. On pension 9. Housewife 10. Student 11. Suspension of Business (Self-Employed) 12. Looking for a Job 13. Other (Please Specify)

(8) Did your occupation change after the earthquake? Please mark one that applies to you. (Single Answer)

1. Regular staff and employee 2. Leased employee 3. Part-time job

4. Hand manufacturing work at home 5. Company executive 6. Self-employed with employees

7. Self-employed without employees 8. On pension 9. Housewife 10. Student 11. Suspension of Business (Self-Employed) 12. Looking for a Job 13. Other (Please Specify)

1. Doing the same job

2. The job was suspended but resumed (when was it resumed?: Year Month)

3. Changed jobs due to the earthquake

4. Lost or closed business due to earthquake

5. Started a business under the direct impact of the earthquake

6. Changed jobs due to my own reason (other than the earthquake)

7. Retired or closed for my own reasons (other than the earthquake)

8. Started a business for my own reasons (other than the earthquake)

9. None of the above

10. Other (Please Specify).

(9) Questions about the sales and performance of your workplace and office
① Did the impact of the earthquake affect the sales and performance of your workplace and workplace? Please mark one that applies to you. (Single Answer).

1. Were affected by the earthquake

2. The impact of the earthquake was hardly seen ⇒Go to question (10)

3. Other (Please specify)

② Which of the following patterns do you think is correct about sales and performance at your workplace/company where you work for compare before and after the disaster? Please mark one that applies to you. (Single Answer)

1. The level has recovered to the level before the earthquake 2. Has not returned to the level before the earthquake 3. Performance continues to deteriorate starting before the earthquake 4. Other(Please specify)

③ The biggest reason why sales and performance decreased (multiple answers allowed)

1. Buildings and equipment were destroyed and production (business) was not possible
2. The number of regular customers has decreased (the trade area has changed
3. Not enough manpower
4. Could not get funding
5. Couldn't buy goods or couldn't get the raw materials
6. Affected by whole Japan's recession
7. Other (Please Specify)
8. Sales and performance have not decreased
9. Don't know

④ When did sales and performance begin to recover? Please mark one that applies to you. (Single Answer)

1. Less than one (1) year after the disaster

2. one (1) year after the earthquake

3. two (2) years after the earthquake
4. three (3) years after the earthquake
5. four (4) years after the earthquake
6. five (5) years after the earthquake
7. six (6) years after the earthquake)
8. seven (7) years after the earthquake
9. eight (8) years or more after the earthquake
10. Not recovered yet ⇒Go to the question below (10)

⑤ Please tell us why sales and business performance have recovered (multiple answers are possible)

1. Orders increased because of earthquake recovery
2. Supported by economic recovery.
3. Results of sales efforts
4. Functions of equipment and machinery damaged by the earthquake have been restored
5. Received support from customers and head office
6. Customers returned
7. There was support from the government
8.Other (Please specify)

(10) How has the management of households changed compared to before the disaster? Please mark one that applies to you

① Income: 1. Increased 2. Did not change 3. Reduced

② Spending: 1. Increased 2. Did not change 3. Reduced

③ Deposits and savings: 1. Increased 2. Did not change 3. Reduced

④ Debt (Loan): 1. Increased 2. Did not change 3. Reduced

II. Questions About Changes in Your Feelings and Behaviors Related to Recovery and Reconstruction.

① When you have grasped the total image of the disaster damage?	· Within 1 year · One year later · Two years later · Three years later · Four years later · Five years later · Six years later · Seven years later · Eight years later · I haven't got it yet · I do not remember
② When you have become thinking yourself safe?	· Within 1 year · One year later · Two years later · Three years later · Four years later · Five years later · Six years later · Seven years later · Eight years later · I haven't got it yet · I do not remember
③ When did you give up if your inconvenient life lasted long?	· Within 1 year · One year later · Two years later · Three years later · Four years later · Five years later · Six years later · Seven years later · Eight years later · I haven't got it yet · I do not remember
④ When your job (including job change) resumed?	· Within 1 year · One year later · Two years later · Three years later · Four years later · Five years later · Six years later · Seven years later · Eight years later · I haven't got it yet · I do not remember
⑤ When the housing problem was finally resolved?	· Within 1 year · One year later · Two years later · Three years later · Four years later · Five years later · Six years later · Seven years later · Eight years later · I haven't got it yet · I do not remember
⑥ When the impact of the disaster on households has ceased?	· Within 1 year · One year later · Two years later · Three years later · Four years later · Five years later · Six years later · Seven years later · Eight years later · I haven't got it yet · I do not remember
⑦ When daily life calmed down?	· Within 1 year · One year later · Two years later · Three years later · Four years later · Five years later · Six years later · Seven years later · Eight years later · I haven't got it yet · I do not remember
⑧ When local activities returned as before?	· Within 1 year · One year later · Two years later · Three years later · Four years later · Five years later · Six years later · Seven years later · Eight years later · I haven't got it yet · I do not remember

(continued)

(continued)

① When you have grasped the total image of the disaster damage?	· Within 1 year · One year later · Two years later · Three years later · Four years later · Five years later · Six years later · Seven years later · Eight years later · I haven't got it yet · I do not remember
⑨ When did you no longer recognize you as a victim?	· Within 1 year · One year later · Two years later · Three years later · Four years later · Five years later · Six years later · Seven years later · Eight years later · I haven't got it yet · I do not remember
⑩ When local economy has survived disaster?	· Within 1 year · One year later · Two years later · Three years later · Four years later · Five years later · Six years later · Seven years later · Eight years later · I haven't got it yet · I do not remember
⑪When local roads have been restored?	· Within 1 year · One year later · Two years later · Three years later · Four years later · Five years later · Six years later · Seven years later · Eight years later · I haven't got it yet · I do not remember
⑫When local school education is restored?	· Within 1 year · One year later · Two years later · Three years later · Four years later · Five years later · Six years later · Seven years later · Eight years later · I haven't got it yet · I do not remember

III. Questions about the recovery situation of the local economy. please mark those that apply

(1) What was the nature of the local economy before the earthquake?

1. Fishing Village 2. Shopping Street 3. Fish Processing 4. Industrial Zone 5. Residential Area 6. Other (Please Specify) 7. I don't know.

(2) What do you think about the recovery situation of regional economic activities?

1. 10% or less recovered 2. 20 to 30% recovered 3. 40–50% recovered 4. 60 to 80% Recovered 5. Almost Completely Recovered 6. More than before the earthquake 7. I don't know

(3) What do you think about the reconstruction status of local shopping streets?

1. 10% or less recovered 2. 20 to 30% recovered 3. 40–50% recovered. 4. 60% to 80% Recovered 5. Almost Completely Recovered

6. More than before the earthquake7. I don't know.

(4) Have you received support for your business/work ? (multiple answers possible)

1. Support for agriculture (Please Specify).

2. Support for fisheries (Please Specify).

3. Group grant (Please Specify).

4. Support for other SMEs (Please Specify).

5. Other (Please Specify).

6. No, Please Proceed to (6)

(5) If you answered for 1. to 5. in (4), were the support measures effective

1. It Was Very Effective 2. Moderately Effective 3. Not Very Effective 4. It Was not Effective at All 5. I don't Know

(6) Have any private or civil organizations participated in the regional economic recovery?

1. Chamber of Commerce 2. Shopping street association 3. Agricultural cooperative 4. Fishing cooperative 5. Town Development Council 6. NGO 7. Other(Please specify) 8. I don't know.

(7) What do you think about the decisive factor in regional economic recovery (multiple answers possible)?

1. Leading of the administration 2. Leading of the Chamber of Commerce 3. Leading of Shopping mall association
4. New working place 5.Other (Please Specify) 6. I don't know.

(8) What are your thoughts on the current situation of regional population recovery?

1. 10% or less recovered 2. 20 to 30% recovered 3. 40–50% recovered 4. 40% to 80% recovered 5. Almost completely recovered 6. More than before the earthquake 7. I do not know ⇒ go to the questions in below IV.

(9) What do you think about the cause of the population outflow (multiple answers possible)?

1. Waiting to live there until the reconstruction public works ended 2. Lack of safety measures 3. Lack of work opportunities and places 4. Lack of living related facilities 5. Poor transportation 6.Other (Please Specify) 7. I don't know

IV. **Questions about the status of local and community activities. Please fill in or mark applicable ones.**

(1) What are the characteristics of the community for you?

(For example, fishing towns, traditional culture towns, etc.)

(2) Questions about the activities that have been conducted in the community. (Multiple answers possible).

① What were the activities performed before the earthquake?

1. Traditional events and festivals 2. Circle activity 3. Athletic events 4. Ceremonies 5. Support for children's activities 6. Senior Citizens' Association 7. Environmental maintenance and cleaning 8. Crime prevention activities 9. Fire and disaster prevention activities 10. Community development 11. Other (Please specify).

② What are the activities being conducted nowadays?

1. Traditional events and festivals 2. Circle activity 3. Athletic events 4. Ceremonies 5. Support for children's activities 6. Senior Citizens' Association 7. Environmental maintenance and cleaning 8. Crime prevention activities 9. Fire and disaster prevention activities 10. Community development 11. Other (Please specify).

③ What activities do you want to be active in the future?

1. Traditional events and festivals 2. Circle activity 3. Athletic events 4. Ceremonies 5. Support for children's activities 6. Senior Citizens' Association 7. Environmental maintenance and cleaning 8. Crime prevention activities 9. Fire and disaster prevention activities 10. Community development 11.Other (Please specify).

(3) Mark the activities you are participating in the community (multiple answers possible)

① Before the earthquake: (Please mark ◎ for activities you often participated in.)

1. Traditional events and festivals 2. Circle activity 3. Athletic events 4. Ceremonies 5. Support for children's activities 6. Senior Citizens' Association 7. Environmental maintenance and cleaning 8. Crime prevention activities. 9. Fire and disaster prevention activities 10. Community development 11. Other (Please specify).

② At present: (Please mark ◎ for activities you frequently participate in.)

1. Traditional events and festivals 2. Circle activity 3. Athletic events 4. Ceremonies 5. Support for children's activities 6. Senior Citizens' Association 7. Environmental maintenance and cleaning 8. Crime prevention activities 9. Fire and disaster prevention activities 10. Community development 11. Other (Please specify).

(4) What is the extent of the area in the activities you often participate in?

① Before the earthquake

1. Range of the municipal level 2. Range of about middle school district 3. Range of elementary school level 4. Neighborhood block 5. Several neighbors 6. Other (Please specify)

② At present

1. Range of the municipal level 2. Range of about middle school district 3. Range of elementary school level 4. Neighborhood block 5. Several neighbors 6.Other (Please specify)

(5) How often do you participate in activities?

① Before the earthquake

1.Every week 2. Every month 3. Every Quarter 4. Once a Six months 5. Once a year 6.Other (Please specify).

② At present

1. Every week 2. Every month 3. Every Quarter 4. Once a Six months 5. Once a year 6.Other (Please specify).

(6) What kind of organization mainly carries out activities that you frequently participate in?

① Before the earthquake

1. (Residents' association) 2. (village Residents' association) 3. (community Residents' association) 4. (Community property management organization) 5. Fishery cooperative 6. Parent &Teachers Association 7. Other (Please specify)

② At present

1. (Residents' association) 2. (village Residents' association) 3.(community Residents' association) 4. (Community property management organization) 5. Fishery cooperative 6. Parent &Teachers Association 7. Other (Please specify)

(7) Do you serve as a board member of the organization that conducts the activities you often participate in?

① Before the earthquake: 1. I was a board member 2. I was not a board member

② At present: 1. I am a board member 2. I am not a board member.

(8) Where are the places where you mostly take part in community activities? (Multiple answers possible)

① Before the earthquake

1. Buildings owned by activity organization 2. School 3. Gymnasium 4. Nearby private homes 5. Pub
6. Cafe 7.Other (Please specify)

② At present

1. Buildings owned by activity organization 2. School 3. Gymnasium 4. Nearby private homes 5. Pub 6. Café 7.Other (Please specify).

(9) Where are the places where you mostly take part in community activities? (Multiple answers possible)

① ① Before the earthquake

1. Within 5 min Walk from Home 2. Within 5–15 min on Foot 3.Other (Please Specify)

② At present

1. Within 5 min Walk from Home 2. Within 5–15 min on Foot 3.Other (Please Specify)

(10) What are the media for the notification in the community (multiple answers possible)?

① Before the earthquake

1. Word of mouth 2. Circular board 3. PR magazine 4. Radio/TV 5. Wireless broadcasting 6. SNS 7. Homepage 8. Other (Please specify)

② At present

1.Word of mouth 2. Circular board 3. PR magazine 4. Radio/TV 5. Wireless broadcasting 6.SNS

7. Homepage 8. Other (Please specify)

(11) Is there any public support for community activities?

① Before the earthquake

1. Yes 2. No 3. I don't know.

② At present

1.Yes 2. No 3. I don't know.

(12) Have you consulted or discussed the following people with regard to reconstruction in the community (multiple answers possible)?

1. Government 2. Community Leaders (Chairpersons, Etc.) 3. Neighbors 4.NPOs and NGOs 5.Construction Company/Consultant 6. Other (Please Specify)

Lastly, please feel free to write about the issues in the future of local economy and community building. Also, if you have any comments about this questionnaire, please write them down.

Thank you for participating in the survey.

When you have completed the form, please enclose the questionnaire in the envelope (no stamps required) and return it.

References

City Population. (n.d.). Philippines: Tacloban City. Retrieved from City Population website https://www.citypopulation.de/en/philippines/tacloban/

National Disaster Risk Reduction and Management Council (NDRRMC). (2013). *Final report re Effects of Typhoon YOLANDA (HAIYAN)*. Retrieved from http://ndrrmc.gov.ph/attachments/article/1329/FINAL_REPORT_re_Effects_of_Typhoon_YOLANDA_(HAIYAN)_06-09NOV2013.pdf

PhilAtlas. (n.d.). Tacloban. Retrieved from https://www.philatlas.com/visayas/r08/tacloban.html

Philippine Statistics Authority (PSA). (n.d.). Census of population and housing report. Retrieved from https://psa.gov.ph/content/census-population-and-housing-report

Tacloban City. (n.d.). *Tacloban city comprehensive land use plan 2013–2022*

GPSR Compliance

The European Union's (EU) General Product Safety Regulation (GPSR) is a set of rules that requires consumer products to be safe and our obligations to ensure this.

If you have any concerns about our products, you can contact us on ProductSafety@springernature.com

In case Publisher is established outside the EU, the EU authorized representative is:

Springer Nature Customer Service Center GmbH
Europaplatz 3
69115 Heidelberg, Germany

Batch number: 08252485

Printed by Printforce, the Netherlands